ADHD IN THE SCHOOLS
Assessment and Intervention Strategies

The Guilford School Practitioner Series

EDITORS

STEPHEN N. ELLIOTT, Ph.D. **JOSEPH C. WITT, Ph.D.**
University of Wisconsin—Madison *Louisiana State University, Baton Rouge*

Academic Skills Problems: Direct Assessment and Intervention
EDWARD S. SHAPIRO

Curriculum-Based Measurement: Assessing Special Children
MARK R. SHINN (Ed.)

Suicide Intervention in the Schools
SCOTT POLAND

Problems in Written Expression: Assessment and Remediation
SHARON BRADLEY-JOHNSON and JUDI LUCAS-LESIAK

Individual and Group Counseling in Schools
STEWART EHLY and RICHARD DUSTIN

School–Home Notes: Promoting Children's Classroom Success
MARY LOU KELLEY

Childhood Depression: School-Based Intervention
KEVIN D. STARK

Assessment for Early Intervention: Best Practices for Professionals
STEPHEN J. BAGNATO and JOHN T. NEISWORTH

The Clinical Child Interview
JAN N. HUGHES and DAVID B. BAKER

Working with Families in Crisis: School-Based Intervention
WILLIAM STEELE and MELVIN RAIDER

Practitioner's Guide to Dynamic Assessment
CAROL S. LIDZ

Reading Problems: Consultation and Remediation
P. G. AARON and R. MALATESHA JOSHI

Crisis Intervention in the Schools
GAYLE D. PITCHER and A. SCOTT POLAND

Behavior Change in the Classroom: Self-Management Interventions
EDWARD S. SHAPIRO and CHRISTINE L. COLE

ADHD in the Schools: Assessment and Intervention Strategies
GEORGE J. DuPAUL and GARY STONER

School Interventions for Children of Alcoholics
BONNIE K. NASTASI and DENISE M. DeZOLT

ADHD IN THE SCHOOLS

Assessment and Intervention Strategies

GEORGE J. DuPAUL, PH.D.
Lehigh University

GARY STONER, PH.D
University of Oregon

Foreword by Russell A. Barkley

THE GUILFORD PRESS
New York   London

© 1994 The Guilford Press
A Division of Guilford Publications, Inc.
72 Spring Street, New York, NY 10012

Printed in the United States of America

This book is printed on acid-free paper.

Last digit is print number: 9 8 7 6 5 4 3

Library of Congress Cataloging-in-Publication Data

DuPaul, George J.
    ADHD in the schools : assessment and intervention strategies
George J. DuPaul, Gary Stoner.
        p.   cm. — (The Guilford school practitioner series)
    Includes bibliographical references (p.   ) and index.
    ISBN 0-89862-245-X
    1. Attention-deficit disordered children—Education—United
States. 2. Attention-deficit hyperactivity disorder—Diagnosis.
I. Stoner, Gary D.   II. Title: Attention-deficit hyperactivity
disorder in the schools.   III. Series.
LC4713.4.D87   1994
371.93—dc20   93-46055
                                                                    CIP

Acknowledgments

This book would not have reached fruition without the support and encouragement of a variety of people. We both owe a great deal to our mentor and major professor, Dr. Mark Rapport of the University of Hawaii. His enthusiasm for the scientific study of ADHD combined with his emphasis on conducting investigations that are clinically and practically relevant provided us with an exemplar of the scientist–practitioner model in action. Further, the high scientific and academic standards that he set for us and other graduate students have led, at least indirectly, to the completion of this book. We also have been inspired by the work of Dr. Russell Barkley of the University of Massachusetts Medical Center. One of the true "giants" in the field of ADHD research, his support and guidance have been critical in the preparation of this text. Next, we would like to acknowledge the assistance of the School Practitioner Series co-editors, Drs. Stephen Elliott and Joseph Witt. Their encouragement and positive feedback about the nature and content of this book at various stages of the process helped to motivate us through several writing hiatuses. We appreciated the patience, support, and suggestions throughout the writing process of our colleagues, Drs. Arthur Anastopoulos, David Guevremont, Edward Shapiro, Terri Shelton, and Mark Shinn. Even greater levels of patience and support were evidenced by our wives, Judy Brown-DuPaul and Joyce Flanagan. Their willingness to tolerate "lost" evenings and weekends will not go unrewarded. In particular, we are grateful to Judy Brown-DuPaul for offering valuable suggestions for preschool teachers working with students with ADHD which we have included in Chapter 8. Finally, we would be remiss if we did not acknowledge the hundreds of students with ADHD, their families, and their teachers whom we have worked with over the past decade or so. Much of this book represents what we have learned from them and we hope that we can now return the favor by advocating for better school-based services and improved educational outcomes for children and adolescents with ADHD.

Foreword

The past decade of research has led us to the inescapable conclusion that ADHD is not primarily a disturbance in attention as its name suggests. It is instead, most likely, a delay in the development of response inhibition. Such a delay may lead to inefficiency in the neuropsychological functions that we believe inhibit responding, such as the ability to (1) fix on and sustain mental images or messages that relate to external events in a person's working memory so that he or she may act (or not act) upon them; (2) reference the past in relation to those events; (3) imagine hypothetical futures that might result from those events; (4) establish goals and plans of action to implement them; (5) avoid reacting to stimuli likely to interfere with goal-directed behavior; (6) use internal speech in the service of self-regulation and goal-directed behavior; (7) regulate affect and motivation in response to situational demands and in the service of goal-directed behavior; (8) separate affect from information (or feelings from facts) in reacting to events; and (9) analyze and synthesize (Barkley, 1994; Bronowski, 1977). Such executive functions are fundamental to self-regulation and future-oriented behavior. Thus, at its core, ADHD represents a profound disturbance in self-regulation and organization of behavior across time—functions known to be subserved by the prefrontal regions of the human brain (Fuster, 1989).

The impairment of response inhibition in ADHD and its consequent impact on the cross-temporal organization of behavior creates a dilemma for school personnel involved in the evaluation, care, and management of children with ADHD. The children's cognitive difficulties are obviously detrimental to their day-to-day ability to meet the demands of real-world performance at school; at the same time they are extremely difficult to detect by standard psychometric tests and measures. The deficits are clear to the child's teachers and parents, who see the nature of the problem unfolding over time, but they are ephemeral to the psychometrist who sees only a small sample of the child's behavior in tests given outside the natural classroom setting. The key to understanding this dilemma is the impact the disorder has on the child's ability to organize behavior *over time* and meet demands for *future* performance. Because psychometric instruments sample brief periods of time, typically no more than 1–2 hours, they do not capture the child's inability to maintain goal-directed behavior and organization over the time necessary to perform well in school for an entire day or week (or even months in the case of middle- and high-school age students). At most, such tests may capture some of the child's problems with response inhibition, though not always reliably, and fail to appreciate the profound negative effects on the nine other components of self-regulation that are linked to the disinhibition.

Conceptualizing ADHD as a disorder of response inhibition that disrupts the executive functions performed during the delay between stimulus and response and that permit self-regulation has a number of implications for addressing the problems of ADHD children within the educational setting:

1. ADHD is a disorder in performance, not in skill; one of dysregulation not of deficit; one of not doing what you know rather than of not knowing what to do. It is an impairment in the execution of behavior as it is organized over time and directed toward future goals rather than in comprehending what those behaviors should be. This is tough for most people to grasp. Professionals in schools are accustomed to dealing with children's deficits in knowledge and skills. To address such problems, they need only teach the child what to do, what to think, and how to execute a skill. But in ADHD we are dealing with a failure in performance, not skill. ADHD children seem to have most or all of the requisite knowledge for normal performance in school (provided that no learning disability coexists with the ADHD). What they cannot do is draw upon this knowledge at the point of performance where the necessary behaviors must be organized and executed over an extended period of time in future- or goal-oriented activities. Hence, it is at the point of performance that the child's failure of self-regulation rests and it is the consequence of inadequate response inhibition.

2. ADHD will therefore have its most profound impact on adaptive functioning—on complex sets of self-regulating behaviors that must be organized over time to meet daily demands, both social and academic, and in accordance with the child's natural development. As such, ADHD will appear as a discrepancy between cognitive ability, or intelligence, and daily adaptive performance, such as is sampled crudely by adaptive behavior inventories or parent/teacher behavior rating scales. In the same way that learning disabilities are reflected in discrepancies between IQ and

tests of academic achievement, ADHD is a disparity between a child's IQ and his or her adaptive performance in school.

3. Given the above, ADHD is not likely to be detected on traditional academic, intellectual, or other psychometric tests. Such tests simply were not designed to assess response inhibition and the nine consequent executive functions that undergird self-regulation. At best, they may come to reflect the long-term side-effects of failure to deal adequately with the disorder, such as a progressive decline in academic achievement scores, mild losses in verbal intelligence estimates over years of schooling, or terribly low self-esteem and demoralization that will eventually appear on projective measures or personality self-reports. A few tests, such as the continuous performance tests discussed in this text, measure to some degree a child's problems with response inhibition. However, such tests identify 10–25% of children as having ADHD who in reality do not, and 20–45% of children as not having ADHD who do. They also do not indicate the more profound impairments that disinhibition creates in the nine executive functions noted above, impairments far more critical to an ADHD child's failure in school than the term "impulsive" can ever hope to capture.

4. Instead, if ADHD is to be captured it must be captured in its lair. It needs to be observed in the child's daily behavior over relatively longer periods of time (days to weeks) than the minutes to hours sampled by psychometric tests. It needs to be observed as behavioral ratings by parents and teachers who report on a child's functioning during the preceding weeks or months. The child's classroom performance should be directly observed on several different occasions over at least a 2–4 week period, with the child being asked to maintain sustained effort, inhibition, organization, and self-regulation. If goal-directed behavior is not required (such as in free play), ADHD is far less likely to be noted than in situations in which it is required (such as in performing extended individual desk assignments and organizing and completing book reports, science projects, etc.).

5. Treatments to be effective must be in place at the points of performance where the desired behaviors are to be executed. The greater the time between an intervention and the point of performance, the less effective the intervention is likely to be (Goldstein & Ingersoll, 1993). Thus, treatments must take place in the natural setting of the classroom, must prompt the type of performance that is desired, must consequate its occurrence as quickly and frequently as permissible, and must be extended over time so as to maintain the performance of the desired behaviors. Behavioral interventions, classroom modification, and medication used in classroom settings fulfill these criteria and, not surprisingly, are most effective at managing ADHD. Psychotherapy, play therapy, social

skills training, cognitive therapy, or family therapy administered in mental health clinics away from the point of performance do not meet these criteria and consequently are less effective interventions for ADHD.

All of these points, and many others, are admirably elucidated in this book by my friends and colleagues George DuPaul and Gary Stoner. Readers will find here rich summaries of the characteristics, subtypes, comorbidities, developmental courses, and outcomes of ADHD children in school, illustrated with instructive case studies. The authors then present a useful model for the screening and evaluation of children thought to have ADHD and guidelines for distinguishing ADHD from learning disabilities, with which it is often confused. This is followed by detailed discussions of the most useful intervention methods in school settings and the critical assumptions on which they should be based. Of special importance is the point, often unrecognized, that intervention must be coupled with specific programs for the support of teachers and the allocation of school resources to assist in helping ADHD children.

Throughout this book the authors take care to extract as much applied knowledge from the existing scientific literature as possible that is relevant to the diagnosis, assessment, and treatment of ADHD within the schools. Moreover, they focus attention on the legal rights of ADHD children under the various public laws that protect those with disabilities against discrimination and define the eligibility of ADHD children for services in public schools. This is critical in view of the recent interpretation by the Department of Education's Office of Special Education, the Office of Civil Rights, and the Social Security Administration that defines ADHD as a developmental disability, eligible for the protection and provision of special services.

In thinking about the useful interventions reviewed in this book, the reader should keep in mind that they are founded on a system of social interaction that includes not only the child, parents, and teachers, but also the school principal and support staff, the special education staff of the school, and any outside professional consultants brought in by the parents or the school, such as pediatricians, psychiatrists, child neurologists, or child clinical psychologists. Add to this the intervention program itself and one begins to appreciate the complex social network in which any intervention must operate. The match, or complementarity, among these participants is often key to the successful implementation of treatment programs for a child with ADHD. To the extent that the match is poor, conflictual, or dysfunctional, the efficacy of the treatment plan is likely to be compromised.

As Greene (1993) has noted, it is not just the complementarity of parent–child, teacher–child, and parent–teacher dyads that must be considered, but also the matchup of these dyads with the requirements of the treatment plan and its underlying philosophy, of the nature of the child's problems, that determines the successful implementation of that treatment plan. For instance, behavior modification methods include certain assumptions about the nature of a behavioral problem (i.e., that it is partially or wholly a function of environmental antecedents and consequents and can be controlled by manipulating these environmental parameters). These may conflict with a teacher's conceptualization of the problem as stemming from an intrapsychic conflict that would be best dealt with in psychotherapy with a mental health service provider. Or, it may be viewed as a manifestation of a dysfunctional family system within the home that would be best treated by a family therapist. Such perspectives are not likely to result in complete cooperation with school intervention plans that are founded on a behavioral model, nor are they likely to be congruent with a medication-based treatment plan. Thus, it is usually helpful to examine the complementarity of people–people and people–program matchups prior to the introduction of an intervention program, in order to detect potential conflicts and address them before imposing the intervention program in that school setting. Often, simply sharing current information on the nature of ADHD will go a long way toward reorienting a person with outmoded perspectives on the problem and ensuring a common conceptual framework among participants before the intervention proceeds.

The authors' extensive experience designing and implementing assessment and treatment protocols within school settings is evident throughout the text. Much pragmatic wisdom is interwoven with the discussions of research studies and yields many specific recommendations for the evaluation and management of ADHD in school. Drs. DuPaul and Stoner are clearly neither armchair philosophers nor Monday-morning quarterbacks but have had to test their conceptual view of ADHD through years of direct experience in school settings, working to improve the plight of those children with ADHD. The reader will be much the wiser for their experience and possesses a desk reference that should prove invaluable for years to come.

Russell A. Barkley, Ph.D.
Professor of Psychiatry and Neurology
University of Massachusetts Medical Center
Worcester, MA

Preface

Students who are inattentive and disruptive present significant challenges to educational professionals. In fact, many children and adolescents who exhibit behavior control difficulties in classroom settings are diagnosed as having an Attention-Deficit Hyperactivity Disorder (ADHD) or are likely to be diagnosed as such. Students with ADHD are at high risk for chronic academic achievement difficulties, the development of antisocial behavior, and problems in relationships with peers, parents, and teachers. Traditionally, this disorder has been identified and treated by clinic-based professionals (e.g., pediatricians, clinical psychologists) on an outpatient basis. Given the fact that children and adolescents with ADHD experience some of their greatest difficulties in educational settings, recently there has been increased attention paid to the needs of these students by school-based professionals. In addition, recent clarifications of federal regulations governing special education eligibility for these students have magnified the need for educators to receive training in assessing and treating individuals with ADHD in the schools. The purpose of this book is to assist school professionals in understanding and treating children and adolescents with ADHD.

A plethora of journal articles, book chapters, and textbooks have been published on the topic of ADHD. Although it could be argued that yet another book on this topic would be superfluous, most of the previous literature on ADHD has been written by and for clinic-based practitioners. We have attempted to address the problems associated with ADHD from a school-based perspective, while recognizing the need for a team effort among parents, community-based professionals, and educators. Specifically, we have focused on how to (1) identify and assess students who might have ADHD; (2) develop and implement classroom-based intervention programs for these students; and (3) communicate with and assist physicians when stimulant medications are employed to treat this disorder. We believe that this is the first book that has attempted to address these issues in a comprehensive fashion for school-based professionals.

This book is intended to meet the needs of a variety of school-based practitioners including school psychologists, guidance counselors, administrators, as well as both regular and special education teachers. Given that students with ADHD are found in nearly every school setting and experience a wide range of difficulties, this text should be of interest to all educators and related professionals. In addition, graduate students who are receiving training in a variety of school-based professions should find this book helpful in understanding this complex disorder. Finally, features of this text have been incorporated to facilitate use by practitioners. For example, we have included a number of appendices containing forms (e.g., handouts, observation coding sheets) that should prove useful for professionals in school settings.

Contents

1

Overview of ADHD

GREG, AGE 7

Greg is a 7-year-old first grader in a general education classroom in a public elementary school. According to his parents, his physical and psychological development were "normal" until about the age of 3 when he first attended nursery school. His preschool and kindergarten teachers reported that Greg had a short attention span, had difficulties staying seated during group activities, and interrupted conversations frequently. These behaviors were increasingly evident at home as well. Currently, Greg is achieving at a level commensurate with his classmates in all academic areas. Unfortunately, he continues to evidence problems with inattention, impulsivity, and motor restlessness. These behaviors are displayed more frequently when Greg is supposed to be listening to the teacher or completing an independent task. His teacher is concerned that Greg may begin to exhibit academic problems if his attention and behavior control do not improve.

AMY, AGE 13

Amy is a 13-year-old eighth grader who receives most of her instruction in general education classrooms. A psychoeducational evaluation conducted when she was 8 years old indicated a "specific learning disability" in math for which she receives resource room instruction three class periods per week. In addition to problems with math skills, Amy has exhibited significant attentional difficulties since at least age 5. Specifically, she appears to daydream excessively and to "space out" when asked to complete effortful tasks either at home or school. Her parents and teachers report that she "forgets" task instructions frequently, particularly if multiple steps are involved. At one time, her inattention problems were assumed to be caused by her math skills deficit. This does not appear to be the case, however, because she is inattentive during most classes (i.e., not just during math instruction), and these behaviors predated her entry into elementary school. Amy is not impulsive or overactive. In fact, she is "slow to respond" at times and appears reticent in social situations.

TOMMY, AGE 9

Tommy is a fourth grader whose schooling occurs in a public elementary school in a self-contained, special education classroom for children identified with "serious emotional disturbance" (SED). His mother reports that Tommy has been a "handful" since infancy. During his preschool years, he was very active (e.g., climbing on furniture, running around excessively, infrequently sitting still) and noncompliant with maternal commands. He has had chronic difficulties relating to peers as he has been both verbally and physically aggressive with others. As a result, he has few friends his own age and tends to play with younger children. Tommy has been placed in an SED class since second grade because of his frequent disruptive activities (e.g., calling out without permission, swearing at the teacher, refusing to complete seatwork) and related problematic academic achievement. During the past year, Tommy's antisocial activities have increased in severity: He has been caught shoplifting on several occasions and has been suspended from school for vandalizing the boy's bathroom. Even in his highly structured classroom, Tommy has a great deal of difficulty attending to independent work and following classroom rules.

Although Greg, Amy, and Tommy are quite different, they share a common difficulty with attention, particularly to assigned schoolwork and household responsibilities. As such, they could all be characterized as displaying an Attention Deficit Disorder (ADD). Further, many children with attention problems, such as Greg and Tommy, display additional difficulties with impulsivity and overactivity. The current psychiatric term for children exhibiting extreme problems with inattention, impulsivity, and hyperactivity is Attention-Deficit Hyperactivity Disorder (ADHD)[1] (Ameri-

---

1. Because multiple labels for Attention Deficit Disorder have been used throughout the years and across disciplines, the term ADHD will be used in this text to promote simplicity. ADHD will be considered synonymous with other terms for the disorder, such as hyperactivity and ADD.

can Psychiatric Association, 1987). As may be discerned from the above case descriptions, the term ADHD is applied to a heterogeneous group of children who are encountered in virtually every educational setting.

The purpose of this chapter is to provide a brief overview of ADHD. Specifically, information will be reviewed regarding the prevalence of this disorder, the school-related problems of children with ADHD, associated adjustment difficulties, methods of subtyping children with this disorder, possible causes of ADHD, the impact of situational factors on symptom severity, and the probable long-term outcomes for this population. This background material will be helpful in providing the context for later descriptions of school-based assessment and treatment strategies for ADHD. Readers who are interested in a more comprehensive discussion of the issues presented in this chapter should consult Barkley (1990) or Matson (1993).

PREVALENCE OF ADHD

Epidemiological (i.e., population survey) studies indicate that approximately 3–5% of children in the United States can be diagnosed with ADHD (Barkley, 1990). Given that most general education classrooms include at least 20 students, approximately one child in every class will have ADHD. As a result, children reported to evidence attention and behavior control problems are referred to school psychologists and other educational and mental health professionals frequently. In fact, children with ADHD may comprise as much as 40% of referrals to child guidance clinics (Barkley, 1990). Boys with the disorder outnumber girls in both clinic-referred (approximately a 6:1 ratio) and community-based (approximately a 3:1 ratio) samples (Barkley, 1990). The higher clinic ratio for boys with this disorder may be a function, in part, of the greater prevalence of additional disruptive behaviors (e.g., noncompliance, conduct disturbance) among boys with ADHD (Breen & Barkley, 1988). Thus, relative to other childhood conditions (e.g., mental retardation, depression), ADHD is a "high-incidence" disorder that is particularly prominent among males.

SCHOOL-RELATED PROBLEMS OF CHILDREN WITH ADHD

Core Behavior Difficulties

The core characteristics (i.e., inattention, impulsivity, and overactivity) of ADHD can lead to myriad difficulties for children in school settings. Specifically, because these children often have problems sustaining attention to effortful tasks, their completion of independent seatwork is quite inconsistent. Their classwork performance also may be compromised by a lack of attention to task instructions. Other academic problems associated with inattention include poor test performance; deficient study skills; disorganized notebooks, desks, and written reports; and a lack of attention to teacher lectures and/or group discussion.

Children with ADHD often disrupt classroom activities and, thus, disturb the learning of their classmates. For example, their impulsivity may be exhibited in a variety of ways including frequent calling out without permission, talking with classmates at inappropriate times, and becoming angry when confronted with reprimands or frustrating tasks. Classwork and homework accuracy also may be affected deleteriously due to an impulsive, careless response style on these tasks.

Problems related to overactivity may be evidenced by children leaving their seats without permission, playing with inappropriate objects (e.g., materials in desk that are unrelated to the task at hand), repetitive tapping of hands and feet, and rocking in their chairs. Although the latter behaviors appear relatively benign, if they occur on a frequent basis they may be a significant disruption to classroom instruction.

Difficulties Associated with ADHD

Students with ADHD are at-risk for significant difficulties in a variety of functional areas. It appears as though problems with inattention, impulsivity, and overactivity predispose children to other difficulties that are, in some cases, more severe than the core deficits of ADHD. Of these difficulties, the three most frequent correlates of ADHD include academic underachievement, high rates of noncompliance and aggression, and disturbances in peer relationships.

Teachers and parents frequently report that children with ADHD underachieve academically compared to their classmates (Barkley, 1990). As stated above, these children exhibit signficantly lower rates of on-task behavior during instruction and independent work periods than those displayed by their peers (Abikoff, Gittelman-Klein, & Klein, 1977). Consequently, children with ADHD have fewer opportunities to respond to academic material, and they complete less independent work than their classmates (Pfiffner & Barkley, 1990). Lower than expected rates of work completion may, in part, account for the association of ADHD with academic underachievement because up to 80% or more of children with this disorder have been found to exhibit academic performance problems (Cantwell & Baker, 1991). Further, a signficant minority (i.e., 20–30%) of children with ADHD are classified as "learning disabled" because of deficits in the acquisition of specific academic skills (see Chapter 3 for details). Finally, the results of prospective follow-up studies of children with ADHD into adolescence and young adulthood indicate heightened risks for chronic academic failure as measured by higher rates of grade retention and dropping out of school relative to their peers (e.g., Barkley, Fischer, Edelbrock, & Smallish, 1990).

The high correlation between hyperactivity and aggression is well documented in the research literature (Loney & Milich, 1982). The problems in the aggressive domain that are most frequently associated with ADHD include defiance or noncompliance with authority figure commands, poor temper control, argumentativeness, and verbal hostility (Loney & Milich, 1982). Problems with noncompliance and temper control presently comprise the psychiatric category of Oppositional Defiant Disorder (ODD) (American Psychiatric Association, 1987). Therefore, it is not surprising that ODD is the most common codiagnosis with ADHD (i.e., associated or comorbid condition), because up to 40% of children with ADHD and 65% of teenagers with ADHD display significant ODD-related behaviors (Barkley, DuPaul, & McMurray, 1990; Barkley, Fischer, et al., 1990). More serious antisocial behaviors (e.g., stealing, physical aggression, truancy) are exhibited by 25% or more of students with ADHD, particularly at the secondary school level (Barkley, Fischer, et al., 1990; Gittelman, Mannuzza, Shenker, & Bonagura, 1985). Children who display aggression and ADHD-related difficulties are at greater risk for interpersonal conflict at home, in school, and with peers than are children who display only ADHD (Barkley, 1990). Further, the combination of conduct problems and ADHD is strongly associated with the abuse of illicit drugs (Gittelman et al., 1985).

It is very difficult for many children with ADHD to initiate and maintain friendships with their classmates (Guevremont, 1990). Studies that have employed sociometric measures have found uniformly high rates of peer rejection for children displaying ADHD-related behaviors (e.g., Milich & Landau, 1982; Pelham & Bender, 1982). The rate of peer rejection is particularly high for children displaying both aggression and ADHD. Typically, peer rejection status is stable over time, implicating the chronic nature of these children's interactional difficulties (Parker & Asher, 1987).

Presumably, the disturbed peer relations of children with ADHD are due to inattentive and impulsive behaviors disrupting their "social performance" (Guevremont, 1990). The most common performance deficits associated with this disorder include inappropriate attempts to join ongoing peer group activities (e.g., barging in on games in progress), poor conversational behaviors (e.g., frequent interruptions, minimal attention to what others are saying), employing aggressive solutions to interpersonal problems, and being prone to losing temper control when conflict or frustrations are encountered in social situations (Guevremont, 1990). Surprisingly, children with ADHD often are able to articulate the proper social behaviors to be exhibited in specific situations. Thus, ADHD-related symptoms lead to social *performance* difficulties for these children, rather than social *skills* deficits per se (see Chapter 6 for details).

SUBTYPES OF ADHD

The current definition of ADHD includes a list of 14 behavioral symptoms; a child must exhibit at least 8 of these symptoms to receive a diagnosis of this disorder (American Psychiatric Association, 1987; see Chapter 2). Given that the symptomatic profile will vary across individuals, children classified with ADHD are a heterogeneous group. Broadening this inherent heterogeneity are the potential correlates of ADHD (i.e., academic underachievement, aggression, and peer relationship difficulties) summarized above. Therefore, attempts have been made to identify more homogeneous subtypes of ADHD to facilitate searches for causal factors, identify potential differences in long-term outcome, and, most importantly, to aid in treatment planning. Although a variety of subtyping schema have been proposed over the years, the most promising have been (1) ADD with versus without hyperactivity and (2) ADHD with versus without aggression.[2]

ADD with or without Hyperactivity

The classification system in the third edition of the *Diagnostic and Statistical Manual of Mental Disorders* (DSM-III) (American Psychiatric Association, 1980) included two different subtypes of ADHD: Attention Deficit Disorder with Hyperactivity (ADD+H) and Attention Deficit Disorder without Hyperactivity (ADDnoH). The latter category included children who exhibited significant problems with inattention and impulsivity in the absence of frequent overactivity. When the DSM-III was revised in 1987 (DSM-III-R), this subtype was removed from the classification schema because of its minimal empirical underpinnings at the time.

Since the publication of the DSM-III-R, a variety of research studies have been conducted that support the existence of an ADDnoH subtype (see Lahey & Carlson, 1992, for a review). In fact, it is highly likely that this subtype, referred to as ADHD—Predominantly Inattentive Type, will reappear in the forthcoming DSM-IV (American Psychiatric Association,

---

2. The advantages and disadvantages of subtyping children with ADHD into those with versus without learning disabilities are discussed in Chapter 3.

in press; see Chapter 2). Children with ADDnoH display significant problems with inattention in the absence of notable impulsivity and hyperactivity (Lahey & Carlson, 1992). There is initial evidence that children with ADDnoH have greater problems with memory retrieval and perceptual–motor speed than their impulsive–hyperactive counterparts (Barkley, DuPaul, & McMurray, 1990). Further, they are described by parents and teachers as being more cognitively "sluggish," prone to daydreaming, and socially withdrawn than children with ADD+H (Barkley, 1990). These and other findings have led some investigators to postulate a greater incidence of learning disabilities among this subtype relative to other children with the full syndrome of ADHD. This hypothesis has not been borne out in any empirical studies, although at least one investigation (Barkley, DuPaul, & McMurray, 1990) found a greater percentage of students with ADDnoH (53%) placed in classrooms for the learning disabled relative to those with ADD+H (34%).

In contrast to the ADDnoH subtype, children with the full syndrome of ADHD exhibit higher rates of impulsivity, overactivity, aggression, noncompliance, and peer rejection (Lahey & Carlson, 1992). Further, they are more likely than their ADDnoH counterparts to be diagnosed with other disruptive behavior disorders (e.g., Conduct Disorder), to be placed in classrooms for students with SED, to obtain a higher frequency of school suspensions, and to receive psychotherapeutic intervention (Barkley, DuPaul, & McMurray, 1990). Although comparative long-term outcome studies have not been conducted, it is assumed that children with the full syndrome of ADHD are at greater risk for antisocial disturbance and behavioral adjustment difficulties. Little is known about the chronicity and longitudinal outcome of ADDnoH in childhood.

A handful of studies have examined the differential response to psychostimulant medication (i.e., Ritalin or methylphenidate) in the two subtypes of ADHD. These generally indicate a positive response to medication among most members of both subtypes, with lower doses found to be sufficient for a greater percentage of children with ADDnoH (e.g., Barkley, DuPaul, & McMurray, 1991). To date, no studies have compared response to nonpharmacological interventions between subtypes.

Although a very small percentage (i.e., approximately 1.3%) of children have ADDnoH relative to those with the full syndrome (Szatmari, Offord, & Boyle, 1989), there is burgeoning evidence to indicate that such children should be identified separately from children with ADD+H. These subtypes clearly differ with respect to associated difficulties and, perhaps, in the areas of treatment response and long-term outcome. Barkley (1990) has argued that children with ADDnoH also may differ from hyperactive–impulsive children in the qualitative nature of their attention deficits. Specifically, children with ADD+H exhibit difficulties with sustained attention, whereas those with ADDnoH are more likely to have problems with focused attention. Thus, different neural mechanisms may be involved leading to discrepant behavioral response styles (Barkley, 1990). It is likely that with the return of this subtype in the DSM-IV classification system, greater professional attention will be devoted to identifying and comparing interventions for the two subtypes. This work is particularly important for school practitioners because, presumably, the latter are more likely to receive referrals for children with ADDnoH than are community-based professionals.

ADHD with versus without Aggression

As stated previously, the term "aggressive" has been used to describe children who display higher than average rates of noncompliance, argumentativeness, defiance, and poor temper control. Many children displaying such behaviors may meet the criteria for the classification of ODD. Although, there is a great deal of overlap or comorbidity between ADHD and ODD (Barkley, 1990; see Difficulties Associated with ADHD section above), children with either disorder by itself are distinct, especially with respect to long-term outcome, from those youngsters who are both hyperactive and aggressive (see Hinshaw, 1987, for a review).

Children with both ADHD and aggression (i.e., ODD or Conduct Disorder) exhibit greater frequencies of antisocial behaviors, such as lying, stealing, and fighting, than those who are hyperactive and not aggressive (Barkley, 1990). Further, hyperactive–aggressive children are at higher risk for peer rejection than those displaying either ADHD or aggression in isolation. Greater levels of family dysfunction and parental psychopathology have been found among youngsters with both disorders as well (Barkley, 1990). Most importantly, children with ADHD and aggression have the highest risk for problematic outcome in adolescence and adulthood (e.g., greater prevalence of substance abuse) relative to any other subgroup of children with ADHD (Barkley, 1990).

Although these subtypes have not been found to exhibit different responses to psychostimulant medication (e.g., Barkley, McMurray, Edelbrock, & Robbins, 1989), there is considerable agreement among professionals that those children with both ADHD *and* aggression will require more intensive and continuous service delivery. The precursors to the combination of ADHD and aggression may hold some clues to the need for comprehensive, multimodal treatment. A combination of within-child (i.e., irritable child temperament, shorter than average attention span, and high activity level) and environmental (i.e., coercive response style of family members, marital discord, and poor parental functioning) factors may lead to the coexistence of these disorders (Barkley, 1990).

To the extent that these factors contribute to child maladjustment throughout development, the later the point of intervention, the greater the need for long-term, intensive service delivery. The protracted and difficult nature of these behavior problems sometimes leads to more restrictive placements outside of the public school and family environments.

POSSIBLE CAUSES OF ADHD

There is no apparent single cause of ADHD. Rather, ADHD symptomatology may result from a variety of causal mechanisms (Barkley, 1990). Most of the research examining the etiology of ADHD is correlational, thus caution is warranted in attributing causal status to identified variables. Nevertheless, empirical data have been gathered regarding the potential causal contributions to ADHD of a number of factors. Within-child variables such as neurological factors, hereditary influences, and toxic reactions have received the greatest attention in the literature (Anastopoulos & Barkley, 1988). The contributions of these variables are summarized briefly, below. Environmental influences (e.g., family stress and poor parental disciplinary practices) appear to modulate the severity of the disorder, but do not play a causal role per se (Barkley, 1990).

Neurological Variables

Over the years, neurological factors have received the greatest attention as etiological factors. The earliest hypotheses postulated that children with ADHD had structural brain damage that contributed to attention and behavior control difficulties (Anastopoulos & Barkley, 1988). However, most children with ADHD *do not* have structural deficits in the central nervous system and structural brain damage is not considered to be a primary cause of ADHD at the present time (Barkley, 1990). More recently, cerebral blood flow, neuropsychological, and psychophysiological findings have provided some evidence of "underreactivity" in specific cortical and subcortical regions of the brain that may be implicated in ADHD (Anastopoulos & Barkley, 1988). Interestingly, one of the sections of the brain that has been studied in this regard is the prefrontal cortex, which purportedly is involved in the inhibition of behavior and mediating responses to environmental stimuli. A final neurological factor that has been studied as an etiological variable is an imbalance or deficiency in certain neurotransmitters (Anastopoulos & Barkley, 1988). Specifically, the neurochemicals dopamine and norepinepherine are presumed to be "less available" in certain regions of the brain, thus contributing to ADHD symptomatology. This hypothesis has been based, in part, on the action of psychostimulants (e.g., Ritalin) in the brain by which the availability of dopamine and norepinepherine is increased.

Hereditary Influences

ADHD appears to be a disorder that runs in families (Barkley, 1990). There is a higher rate of concurrent and past ADHD symptoms in immediate family members of children with ADHD relative to their non-ADHD counterparts (Anastopoulos & Barkley, 1988). Further, the results of behavioral genetics studies have provided evidence in support of a hereditary contribution to ADHD. For example, there is a higher incidence of ADHD among first-degree biological relatives relative to adoptive parents and siblings for children with ADHD that were adopted at an early age (Anastopoulos & Barkley, 1988). Thus, initial evidence is supportive of a genetic contribution to ADHD, however more definitive investigations that include chromosomal analyses must be conducted.

Environmental Toxins

A variety of environmental toxins have been hypothesized to account for ADHD symptoms. Some of the more popular theories have implicated nutritional factors, lead poisoning, and prenatal exposure to drugs or alcohol (Ross & Ross, 1982). For example, Feingold (1975) argued that certain food additives (e.g., artificial food colorings, salicylates) led to childhood hyperactivity. Well-controlled studies that have examined this hypothesis, as well as similar assumptions about sugar, indicate that dietary factors play a minimal role in the genesis of ADHD (Barkley, 1990). In fact, this is generally true for the whole area of environmental toxins. Specifically, their relationship to ADHD has been explicated through correlational studies. The exact role that these factors play in causing ADHD is presumed to be minimal, at least for the majority of youngsters receiving this diagnosis (Anastopoulos & Barkley, 1988).

Conclusions

The most prudent conclusion regarding the etiology of ADHD is that multiple biological factors may predispose children to exhibiting shorter than average attention spans along with higher rates of activity and impulsivity compared to other children. The most promising evidence points to a hereditary influence that may alter brain (i.e., neurochemical) functioning. Several caveats should be kept in mind about the above conclusions. First, research in this area has been fraught with methodological difficulties that reduce confidence in interpreting results (Anastopoulos & Barkley, 1988). Second, despite the fact that within-child variables appear to be primary causal factors, this does not denigrate the role of the environment in the maintenance of ADHD symptoms. For instance, as discussed in Chapters 4 and 6, interventions that involve the manipulation of environmental conditions can be quite effective in enhancing the functioning of children with this disorder. Finally, at present, there is no known connection between the cause of an individual's ADHD and treatment planning. As such, determination of etiology is minimally related to enhancing successful outcomes. Perhaps as the use of advanced assessment technologies (e.g., *magnetic resonance imaging* [MRI]) becomes more widespread, clinically useful information about the etiology of ADHD will be forthcoming.

THE IMPACT OF SITUATIONAL FACTORS ON SYMPTOM SEVERITY

Although biological variables are hypothesized to be the primary causes for ADHD, environmental factors, which may provoke or reduce the probability of ADHD-related behaviors, remain important for professional service delivery. Both antecedent and consequent stimuli are critical in determining the severity of attention problems, impulsivity, and behavior control. Important antecedent events that affect the probability of ADHD-related behaviors occurring include the type of commands or instructions a child is given, the degree to which a child is supervised during independent work, and the number of children present during instruction (Barkley, 1990). A variety of factors impact on the degree to which consequences control the behavior of children with ADHD. These include the latency between behavior and its consequences, the frequency of reinforcement, how salient or motivating the consequences are to the child, and the manner in which verbal reprimands are delivered (Pfiffner & Barkley, 1990). The environmental factors listed above affect the behavior of all children, however the performance of children with attention and behavior control problems is much more sensitive to these events.

Children with ADHD are more likely to attend to commands that are given in a straightforward, declarative manner (e.g., "Get back to work") than those delivered as a question or request for a favor ("Will you please get back to work?") (Anastopoulos & Barkley, 1990). Further, instructions are more likely to be followed when they are delivered once potential distractors (e.g., toys, television) have been removed and the student has made eye contact with the instructor. Finally, compliance with instructions is enhanced by continued supervision of the child during the initial minute or so after giving the command (Barkley, 1987).

Teachers often state that children with attention problems are able to complete more accurate work if they interact one-to-one with a supervisor (e.g., teacher, aide, peer). When asked to attend to seatwork or instruction in group settings, however, students with ADHD encounter frequent difficulties (Barkley, 1990). In a similar fashion, when independent work is closely supervised, children with ADHD are able to produce a greater quantity and quality of output relative to minimal supervision situations. Thus, the antecedent conditions that will promote better behavior control and academic performance include provision of effective commands along with supervision of the child's work on a one-to-one basis.

Children with ADHD perform akin to their classmates under conditions of relatively immediate and frequent reinforcement (Pfiffner & Barkley, 1990). This is particularly the case when the type of reinforcement is highly salient and meaningful to the child. However, reinforcement is delayed and infrequent in most general education classrooms. Further, the typical reinforcers (e.g., grades, teacher praise) provided in schools are usually on the low end of the saliency continuum.

Verbal reprimands are commonly used by teachers to reduce students' disruptive behaviors (White, 1975). Usually, reprimands are delivered in a loud voice in front of the class, while the teacher exhibits nonverbal cues (e.g., frown, ruddy complexion) that indicate anger with the perpetrating student(s). However, an impressive body of research indicates that reprimands are more likely to reduce behavior when delivered privately to the child, relatively immediately following a transgression, and with a minimum of discussion and affect (e.g., Pfiffner & O'Leary, 1987). The latter factors are particularly important when attempting to reduce the disruptive behavior of an inattentive student.

The crucial role that environmental events play in determining the severity of ADHD symptoms has led to recent changes in the conceptualization of the deficits underlying this disorder. For example, Barkley (1990) defines ADHD as consisting of

> . . . developmental deficiencies in the regulation and maintenance of behavior by rules or consequences. These deficiencies give rise to problems with inhibiting, initiating, or sustaining responses to tasks or stimuli, and adhering to rules or instructions, particularly in situations where consequences for such behavior are delayed, weak, or nonexistent. (p. 71)

In particular, the central feature of ADHD may be an impairment in delayed responding (i.e., behavioral inhibition) rather than a deficit in attention per se (Barkley, in press). Many important settings (e.g., class-room) and abilities (e.g., internalization of speech) require the capacity to delay responding to the environment. Thus, deficits in delayed respond-ing lead to the exhibition of ADHD symptoms in multiple settings and deleteriously affect the development of rule-governed behavior.

The implications of this conceptualization of ADHD are clear. In-terventions for this disorder must include changes in antecedent and consequent stimuli to increase the probability of delayed responding, thereby leading to attentive, productive behavior (Barkley, in press). Unfortunately, most classrooms are structured to provide delayed, infre-quent reinforcement under the assumption that students become "inter-nally motivated" to conform with rules and complete academic tasks. These are precisely the conditions that are most likely to lead to inatten-tive, disruptive behaviors (i.e., impaired response inhibition) in children with ADHD. Thus, the challenge to education professionals is to incor-porate environmental stimuli that are known to enhance student success into all classrooms where inattentive, disruptive students are being taught (see Chapter 4).

LONG-TERM OUTCOME OF CHILDREN WITH ADHD

Historically, it has been assumed, particularly by members of the lay community, that children with ADHD will outgrow their behavior con-trol difficulties upon reaching adolescence or early adulthood. Unfortu-nately, this assumption has not been borne out by longitudinal investiga-tions of the disorder (see Weiss & Hechtman, 1993). As children with ADHD progress into their teenage years, the *absolute* frequency and in-tensity of their symptoms decline (Barkley, 1990). That is, they improve with respect to attention, impulsivity, and especially overactivity as com-pared to their own behavior during preschool and elementary school years. Of course, their peers are exhibiting similar improvements in be-havior control, which contributes to an ongoing discrepancy between ado-lescents with ADHD and their classmates. In fact, 70–80% of children with ADHD will continue to exhibit significant deficits in inattention and impulsivity *relative* to their agemates during their adolescence (Barkley, Fischer, et al., 1990).

In addition to continued ADHD symptomatology, teenagers with ADHD display adjustment problems in a variety of areas of functioning. First, over 60% of adolescents with this disorder have been found to exhibit frequent defiance and noncompliance with authority figures and rules (Barkley, Fischer, et al., 1990). Further, more than 40% of teens with ADHD display significant antisocial behaviors such as physical fighting, stealing, and vandalism (Barkley, Fischer, et al., 1990; Gittelman et al., 1985). When compared with their non-ADHD classmates, adolescents with this disorder are at higher risk for grade retentions, school suspensions, school drop out, and substance abuse. The risk for drug use seems to be attributable to the presence of significant conduct problems in addition to ADHD-related behaviors (Gittelman et al., 1985). Thus, for a large percentage of children with ADHD, it is unrealistic to assume that they will outgrow experiencing problems in daily living simply as a function of maturation.

Several prospective, longitudinal investigations have followed children with ADHD into young adulthood (i.e., 18–25 years old). In general, these have found that over 50% of children with ADHD will continue to evidence symptoms of the disorder into adulthood, especially with respect to inattention and impulsivity (Barkley, Fischer, et al., 1990; Gittelman et al., 1985; Weiss & Hechtman, 1993). Problems in the domains of academic achievement and antisocial behavior that were noted for adolescents with this disorder continue to be the highest risks for this group in adulthood. Almost a third of these adults will have dropped out of high school, with only 5% completing a university degree program as compared to over 40% of control group subjects (Barkley, Fischer, et al., 1990). Approximately 25% or more of these children will develop chronic patterns of antisocial behavior that persist into adulthood and are associated with other adjustment problems (e.g., substance abuse, interpersonal difficulties, occupational instability). On a positive note, approximately one-third of children followed into adulthood are seen as symptom free and relatively well adjusted (Barkley, 1990). Yet, the risks that this childhood disorder carries for long-term outcome are quite high relative to the non-ADHD population.

Investigators have searched for childhood variables that can reliably predict the adolescent and adult outcomes of individuals with ADHD. Few specific predictors have been identified beyond those variables (e.g., intelligence test scores, socioeconomic status) that are predictive of outcome for the general population. Nevertheless, there are two classes of predictors that are noteworthy for practitioners. First, an early onset of antisocial behaviors, especially lying, stealing, and fighting, is predictive of later antisocial outcome and perhaps continued ADHD (Barkley, 1990). Early onset is defined as prior to the ages of 8–10 years old. Second, being rejected by one's peers in childhood is predictive of continued interpersonal adjustment problems in later years (Barkley, 1990; Parker & Asher, 1987). Therefore, at the present time, the combination of the child's cognitive ability, the child's level of aggressiveness and peer rejection, family stability, and child-rearing practices represents the best predictive scheme (Barkley, 1990).

Given the protracted nature of the disorder and the attendant long-term risks for a large percentage of children with ADHD, there is an emerging consensus that multiple treatment modalities are necessary throughout the school years (Barkley, 1990). A shift in focus from attempting to cure the disorder to endeavoring to help children compensate for their behavior control problems is warranted. Thus, treatment may entail modifications to school and home environments as well as attempts to change within-child variables through the use of psychostimulant medication. The emphasis throughout this book is to promote methods to create and maintain "prosthetic environments" (Barkley, 1990) that will allow children with ADHD to succeed academically, emotionally, and socially. To achieve these outcomes a concerted effort must be made by school professionals, parents, and other health practitioners over the course of multiple school years.

OVERVIEW OF SUBSEQUENT CHAPTERS

The purpose of this book is to provide school-based professionals with a guide to the assessment and treatment of students with ADHD. We attempt to identify evaluation and intervention techniques that have a sound empirical basis and are practical for "real-world" application. Although several texts are available that provide similar information from clinical (e.g., Barkley, 1990) and/or research (e.g., Ross & Ross, 1982) perspectives, few guides for school-based services for this population have been produced.[3]

A model for the school-based screening and assessment of ADHD is presented in Chapter 2. It is proposed that the evaluation of students who might exhibit ADHD-related behaviors involves the use of multiple assessment techniques across home and school settings. The purpose of assessment is not simply to arrive at a diagnosis but, more importantly, to guide the development of an effective treatment plan.

The relationship between ADHD and academic performance difficulties is examined in detail in Chapter 3. Although ADHD is not a learning disability per se, a significant minority of children with attention and behavior control problems display academic skills deficits. It is unclear whether ADHD causes academic skills deficiencies or vice versa; it is more likely that these disorders are simply correlated rather than one causing the other. Suggestions are offered for making special education eligibility decisions for students with ADHD.

3. Recently, Fowler (1992), Parker (1992), and Swanson (1992) have written guides to ADHD for teachers and other education professionals.

One of the most effective interventions for ADHD is the manipulation of antecedent and consequent events in the classroom environment. In Chapter 4, behaviorally based methods that have been found to enhance behavior control, academic performance, and social behavior are described. Such techniques include token reinforcement programming, response cost, and self-management interventions.

The most widely studied and cost-effective treatment for ADHD is the prescription of psychostimulant medication, such as Ritalin (methylphenidate). These medications can lead to improvements in on-task behavior, impulsivity, social behavior, compliance, and academic productivity in as many as 70–80% of children with ADHD. Descriptions of the specific medications, behavioral effects, side effects, and dose–response factors are provided in Chapter 5. Further, methods for school-based practitioners to aid physicians in evaluating medication response are delineated.

Multiple interventions across settings are frequently necessary to ameliorate ADHD symptomatology. Thus, medication and classroom-based behavioral interventions may be supplemented by social skills training, parent training, and/or behavioral family therapy. These treatments are described in Chapter 6. Additional classroom-based interventions (e.g., peer-mediated strategies, computer-assisted instruction) that hold some promise for the treatment of ADHD are discussed as well. Finally, suggestions are provided on how to advise parents regarding treatments for ADHD that have minimal or no empirical support (e.g., EEG biofeedback training).

A team approach to treatment of ADHD is crucial to successful outcome. Communication among professionals and parents is discussed in detail in Chapter 7. All too often, miscommunication between school and home or school professionals and community-based professionals (e.g., physicians) results in inefficient service delivery. Methods to foster appropriate communication among treatment team members are delineated in this chapter as well.

Potential future directions for school-based programming and research on ADHD are discussed in Chapter 8. Greater attention to early childhood intervention, direct instruction in study and organization skills, and vocational counseling/programming is clearly needed for children with this disorder. The suggestions offered in this book are merely a starting point and indicate an obvious need to develop school-based strategies that lead to more successful outcomes for students exhibiting ADHD-related difficulties.

2

Assessment of ADHD
in School Settings

Multiple assessment techniques are typically employed across home and school settings in the comprehensive evaluation of children who may have ADHD (Barkley, 1990; DuPaul, 1992; Schaughency & Rothlind, 1991). Although the diagnostic criteria for this disorder have been developed and published primarily by physicians (i.e., American Psychiatric Association, 1987), school professionals must be knowledgeable regarding appropriate evaluation procedures for a number of reasons. First, problems with attention and behavioral control are two of the most common reasons for referral to school and clinical child psychologists (Barkley, 1988a). Thus, school psychologists must be in a position to conduct an assessment of ADHD themselves or, at least, be cognizant of community-based professionals who could provide an appropriate evaluation. Second, school psychologists have direct access to sources of information and data (e.g., teachers, observations of child behavior in natural settings) crucial to the differential diagnosis of ADHD. Third, ADHD is prevalent among certain populations (e.g., children with learning disabilities) frequently served by school psychologists (Barkley, 1990). Finally, children with ADHD may be eligible for special education services under the "other health impairment" category of the Individuals with Disabilities Education Act (see Hakola, 1992). Thus, school psychologists will be called upon to help determine whether referred children are eligible for such services under this category.

The purpose of this chapter is to describe a school-based assessment approach to the evaluation of ADHD that incorporates those techniques having the greatest empirical support in the literature. Proper use of this evaluation methodology assumes that the professional conducting the assessment will have received appropriate professional training in the use of the DSM-III-R (American Psychiatric Association, 1987) classification system as well as clinical assessment techniques. First, the DSM-III-R criteria for ADHD will be reviewed in the context of a school-based assessment paradigm and its limitations for this purpose will be delineated. Second, a behavioral assessment approach to the evaluation of ADHD will be described incorporating multiple sources of data collected across school and home settings. Finally, the specific steps of the assessment process will be detailed in the context of an educational decision-making paradigm based on a model proposed by Salvia and Ysseldyke (1991). The stages of the ADHD evaluation described include screening, multimethod assessment, interpretation of obtained results to reach a diagnostic decision, development of a treatment plan based on assessment data, and ongoing evaluation of the success of the intervention program.

THE USE OF DIAGNOSTIC CRITERIA IN THE SCHOOL-BASED ASSESSMENT OF ADHD

Current Definition of ADHD

ADHD has been defined and conceptualized in a variety of ways over the past several decades, thus leading to confusion among professionals regarding proper diagnosis and evaluation procedures (Barkley, 1990). More recently, there is an emerging consensus that ADHD is characterized by the display of developmentally inappropriate frequencies of inattention, impulsivity, and overactivity (American Psychiatric Association, 1987). This constellation of behaviors leads to impairment in functioning wherein the child with ADHD demonstrates difficulties with rule-governed behavior and maintaining consistent work performance over the course of time (American Psychiatric Association, 1987; Barkley, 1990). The behaviors or symptoms comprising ADHD according to DSM-III-R criteria (American Psychiatric Association, 1987) are listed in Table 2.1. To be considered symptoms of ADHD, the behaviors must have been initially exhibited in early childhood (i.e., prior to the age of 7 years old) and are chronically displayed across a variety of settings (American Psychiatric Association, 1987). The ADHD diagnosis is usually arrived at by establishing the developmental deviance and pervasiveness of symptoms. At the same time, it is important to rule out alternative causes for the child's inattention, impulsivity, and motor restlessness including poor academic instruction and management practices; gross neurological, sensory, motor, or language impairment; mental retardation; or severe emotional disturbance (Barkley, 1990).

TABLE 2.1. DSM-III-R Diagnostic Criteria for ADHD

A disturbance of at least six months during which at least eight of the followng are present:

(1) Often fidgets with hands or feet or squirms in seat (in adolescents, may be limited to subjective feelings of restlessness).
(2) Has difficulty remaining seated when required to do so.
(3) Is easily distracted by extraneous stimuli.
(4) Has difficulty awaiting turn in games or group situations.
(5) Often blurts out answers to questions before they have been completed.
(6) Has difficulty following through on instructions from others (not due to oppositional behavior or failure of comprehension).
(7) Has difficulty sustaining attention in tasks or play activities.
(8) Often shifts from one uncompleted activity to another.
(9) Has difficulty playing quietly.
(10) Often talks excessively.
(11) Often interrupts or intrudes on others (e.g., butts into other children's games).
(12) Often does not seem to listen to what is being said to him or her.
(13) Often loses things necessary for tasks or activities at school or at home (e.g., toys, pencils, books, assignments).
(14) Often engages in physically dangerous activities without considering possible consequences, not for the purpose of thrill-seeking (e.g., runs into street without looking).

Note. From the *Diagnostic and statistical manual of mental disorders* (3rd ed., rev., pp. 52–53) by the American Psychiatric Association, 1987, Washington, DC: Author. Copyright 1987 by the American Psychiatric Association. Reprinted by permission.

At the time that this chapter was written, the American Psychiatric Association was in the process of preparing the DSM-IV for publication. It appears that several changes will be made to the diagnostic criteria for ADHD (American Psychiatric Association, 1991). First, two separate symptom lists (i.e., inattention and hyperactive–impulsive) will be used rather than a single list. This change was made to conform with the results of several studies that have subjected the ADHD symptom list to principal components analysis resulting in two separate factors (e.g., DuPaul, 1991a). Second, to be diagnosed with ADHD–Combined Type, a child must be reported to exhibit at least six of the nine inattention symptoms and at least four of the six hyperactive–impulsive behaviors (see Table 2.2). Third, ADHD–Predominantly Inattentive Type (previous terms have included Undifferentiated ADD and ADDnoH) will be diagnosed in those children exhibiting at least six of the nine inattention symptoms and *no more than* three of the hyperactive–impulsive behaviors. The latter change has been made to conform with empirical work demonstrating that there are some children who demonstrate significant

TABLE 2.2. Possible DSM-IV Criteria for ADHD

A. At least six of the following symptoms of inattention have persisted for at least six months to a degree that is maladaptive and inconsistent with developmental level:

(1) Often fails to give close attention to details or makes careless mistakes in schoolwork or other activities.
(2) Often has difficulty sustaining attention to tasks or play activities.
(3) Often does not seem to listen to what is being said to him or her.
(4) Often does not follow through on instructions and fails to finish schoolwork, chores, or duties in the workplace (not due to oppositional behavior or failure to understand instructions).
(5) Often has difficulty organizing tasks and activities.
(6) Frequently has difficulty becoming engaged in tasks, such as schoolwork or homework, that require sustained mental effort.
(7) Often loses things necessary for tasks or activities (e.g., school assignments, pencils, books, tools, or toys).
(8) Often is easily distracted by extraneous stimuli.
(9) Often is forgetful in daily activities.

B. At least four of the following symptoms of hyperactivity–impulsivity have persisted for at least six months to a degree that is maladaptive and inconsistent with developmental level:

(1) Often fidgets with hands or feet or squirms in seat.
(2) Often leaves seat in classroom or in other situations in which remaining seated is expected.
(3) Often runs about or climbs excessively in situations where it is inappropriate (in adolescents or adults, may be limited to subjective feelings of restlessness).
(4) Often has difficulty playing or engaging in leisure activities quietly.
(5) Often blurts out answers to questions before the questions have been completed.
(6) Often has difficulty waiting in lines or awaiting turn in games or group situations.

Note. Adapted from the *DSM-IV options book: Work in progress* (pp. 16–17) by the American Psychiatric Association, 1991, Washington, DC: Author. Copyright 1991 by the American Psychiatric Association. Adapted by permission.

difficulties with attention but are not impulsive or hyperactive (e.g., Barkley, DuPaul, & McMurray, 1990). Fourth, symptoms of ADHD must be present in two or more situations (e.g., at school, at home, etc.) to be considered significant. This implicates the need for both parents and teachers to be involved in the diagnostic process. Finally, other aspects of the diagnostic criteria from the DSM-III-R (e.g., age of onset) will probably be retained.

There are several issues relative to the DSM-IV criteria for ADHD that were not resolved at the time that this chapter was written. First, the wording of items on the symptom lists has not been finalized and may be changed in the final version of DSM-IV. Second, it is possible that some children may be diagnosed with ADHD—Predominantly Hyperactive–Impulsive Type on the basis of exhibiting only four of the six hyperactive–impulsive behaviors. It is likely that this subtype will apply primarily to children under the age of 7 years old because determining the deviance of attentional behaviors in young children is very difficult to accomplish. Further, the results of initial field trials of the DSM-IV criteria indicated that any child exhibiting four or more hyperactive–impulsive behaviors was clinically impaired irrespective of whether or not he or she met the criteria for inattentive behaviors (Lahey, 1993). Practitioners should consult the DSM-IV (American Psychiatric Association, in press) for final details about these diagnostic criteria.

Advantages of the DSM Approach

Although the diagnostic criteria for ADHD have been developed in the context of a medical model for child behavior problems, there are several reasons why these criteria are useful in educational settings. First, the symptom list describes a set of problem behaviors that reliably covary in some children. The diagnosis (i.e., constellation of covariant behaviors) can be used to predict the relative success of possible interventions, the risk for concurrent or future behavioral difficulties, and suggest possible controlling variables (Barlow, 1981). Second, the use of DSM criteria structures the assessment in a standardized fashion, thus potentially increasing interprofessional agreement regarding diagnostic status. Further, such criteria guide the selection of competing hypotheses (i.e., other disorders or problems) that could potentially account for apparent symptoms of ADHD. Conclusions based on differential diagnosis may increase the chances of planning a successful intervention program in the classroom. For instance, if a child's attention problems were found to be related to an anxiety disorder rather than to ADHD, initial treatment strategies would be quite different.

An additional factor supporting the use of DSM criteria in the assessment protocol is that these symptom lists may indicate the problem behaviors that should be targeted for intervention. For example, those symptoms that are most frequently endorsed or are deemed most important by parents and teachers might become the initial focus of treatment. Finally, incorporating agreed-upon diagnostic criteria into the evaluation will ultimately enhance communication with other mental health (e.g., clinical child psychologists) or medical professionals regarding the child's psychological status, thus fostering a team approach to treatment.

Limitations of the DSM Approach

Although DSM criteria are important components of the evaluation process, there are several limitations to this approach that must be considered. First, the criteria for ADHD were developed in the context of a medical model, thus implying that the location of the problem is within the child. The characterization of the child as having a disorder could diminish attempts to assess environmental variables that may play a role in causing or maintaining the problem behaviors. A second, related limitation is that the use of a psychiatric classification system promotes a search for pathology that could, under certain conditions, result in over-identification of children with behavior disorders (i.e., identification of "false positives"). These circumstances suggest the need for a multimethod assessment approach wherein objective measures (e.g., behavioral observations) supplement the use of more subjective assessment techniques, such as diagnostic interviews. A third potential drawback to the use of a psychiatric classification system is that the receipt of a diagnostic label may compromise a child's self-esteem as others come to view him or her as "disordered." The possible iatrogenic effects of being diagnosed ADHD have not been empirically investigated to date. A final, important limitation of the DSM is that the psychometric properties (e.g., reliability, validity) of the various diagnostic criteria are not well established (Gresham & Gansle, 1992a).

A number of skills are necessary to ensure the proper use of the DSM classification paradigm (adapted from Barlow, 1981). First, the school psychologist should have enough familiarity with child psychopathology to know which problem behaviors typically covary (e.g., inattention, impulsivity, and overacitivity). Second, a working knowledge of current DSM criteria for most childhood disorders, not just ADHD, is necessary. This requires not only familiarity with symptom lists but also with criteria regarding age of onset and minimum duration of problem behaviors. Finally, the psychologist must have had training in the use of a comprehensive assessment protocol to determine which symptoms are present in a specific student's repertoire.

ADHD is best viewed as a result of a poor "fit" between the biological endowment and characteristics of the child and the environment, such as the structure and prevailing contingencies in the classroom. In this context, diagnostic criteria provide only nomothetic suggestions about problem behavior covariation, controlling variables, and effective interventions (Barlow, 1981). Therefore, DSM criteria are supplemented with multiple assessment methods conducted across settings to determine the specific problem behaviors, controlling variables, and possible intervention strategies that are applicable for an individual student. The diagnosis of ADHD is but one step in the process of designing and evaluating interventions to promote greater classroom success.

OVERVIEW OF ASSESSMENT METHODS

A behavioral assessment approach is typically employed in the evaluation of ADHD wherein multiple methods of data collection are utilized across informants and settings (see Atkins & Pelham, 1991; Barkley, 1990; Guevremont, DuPaul, & Barkley, 1990, 1993; Schaughency & Rothlind, 1991, for reviews). In particular, emphasis is placed upon obtaining reliable information regarding a child's behavior from parents and teachers as well as from first-hand observations of student performance. Therefore, the major components of the evaluation include interviews with the child's parent(s) and teacher(s), questionnaires completed by parents and teachers, and observations of child behavior across multiple settings and under variant task conditions (Barkley, 1988a, 1990). Although many of these same procedures are used when evaluating adolescents, some modifications (e.g., inclusion of self-report data) are necessary to maintain the reliability and validity of the assessment data (see Developmental Considerations section below).

Each of the evaluation techniques will be discussed in detail in the context of the stages of the assessment process in the next section. Interviews with the parent(s), teacher(s), and child are conducted to determine the presence or absence of various DSM symptoms as well as to enumerate possible historical and/or current factors that may be maintaining identified problem behaviors. Behavior rating scales completed by the student's parent(s) and teacher(s) provide data that establish the severity of ADHD-related behaviors relative to a normative sample. To supplement parent and teacher reports, several direct measures of student behavior are used. The child's behavior is observed across settings (e.g., classroom and playground) on several occasions to establish the frequency and/or duration of various target behaviors. Behavioral frequencies are usually compared to those displayed by several of the student's classmates to determine the deviance of the referred child's behavior. Finally, the products of the child's behavior (e.g., academic productivity and accuracy, quality of desk organization) may be collected and/or examined.

Although each of these techniques is limited in some manner, when used in a multimodal assessment package, a system of checks and balances develops such that the drawbacks of any single measure are balanced by data obtained through other means (Barkley, 1988a).

Several assessment techniques typically employed by school psychologists have limited utility in the diagnostic evaluation of ADHD. The results of cognitive, neuropsychological, and educational tests typically are not helpful in determining whether a child has ADHD or not. To date, no individually administered test or group of tests has demonstrated an acceptable degree of ecological validity to be helpful in the diagnostic process (Barkley, 1991a). For example, the test most frequently employed by school psychologists (i.e., Wechsler Intelligence Scale for Children–Revised [WISC-R] and now the WISC-III) has not been found to reliably discriminate ADHD from normal children or students with learning disabilities (Barkley, DuPaul, & McMurray, 1990). More importantly, scores on the Freedom from Distractiblity factor (i.e., Arithmetic, Digit Span, and Coding subtests) of the WISC-R are not reliable diagnostic indicators of ADHD (Cohen, Becker, & Campbell, 1990). Poor performance on this factor may be due to a variety of possible causes, including performance anxiety (Cohen et al., 1990; Wielkiewicz, 1990). Further, children with ADHD often display appropriate levels of attention and behavioral control under task conditions that are highly structured and involve one-to-one interaction with a novel adult as is found in most testing situations (Barkley, 1990). Thus, although individually administered tests may be helpful in determining the child's intellectual and educational status, they are not necessary components of the diagnostic evaluation of ADHD.

Standardized measures of sustained attention and impulse control have been incorporated routinely into the diagnostic evaluation of ADHD (Barkley, 1990). Purportedly, they provide objective data that are less influenced by factors (e.g., parental psychopathology) that may bias parent and teacher report (Barkley, 1987; Gordon, 1986). Two of the more popular standardized measures are the Continuous Performance Test (CPT) (Rosvold, Mirsky, Sarason, Bransome, & Beck, 1956) and the Matching Familiar Figures Test (MFFT) (Kagan, 1966).

Although scores on the CPT and MFFT appear to discriminate between children with ADHD and their normal counterparts at a group level, the utility of these measures in assessing individual children is limited by several factors. First, several investigations have failed to obtain significant correlations between criterion measures (e.g., teacher ratings) and scores on various CPTs (Halperin, Sharma, Greenblatt, & Schwartz, 1991; Lovejoy & Rasmussen, 1990) or the MFFT (Barkley, 1991a; Milich & Kramer, 1984). Second, when the effects of age, sex, and receptive vocabulary skills are partialled out, scores on these measures have failed to discriminate among children with ADHD, Conduct Disorder, Anxiety Disorder, and their normal peers (Werry, Elkind, & Reeves, 1987). Even when significant correlations are obtained between MFFT and CPT scores and criterion measures, these typically are of low magnitude (i.e., absolute values of .21–.50) suggesting that the results of clinic-based tasks account for minimal variance of criterion indices (Barkley, 1991). Finally, CPT and MFFT scores, either alone or in combination, have been found to result in classification decisions that are frequently discrepant with a diagnosis of ADHD based on parent interview and behavior rating scale data (DuPaul, Anastopoulos, Shelton, Guevremont, & Metevia, 1992). Thus, the use of such instruments in the evaluation of ADHD is limited by rather suspect ecological validity (Barkley, 1991a).

Measures that are typically used by school psychologists to assess a student's emotional functioning are not useful in evaluating whether a child has ADHD. Projective techniques, such as the Thematic Apperception Test (Murray, 1943) or Kinetic Family Drawing (see Hammer, 1975), are based on a theoretical assumption that problem behaviors are caused by underlying emotional difficulties. This assumption has no empirical support in relation to the behaviors comprising ADHD. Further, projective tests have been criticized for their questionable levels of reliability and validity (Prout & Ferber, 1988).

Self-report questionnaires completed by the child have become increasingly popular in recent years (LaGreca, 1990). Although a number of psychometrically sound self-report checklists are available (e.g., Youth Self-Report; Achenbach, 1991), at least two factors limit their use in the assessment of ADHD. First, children with disruptive behavior disorders are typically poor reporters of their own behavior (Landau, Milich, & Widiger, 1991). The reliability and validity of self-report data provided by children with ADHD have not been established. Second, many of the self-report measures available do not have separate factors or subscales specific to ADHD, thus limiting their diagnostic utility. Nevertheless, self-report data are important to collect when evaluating adolescents who may be diagnosed with ADHD so as to facilitate assessment of covert areas of functioning (e.g., depressive symptoms) and engender cooperation with the evaluation and treatment process (see Developmental Considerations section below).

STAGES OF ASSESSMENT OF ADHD

Following a teacher referral for attention and behavior control difficulties, the school-based evaluation of ADHD is conducted in five stages (DuPaul, 1992; see Figure 2.1). These stages are based on the educational

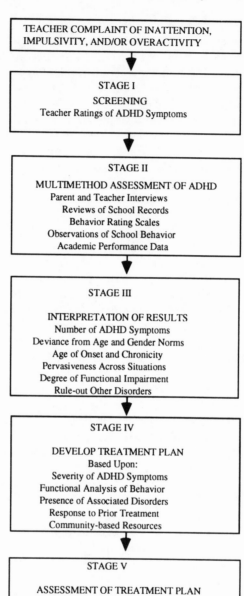

FIGURE 2.1. Five stages of the school-based assessment of ADHD.

decision-making model proposed by Salvia and Ysseldyke (1991). First, teacher ratings are obtained and a brief interview is conducted with the teacher to screen for the severity and frequency of possible ADHD symptoms. Next, if the findings of this screening are significant, then multiple assessment methods are used across sources and settings to document the child's functioning across a number of areas. Third, the evaluation results are interpreted such that classification and diagnostic decisions can be made. Fourth, a treatment plan is developed based on the obtained assessment data. Finally, the child's school behavior and academic performance are assessed on an ongoing basis to determine the success of and the need for changes in the intervention program.

Each of the stages of assessment are discussed in detail below. Initially, for each phase of the assessment, a series of questions to be addressed will be identified, based in part on guidelines for behavioral assessment provided by Barrios and Hartmann (1986). Next, the process of assessment during each stage of the evaluation will be delineated. Finally, the manner in which specific techniques are used to answer the assessment questions at each phase of the evaluation will be reviewed.

Stage I: Screening

Questions to Be Addressed

The screening process is designed to answer the following questions:

1. Does this student have a problem related to possible ADHD?
2. Is further assessment of ADHD required?

Screening Process

Screening for possible ADHD should be conducted whenever a teacher seeks assistance because of a student's difficulties paying attention during instruction, inconsistent completion of independent tasks, inability to remain seated at appropriate times, or display of impulsive, disruptive behavior. A brief interview with the teacher is conducted to specify the behavioral concerns and to identify environmental factors that may be eliciting and/or maintaining the child's problem behaviors. Teacher ratings of the frequency of ADHD symptoms are then obtained.

Screening Techniques

The initial interview with the teacher should address the frequency, intensity, and/or duration of specific problem behaviors. The role of various environmental factors (e.g., task parameters, method of instruction, behaviors of classmates) also should be explored to establish antecedent and consequent events for the problem behaviors. In an effort to establish whether the problem behaviors may be related to ADHD, the presence or absence of the 14 DSM-III-R symptoms of this disorder should be established as well as the chronicity of the apparent ADHD-related behaviors.[1] If 8 or more of these symptoms are reported to occur on a frequent basis, further assessment of ADHD is warranted. Even if fewer than 8 symptoms are reported, further assessment of ADHD may be warranted, especially for students at the secondary level.

The most efficient screening method is for the teacher to complete the ADHD Rating Scale (DuPaul, 1991a) regarding the child's typical behavior over the course of the school year. The teacher indicates on a 4-point Likert scale the frequency of the 14 behavioral symptoms of ADHD directly adapted from the DSM-III-R (American Psychiatric Association, 1987). As with the teacher interview, if 8 or more of these items are rated as occurring "pretty much" or "very much" of the time, then further assessment of possible ADHD is warranted. If a lesser number of items is endorsed in this frequency range, this does not rule out further assessment of ADHD but does necessitate strong consideration of other explanations (e.g., academic skills deficits) for teacher concerns.

Stage II: Multimethod Assessment of ADHD

Questions to Be Addressed

Data from multiple assessment techniques are gathered to answer the following questions:

1. What is the extent and nature of the ADHD-related problems?
2. What factors (e.g., organismic, environmental) maintain these problems?
3. What is the frequency, duration, and/or intensity of the problem behaviors?
4. In what settings do the ADHD-related behaviors occur?

---

1. Screening criteria will be different for the DSM-IV. For the latter, the presence or absence of each of the inattention and hyperactive–impulsive behaviors should be ascertained from the teacher. If the child is reported to exhibit a number of symptoms that is near the cutoff of each of the symptom lists (i.e., six inattention symptoms and/or four hyperactive–impulsive symptoms), then further assessment would be necessary.

Assessment Process

If the initial screening results are indicative of possible ADHD, then a more comprehensive evaluation of the child's overall functioning is warranted. Initially, the child's parent(s) and teacher(s) are interviewed to specify problem behaviors, identify possible antecedent and consequent events for these behaviors, and to explore the causal role of various historical variables. A review of archival data (e.g., school records) is completed to provide additional historical data. Thus, the initial phase of the evaluation process is designed to identify specific problem behaviors, environmental factors, and historical variables which require further assessment.

The student's parent(s) and teacher(s) complete several questionnaires to provide more specific data regarding the frequency and/or severity of problem behaviors. These ratings help to establish the developmental deviance of ADHD-related behaviors relative to normative data as well as to identify whether such behaviors are evident across settings and caregivers. The specific questionnaires utilized vary as a function of the target behaviors to be assessed and the age of the child, as discussed below.

The final phase of the formal evaluation of ADHD is comprised of direct observations of child behavior across settings and the collection of academic performance data. These techniques can provide crucial information regarding the frequency and duration of target behaviors, whether specific antecedent and consequent events elicit or maintain the problem behaviors, and the degree to which the ADHD-related behaviors compromise the child's social and academic functioning. Further, data derived from these procedures will be most helpful in the identification and design of intervention strategies.

Assessment Techniques

Teacher Interview The teacher should be asked to describe the student's difficulties in specific, behavioral terms in the context of a problem identification interview as described by Bergan and Kratochwill (1990). Further, the current DSM diagnostic criteria for a variety of child behavior disorders should be reviewed with the teacher. In addition to ADHD, the presence or absence of behaviors associated with ODD, Conduct Disorder, Overanxious Disorder, Separation Anxiety Disorder, and Depression should be ascertained. It is important to review this set of problems for two reasons. First, apparent symptoms of ADHD actually may be manifestations of another disorder. For instance, a child who is depressed may exhibit problems with concentration. Thus, the diagnosis of ADHD is arrived at by ruling out competing hypotheses (i.e., disorders) for the problem behaviors. A second reason to review these diagnostic criteria is that many children with ADHD also exhibit symptoms of other disorders (Abikoff & Klein, 1992). The most frequent associated diagnosis is ODD; approximately 40–65% of children with ADHD exhibit symptoms of this disorder (e.g., Barkley, DuPaul, & McMurray, 1990). Further, the combination of ADHD and other behavior or emotional disorders implicates the need for multiple interventions, as discussed below.

While ascertaining the presence or absence of each of the behavioral symptoms, the teacher also is asked to provide specific examples of those behaviors indicated to be present as well as an estimate of their frequency. The typical antecedent (e.g., type of instruction) and consequent (e.g., teacher response to child misbehavior) events surrounding each problematic behavior should also be identified as these may be serving to maintain and/or exacerbate behavioral difficulties. Current management techniques and their relative degree of success then should be discussed.

It is imperative that information regarding the quality of the child's academic performance and social status be gathered. Some children with ADHD may exhibit significant academic skills deficits beyond task completion difficulties. Of course, an academic skills assessment (e.g., curriculum-based measurement) would be warranted in such situations. Teacher observations regarding the child's social interaction style and acceptance by peers are helpful in determining whether further assessment (e.g., sociometrics) in this area is necessary. Many children with ADHD will exhibit a controlling, aggressive interaction pattern with others resulting in low acceptance or overt rejection by their classmates (Pelham & Bender, 1982). Teacher interview data are used to identify possible social skills deficits that could be targeted for further assessment and intervention as well as delineating those settings and/or times of the school day where social relationship difficulties are most likely to be exhibited.

Review of School Record   The student's school record should be reviewed to obtain data that may be helpful in pinpointing the onset and course of classroom ADHD-related difficulties. For instance, teachers often grade the quality of a child's work habits and conduct on report cards. Not surprisingly, most students with ADHD are found to obtain below average rankings in these areas across grade levels. These below-average grades are often supplemented with teacher comments regarding poor task completion, high degrees of restlessness, or frequent talking to peers without permission. The specific grade level where such grades and comments first appear is important to note so that it can be cross-referenced with the age of onset as reported by the parents.

Parent Interview   A brief (i.e., 30–45 minutes) interview with the student's parent(s) should be conducted either in person or by telephone. Although discussion of the child's past and current functioning across a variety of areas (e.g., medical history) is possible, the most important lines of questioning are as follows.

First, the presence and frequency of behavior control difficulties at home should be identified. This is best accomplished by reviewing the current DSM diagnostic criteria for ADHD and related disruptive behavior disorders (ODD, Conduct Disorder) with the parent. In addition, the presence of symptoms associated with internalizing disorders (e.g., anxiety disorders) that could be causally related to a child's inattention and overactivity should be identified. As with the teacher interview, a review of DSM criteria will aid in ruling out the presence of other disorders that may be causally related to the exhibition of ADHD symptoms.

A second area of discussion for the parent interview is information regarding the child's early childhood development. It is important to pinpoint the onset of the ADHD-related behaviors as well as their chronicity over time. The early childhood behavior of children with ADHD typically is characterized as highly active and difficult to control (Campbell, 1990). In some cases, however, the child's behavior is not seen as problematic until school entry, when independent task demands increase. This is particularly the case when the parents have little previous experience with children (e.g., only or oldest child) and/or have unrealistic expectations regarding child behavior.

A third area of investigation is the child's family history of behavioral, emotional, and learning problems. Although this may be uncomfortable for a parent to discuss, it is important for two reasons. First, research indicates that ADHD may have a genetic or familial component (Lahey et al., 1988) and thus tends to run in families. The presence of ADHD in the family increases the odds that the identified child has ADHD. Second, in 27–32% of cases, the child's mother may be depressed or have a history of depression (Biederman et al., 1987). There also is a greater incidence of paternal antisocial behavior in the families of children with ADHD (Lahey et al., 1988). The presence of such difficulties in the family has direct implications for treatment because home-based interventions for ADHD are more likely to be successful when implemented following amelioration of parental psychopathology and problems related to family functioning. For example, depressed mothers of children with behavior disorders evidence a higher failure rate in response to training in behavior modification strategies (McMahon & Wells, 1989).

Parent Ratings   One or both parents should complete several questionnaires to aid in determining the developmental deviance of the child's ADHD-related behaviors as well as to establish the pervasiveness of problem behaviors across settings. There are a variety of general behavior rating scales which have adequate normative data and sound psychometric properties (see Barkley, 1988b, for a review). Chief among these questionnaires are the Child Behavior Checklist (CBCL) (Achenbach, 1991) and Conners Parent Rating Scale—Revised (CPRS-R) (Goyette, Conners, & Ulrich, 1978). Under most circumstances, the CBCL is preferred for two reasons. First, it contains a larger item pool and, hence, wider coverage of both internalizing and externalizing disturbances. This large item pool facilitates differential diagnosis as competing hypotheses (e.g., presence of other disorders) for the exhibition of ADHD symptoms can be explored. Second, because the item pool and factor structure of the parent and teacher versions of the CBCL are quite similar, cross-informant agreement can be specifically examined. Because parent and teacher agreement is important in making a diagnosis of ADHD, such information is invaluable.

In addition to the CBCL, the parent(s) should complete two questionnaires containing items more specific to ADHD-related behaviors: the ADHD Rating Scale and the Home Situations Questionnaire (HSQ) (Barkley, 1990). The ADHD Rating Scale provides information regarding the frequency of occurrence of each of the 14 symptoms of this disorder in the home setting. The number of items rated as occurring "pretty much" or "very much" of the time is tallied. The total score on this scale can be compared to normative data to determine the developmental deviance of ADHD symptomatology (DuPaul, 1991a). Parental responses on the HSQ allow determination of the number of home settings where behavior problems are exhibited by the child. In addition, the severity of behavior problems within each situation is rated on a 1 (mild) to 9 (severe) Likert scale. The revised version of the HSQ (HSQ-R) (DuPaul & Barkley, 1992a) provides more specific information regarding the pervasiveness of attention problems across home situations. Thus, the HSQ will be helpful in determining the situational specificity and severity of conduct problems, whereas the HSQ-R provides data regarding these same variables for attentional difficulties.

Many children with ADHD symptoms exhibit significant difficulties with homework completion and study skills. When such problems are reported by the parents or teacher, then additional assessment is necessary to determine which homework-related behaviors need to be addressed. Initially, the parent is asked to complete the Homework Problem Checklist (Anesko, Shoiock, Ramirez, & Levine, 1987), which provides data regarding the frequency of various problems (e.g., denies having homework assignment, fails to complete homework) related to homework. Parent responses on this questionnaire can lead to further inquiry as to the specific problems that may be present at each step of the homework completion process.

Teacher Ratings   As is the case with parent questionnaires, there are a plethora of well-standardized teacher rating scales available. The teacher(s) should complete a comprehensive questionnaire such as the Teacher Report Form of the Child Behavior Checklist (TRF-CBCL) (Achenbach, 1991) in combination with several briefer rating scales that are more specific to ADHD-related behaviors. The Conners Teacher Rating Scale–Revised (Goyette et al., 1978) is preferred for children under the age of 5 as the TRF-CBCL does not have normative data for the preschool age group. As mentioned above, the advantages of the TRF-CBCL over other general behavior questionnaires are its breadth of item coverage and the opportunity to examine cross-informant consistency between parent and teacher report of problem behaviors.

In conjunction with a general behavior questionnaire, the School Situations Questionnaire (SSQ) (Barkley, 1981) and/or the School Situations Questionnaire–Revised (SSQ-R) (DuPaul & Barkley, 1992a) should be completed. The SSQ and SSQ-R provide information regarding the pervasiveness across situations and severity level of conduct and attention problems, respectively. If the teacher has not already completed the ADHD Rating Scale during the screening process, it should be filled out at this stage of the assessment process.

In many cases, students referred for an ADHD evaluation also are reported to evidence social relationship and academic performance difficulties. Thus, teacher perceptions of student functioning in these areas may need to be assessed as well. There are a number of psychometrically sound social skills questionnaires that are available, including the Social Skills Rating System (Gresham & Elliott, 1990) and the Walker–McConnell Scale of Social Competence and School Adjustment (Walker & McConnell, 1988). Where indicated, teacher ratings of social competence should be supplemented by peer ratings and/or sociometric data. Teacher ratings of academic achievement difficulties can be obtained through use of the Academic Performance Rating Scale (DuPaul, Rapport, & Perriello, 1991). Ratings on the latter questionnaire may indicate the need for further assessment of academic skills deficits.

Direct Observations of Behavior   Interview and rating scale data are subject to a number of limitations including the inherent biases of those answering the interview questions and completing the questionnaires (Barkley, 1988b). Thus, these data should be supplemented with assessment of child behavior that is potentially less subject to such biases. Direct observation of student behavior on several occasions and across settings and situations is one of the best methods to achieve this goal. In many cases, direct observations will provide the most fruitful data when conducted during independent seatwork situations. Typically, observation sessions are 10–30 minutes in length and are repeated across several days to establish a consistent estimate of behavioral frequency. Further, observations are conducted on a repeated basis in several situations (e.g., math work time, language arts instruction) in the classroom, as well as in other school settings such as the playground and cafeteria. The latter provides the opportunity to observe interactions between the referred child and his or her peers.

A number of behavior observation coding systems have been developed to determine the frequencies of various ADHD-related behaviors during classroom task periods (see Platzman et al., 1992, for a review). These include the ADHD Behavior Coding System (Barkley, 1990; Barkley, Fischer, Newby, & Breen, 1988), the Hyperactive Behavior Code (Jacob, O'Leary, & Rosenblad, 1978), and the Classroom Observation Code (Abikoff et al., 1977). Each of these systems requires observers to classify behaviors into a variety of categories (e.g., off-task behavior, fidgeting) using interval recording procedures. For example, the coding criteria and a sample observation sheet for the Revised ADHD Behavior Coding System are provided in Appendix 2.1 and Figure 2.2, respectively.

Recently, Platzman and colleagues (1992) reviewed the various observational methods that have been developed to aid in the assessment of ADHD. Several of their findings are noteworthy for practitioners. First, they found that observations conducted in the classroom provided data that were better at discriminating children with ADHD from controls than were observations conducted in clinic analog settings. This further attests to the need for school-based practitioners to be involved in ADHD evaluations. Second, three categories of behavior were found to consistently discriminate between ADHD and non-ADHD samples. Thus, observation systems that include measures of off-task behavior, excessive gross motor activity, and negative vocalizations (e.g., refusal to obey commands) are most likely to provide sensitive diagnostic data. Finally, they found very few studies that included female participants. Because a smaller percentage of girls with ADHD are defiant and aggressive (Barkley, 1990), certain observation categories (e.g., negative vocalization) may be less discriminatory between girls with and without ADHD. As a result, practitioners may need to emphasize differences in off-task behavior when evaluating girls suspected of having this disorder.

Because normative data based on large, representative samples are lacking for most of these observation systems, the behavior of the referred

RESTRICTED ACADEMIC SITUATION CODING SHEET

Child's Name _____   Date _____

Observer _____

Interval #:	1	2	3	4	5	6	7	8	9	10	11	12	13	14	15
Off-task															
Fidgeting															
T-R Vocal.															
T-I Vocal.															
Out-of-seat															
Interval #:	16	17	18	19	20	21	22	23	24	25	26	27	28	29	30
Off-task															
Fidgeting															
T-R Vocal.															
T-I Vocal.															
Out-of-Seat															

COMMENTS:

BEHAVIOR	TOTAL
Off-Task	/30
Fidgeting	/30
T-R Vocal.	/30
T-I Vocal.	/30
Out-of-Seat	/30
TOTAL	/150

FIGURE 2.2. Sample recording form for the Revised ADHD Behavior Coding System. See Appendix 2.1 for code definitions. Adapted from *Attention-Deficit Hyperactivity Disorder: A clinical workbook* (p. 75) by R. A. Barkley, 1991, New York: Guilford Press. Copyright 1991 by The Guilford Press. Adapted by permission.

student should be compared to one or two classmates who have been identified as "typical" or "average" by the classroom teacher. In this fashion, each child would be evaluated relative to a classroom-based standard of behavior. If possible, another person (e.g., classroom aide) should simultaneously conduct these observations every so often to ensure adequate levels of interobserver reliability. Regardless of the coding system used, the two goals of this phase of the assessment process are to (1) establish the frequency of inattentive, restless behaviors relative to classmates and (2) obtain stable estimates of these frequencies by conducting observations on several occasions in the same classroom setting.

In addition to coding the child's behavior during task situations, it is sometimes helpful to collect supplemental observation data. For instance, teacher behaviors (e.g., prompts, reprimands, feedback) could be coded as possible antecendent and/or consequent events for child behavior (Whalen, Henker, & Dotemoto, 1981). The specific teacher or classmate behaviors to be observed might be identified in the course of the teacher interview discussed above. An example of a coding system (adapted from Saudargas & Creed, 1980) that incorporates observation of teacher behavior is included in Appendix 2.2. Usually, teacher behaviors such as positive attention and/or negative reprimands are coded on an interval recording basis simultaneous with observations of child behavior as displayed in the sample coding form in Appendix 2.2. Such recording makes it possible to determine the percentage of observation intervals where specific teacher and child behaviors have occurred contiguously. For example, one might find that teacher positive attention occurred during a very low percentage of intervals where the child was on-task, while negative reprimands from the teacher were quite frequent when the child was off-task. In such cases, it might be hypothesized that teacher attention is reinforcing off-task rather than on-task behavior. Suggestions for modifications in teacher behavior (e.g., increasing positive attention to on-task behavior) can be generated readily from observations of this type.

If social relationship difficulties are identified, then observations of the child's interpersonal behaviors should be conducted in the identified settings. An example of an observation system that can be used to determine the frequency of specific social behaviors (e.g., aggressive, negative, and positive) in settings such as the playground and cafeteria is provided in Appendix 2.3. Another observation system that has been found useful is the Code for Observing Social Activity (COSA) (Sprafkin, Grayson, Gadow, Nolan, & Paolicelli, 1986). Typically, children with ADHD exhibit higher than average frequencies of aggressive and negative behaviors (Guevremont, 1990). In most cases, their rates of positive social behavior are not substantially different from their normal counterparts (Pelham & Bender, 1982). Results of these observations not only document the type and severity of social relationship difficulties, but also help to target specific behaviors for intervention.

Assessment of Academic Performance   Although children with ADHD usually perform similar to their peers on traditional, individually administered achievement tests (Barkley, DuPaul, & McMurray, 1990), their day-to-day performance on classroom tasks and homework is often inconsistent and inferior relative to their classmates (Barkley, 1990). It is helpful to obtain relatively direct measurements of academic behavior prior to intervention, as changes in scholastic status can be considered one of the more socially valid outcomes of treatment. Some of the more important academic behaviors to assess include the completion and accuracy of independent classwork, completion and accuracy of homework, and organizational skills.

Completion and accuracy rates on assigned work should be calculated. First, the amount of written work (i.e., percentage of items) completed relative to the amount of work assigned (Rapport, 1987a) or relative to typical classmates during observation sessions should be calculated. Second, the percentage of items completed correctly (i.e., academic efficiency score; Rapport et al., 1987) are calculated to determine task accuracy. It is expected that students with ADHD will complete significantly less work or complete tasks in a less accurate fashion due to problems with inattention and/or carelessness. Such data are relatively straightforward to collect in conjunction with the observations of classroom behavior discussed above. Similar data regarding homework completion and accuracy could be collected by the teacher over a short time interval (e.g., 2–3 weeks) contemporaneous with the ADHD evaluation. Parents also may be asked to record the frequency of completion of various steps in the homework process over a similar time period. Further, items indicated to be problematic on the Homework Problem Checklist can be used to generate possible targets for intervention.

The organization of the child's desk (i.e., neatness and preparedness) can be examined directly on a regular basis over a short time interval (e.g., 2–3 weeks) and compared to classmates' desks (Atkins, Pelham, & Licht, 1985). A frequent complaint of teachers is that children with ADHD have unorganized, messy desks with a resultant loss of task and text materials.

Stage III: Interpretation of Results (Diagnosis/Classification)

Questions to Be Addressed

The results of multimethod assessment data are used to determine the diagnostic status of the referred child by reviewing the following questions:

1. Does the child exhibit a significant number of behavioral symptoms of ADHD according to parent and teacher report?
2. Does the child exhibit ADHD symptoms at a frequency that is significantly greater than that demonstrated by children of the same gender and chronological age?
3. At what age did the child begin demonstrating significant ADHD-related behaviors and are these behaviors chronic and evident across many situations?
4. Is the child's functioning at school, at home, and with peers significantly impaired?
5. Are there other possible problems (e.g., academic skills deficits) or factors (e.g., teacher intolerance for active behavior) that could account for the reported display of ADHD symptoms?

Interpretation Process and Procedures

The data obtained with the previously described techniques can be used to address the above questions. Although each of the assessment techniques has limitations, the advantage of using a multimethod approach is that each technique's strengths and weaknesses will be balanced out as part of the larger evaluation package. The overriding goals are to derive consistent information regarding the frequency and severity of ADHD-related behaviors across caregivers and settings, as well as to determine possible causes for these difficulties. To the exent that these goals are achieved, relative confidence can be placed in conclusions drawn as a result of the assessment. The interpretation of evaluation data is discussed relative to each of the major assessment questions.

Number of ADHD Symptoms? This is determined based on parent and teacher interview data in conjunction with ADHD Rating Scale results. If eight or more symptoms are reported by each caregiver (particularly during the interviews), this is considered diagnostically significant for ADHD according to DSM-III-R guidelines (American Psychiatric Association, 1987). If the five or six items pertaining to inattention are endorsed in the absence of significant impulsivity and hyperactivity, then the possibility of the child having ADDnoH or Undifferentiated ADD (American Psychiatric Association, 1987) should be considered.

Using the newly developed DSM-IV criteria, a child's behavior must be evaluated in the context of both inattentive and hyperactive–impulsive behaviors. Specifically, to receive a diagnosis of ADHD, the child should be reported to evidence at least six of the nine inattentive symptoms and four of the six hyperactive–impulsive behaviors (see Table 2.2). For a diagnosis of ADHD–Predominantly Inattentive Type, six of the nine inattentive symptoms must be reported combined with a *maximum* of three hyperactive–impulsive behaviors. It should be noted that these cut-off scores may be different in the final version of DSM-IV, which is scheduled to be published soon.

Frequency of ADHD-Related Behaviors?   The parent and teacher questionnaires discussed above all contain at least one factor related to ADHD (e.g., labeled "Hyperactivity," "Attention Problems," "Overactive–Restless"). If a child's score on this factor is greater than 2 standard deviations above the mean for his or her gender and chronological age, this is considered significant for ADHD (Barkley, 1988a). Scores on these same factors that are between 1.5 and 2 standard deviations above the mean are considered to be in the borderline significant (i.e., mild) range for ADHD. Thus, children receiving scores in the upper 2–7% of ADHD symptoms for their age and gender may be identified as having ADHD (depending upon other assessment findings).

Behavioral observation data are used to determine the frequencies of ADHD-related behaviors displayed by the referred student as compared to his or her classmates. If a large enough sample of observations is collected, the difference in behavioral frequencies between the referred and nonreferred students could be tested statistically using a *t*-test, for example. The child with ADHD should be exhibiting inattentive and restless behaviors at a significantly higher frequency than classmates. If this is not observed, other lines of investigation (e.g., inadequate methods of behavior management) may need to be pursued.

Age of Onset and Chronicity of Problem Behaviors?   Parent report of the onset of ADHD symptoms is obtained during the interview. Typically, the age of onset is reported to be when the child begins formal schooling (i.e., kindergarten or first grade) or earlier. The consistency of ADHD-related behaviors across grades or time can be confirmed through inspection of the child's previous report cards in the school record. The onset of ADHD symptoms should be reported to be prior to the age of 7 (American Psychiatric Association, 1987) and must be occurring on a daily basis for at least 1 year (Barkley, 1990). Longitudinal investigations consistently have found that ADHD symptoms typically begin early in life and, in many cases, are present throughout the lifespan (Barkley, Fischer, et al., 1990; Gittelman et al., 1985; Weiss & Hechtman, 1993).

Under some circumstances, the child's ADHD symptoms will not be problematic until the fourth or fifth grade. This may be the case when a child is bright enough to compensate for his or her difficulties during the earlier grades and encounters more problems when demands for independent task completion increase. Alternatively, students with academic problems may develop ADHD-like symptoms as a function of continued frustrations in educational settings. The latter would not be diagnosed and treated as a child with true ADHD as the academic skills deficit or learning disability would be the primary focus of intervention (Barkley, 1990).

Problem Behaviors Occurring across Situations?   Generally, if both the parent(s) and teacher(s) are reporting significant display of ADHD-related behaviors across home and school environments, then this criterion is met. The pervasiveness of inattentive behaviors and/or conduct problems across situations within home and school environments can be determined using the original and revised versions of the HSQ and SSQ. If attention or conduct problems are reported in 50% or more of identified situations, this is considered significant (Barkley, 1981). In addition, if scores on these rating scales are 1.5 to 2 standard deviations above the mean using normative data (see Barkley, 1990), a more stringent criterion is reached.

To the degree that significant ADHD-related behaviors are reported to occur across home and school settings, relative confidence may be placed in the conclusion that within-child variables (i.e., presence of ADHD) account for the behavioral control difficulties to a large degree. When inconsistencies between parent and teacher report are obtained, confidence in the diagnosis of ADHD is reduced. In general, teacher ratings are given more credence because the school is the more problematic setting for children with ADHD and teachers have greater exposure to children within a specific age range.

Functional Impairment?   The degree to which the child's academic, social, and emotional functioning is impaired is determined through examination of all of the measures discussed above. The most frequently encountered signs of impairment associated with ADHD are academic achievement below expectations for the child and poor acceptance by peers (Barkley, 1990). Thus, the child would be expected to produce less complete and accurate work than classmates based on observational data and teacher ratings. Further, ratings for the child on scales of social competence and peer relationships would be below average for his or her age and gender. Observational data may confirm the latter, as the child may exhibit high rates of aggressive behavior on the playground or may be ignored by classmates during free-play periods.

Other Factors Accounting for ADHD-Like Behavior?   The ADHD diagnosis is usually arrived at by establishing the developmental deviance and pervasiveness of symptoms by addressing the previous questions. At the same time, it is crucial to consider alternative causes for the child's inattention, impulsivity, and motor restlessness. One possibility is that these behaviors are secondary to the frustrations encountered due to a child's academic difficulties, as discussed above. If, for instance, the child begins to exhibit ADHD symptoms later in childhood after several years of learning difficulties or only exhibits problem behaviors during academic instruction in their weaker subjects, then this possibility must be entertained strongly. Alternatively, if ADHD symptoms began early in life and are pervasive across settings, then a more plausible conclusion is that the child has both ADHD and academic skills deficiencies (see Chapter 3 for additional details).

A second possibility is that the child is encountering emotional difficulties that have led to inattentive, restless behaviors. If this were the case, then interview and questionnaire data would indicate significant symptoms of an alternative disorder (e.g., Anxiety Disorder, Conduct Disorder) in addition to or in lieu of ADHD symptoms. Further, the symptoms of emotional disturbance would predate the onset of ADHD-related behaviors. The latter would be of relatively recent onset and would probably not be exhibited on a chronic and cross-situational basis.

Poor or inconsistent academic instruction and/or behavior management practices are other possible causes of apparent ADHD symptoms. This hypothesis should be explored whenever assessment data are inconsistent across sources and settings, as when parents and teachers disagree about the severity and frequency of ADHD symptoms. This is particularly true when there are discrepancies among several teachers regarding the presence or absence of ADHD symptoms. If the latter are reported by a single teacher in the absence of a developmental history of ADHD-related difficulties and other data supporting the diagnosis of ADHD, then closer inspection of instructional and management variables is necessary. Rather than classifying the problem behaviors as resulting from within-child variables (i.e., ADHD), the faulty teaching practices would warrant modification.

Once a diagnostic decision is reached, the findings and resultant treatment recommendations must be communicated to the student's teachers and parents, as well as any community-based professionals (e.g., pediatrician) who may be working with the child. Typically, a written report is generated and results and recommendations are orally reviewed with pertinent school personnel and parents. Issues and procedures related to communication of assessment results are discussed in greater detail in Chapter 7.

Stage IV: Designing the Treatment Plan

Questions to Be Addressed

The following questions should be addressed when designing an intervention program for students with ADHD:

1. What are the behavioral objectives?
2. What are the student's strengths and weaknesses (e.g., motivation and skills)?
3. What are the optimum intervention strategies?
4. What additional resources are available to address the child's ADHD-related problems?

Intervention Planning Process and Procedures

The assessment process does not conclude with a diagnosis, as the latter is only one part of a process to determine which intervention strategies are most likely to be successful. Thus, the assessment data are used to generate an appropriate treatment plan. The intervention strategies that have the greatest research support in the treatment of ADHD are the prescription of psychostimulant medication (e.g., Ritalin) and behavior modification procedures (Barkley, 1990; Pelham & Murphy, 1986). The specifics of these interventions are reviewed in greater detail in Chapters 4, 5, and 6. In addition, further information regarding these interventions can be obtained through several recent reviews (e.g., Abramowitz & O'Leary, 1991; Barkley, 1990; Pfiffner & O'Leary, 1993).

Interventions for ADHD typically are designed to impact target behaviors across academic and social domains. Because ADHD symptoms are, by definition, exhibited across settings, then treatment strategies must be outlined for multiple caregivers (e.g., parents and teachers) to use across a number of situations. Although an explicit goal of the intervention program is to decrease the frequency of various ADHD-related behaviors (e.g., inattention to task materials), the primary emphasis is on enhancing competencies in a number of areas. Thus, treatment targets are behaviors that should increase in frequency as a function of treatment, such as completion of independent work, compliance with teacher directives, accuracy of academic responding, and positive interactions with peers. Behavioral objectives must be designed on an individual basis using data from direct observations of classroom behavior as well as the results of parent and teacher ratings. Assessment results also will identify behavioral competencies (e.g., adequate peer relations) that possibly could aid in the amelioration of the child's deficits. Those behaviors occurring at the lowest frequencies and/or deemed most crucial to classroom functioning by the teacher usually serve as initial intervention targets.

A number of factors are considered in the process of choosing appropriate interventions for an individual child with ADHD. First, the severity of the child's ADHD should be categorized into one of four levels (i.e., borderline, mild, moderate, severe) based upon the number of symptoms reported on the ADHD Rating Scale and the degree of functional impairment evidenced (American Psychiatric Association, 1987). The greater the severity of ADHD symptoms, the more likely that a referral to a physician for a medication assessment will be warranted.

In general, the treatment of first resort will be the implementation of a behaviorally based intervention employing positive reinforcement techniques designed to increase task-related attention and completion of assigned work (DuPaul, 1991b; DuPaul, Stoner, Tilly, & Putnam, 1991). Observation results will aid in this process by providing baseline data and helping to identify antecedent and consequent events that could be manipulated as part of the intervention. Thus, functional analysis data are used to determine the specific parameters (e.g., possible reinforcers) of the behavioral intervention (Kazdin, 1989). In addition, the specific settings where intervention procedures are to be implemented are identified based on observation data. For example, a student with ADHD may be found to exhibit the lowest frequencies of desired behaviors in classroom rather than playground settings. Further, task-related attention and work completion rates may be different across academic subject areas. Initial interventions may be designed, therefore, to increase attention and work completion frequencies during instruction in those academic areas where the child exhibits the greatest ADHD-related difficulties and in the classroom setting only. As progress is achieved, target behaviors in other academic settings may be addressed.

A third factor to consider in developing treatment strategies is the presence of additional behavior or learning disorders. For example, many children with ADHD are also oppositional and defiant in response to authority figure commands (Loney & Milich, 1982). Noncompliant and aggressive behaviors would then become additional targets of the classroom intervention program. A referral to a community-based professional (e.g., clinical child psychologist) may be necessary so that parents can receive training in appropriate behavior management strategies at home.

An additional consideration in designing the treatment plan is a child's response to previous interventions. If, for example, a behavioral program has been implemented in the classroom and yet the child continues to exhibit a high frequency of ADHD-related behaviors, then other treatment modalities (e.g., prescription of stimulant medication) may need to be recommended. As is the case for most children with special needs, the preference is for placement and treatments considered to be least restrictive. In fact, most children with ADHD are placed primarily within regular classroom settings (Lambert & Sandoval, 1980; Pfiffner & Barkley, 1990). Thus, resistance to previous intervention should be the major criterion in determining whether a child's behavior control problems are severe enough to warrant special education placement (Gresham, 1991; see Chapter 3 for further discussion of this issue).

A final factor to consider is the availability of treatment resources in the community. For instance, this availability will determine whether the child and his or her family are referred to a community-based professional such as a clinical child psychologist or whether home-based interventions are to be designed by the school psychologist. When both parents and teachers are actively involved in the treatment process (e.g., through implementation of behavior modification strategies), there is a greater probability of success. Thus, in most cases, parents will be referred for training in behavior management strategies when such services are available.

Stage V: Program/Intervention Evaluation

Questions to Be Addressed

Once the intervention program is designed and implemented, ongoing assessment is conducted to answer the following questions:

1. Are changes occurring in the target and collateral behaviors?
2. Are the treatment changes socially valid and clinically significant?
3. Are target behaviors normalized?

Intervention Evaluation Process

The assessment of the child with ADHD does not conclude with the diagnosis, but continues on an ongoing basis as intervention procedures are implemented. In this context, the initial evaluation data not only contribute to diagnostic decisions but also serve as baseline or preintervention measures. If assessment data are not collected once treatment begins, one can never be sure that the intervention is successful, or if it requires adjustments. Single-subject design methodology is typically employed to evaluate treatment-related changes in target behaviors (DuPaul, Stoner, et al., 1991). More details regarding the use of single-subject methodology to evaluate behavioral change can be obtained by consulting several excellent texts on this topic (e.g., Hersen & Barlow, 1982; Kazdin, 1992).

Throughout the treatment process, the student serves as his or her own "control" and behavioral change is evaluated in comparison to baseline or nonintervention conditions. This process requires the repeated acquisition of assessment data across settings and caretakers at various points in the intervention program. In addition, treatment integrity is evaluated to ensure the accurate application (e.g., treatment compliance) of the prescribed intervention. If the intervention is implemented as designed and reliable behavior change occurs, then one can assume that the treatment is working as planned. If not, then changes to the intervention or the way that it is implemented by teachers or parents must be made. Thus, ongoing assessment is crucial to the treatment process, and the two are inexorably linked.

Intervention Evaluation Techniques

In most cases, narrow-band assessment techniques, such as the direct observations of behavior and academic performance data discussed above, are used to evaluation treatment-related change. Such data contribute to addressing whether behavioral changes are occurring as planned in association with intervention. For example, direct observations and performance data are collected on a daily or weekly basis in the context of a reversal (i.e., ABA) or multiple baseline across settings design. Changes in the mean, intercept, and trend of the data are used to determine whether the intervention has led to increases in task-related attention, compliance with classroom rules, and academic productivity and accuracy (see Chapter 4 for specific examples of the evaluation of a classroom intervention program). Occasionally, interobserver agreement is assessed by having a classroom aide, teacher, or other observer present when data are collected. Interobserver agreement should be assessed at least several times per treatment phase to ensure that observation and performance data are reliable.

Several additional assessment techniques are used to determine whether reliable behavior change has occurred as a function of the intervention. First, teacher ratings on the CBCL or Conners Rating Scales are collected at several points including prior to the intervention, during the treatment phase, following the return to baseline phase (if applicable), and approximately 1 month after the formal intervention has ceased. Thus, general behavior ratings are obtained once per treatment phase. Even though these ratings were collected during the initial evaluation, it is important to obtain them on an additional occasion prior to treatment implementation, as "practice" effects on these measures have been found (Barkley, 1988a). A second administration of teacher ratings during baseline would reduce the possibility of attributing change to the treatment when it was actually due to a regression to the mean artifact. Teacher ratings that contain fewer items, such as the ADHD Rating Scale or the Academic Performance Rating Scale (APRS), may be collected on a weekly basis throughout all treatment phases. Typically, the means of the various teacher ratings are compared across phases to determine whether the teacher perceives any treatment-induced improvements in performance and behavior control.

A second assessment component necessary to document treatment-related change is a method to determine whether the intervention has been implemented as prescribed (Peterson, Homer, & Wonderlich, 1982; Gresham, 1989). If medication effects are being assessed, then pill counts are conducted on a regular basis (e.g., weekly) to ensure that the medicine has been administered. Alternatively, when a parent or teacher is carrying out the intervention (e.g., classroom-based token reinforcement program), treatment integrity is more difficult to determine. Ideally, direct observations of teacher behavior would be conducted occasionally throughout treatment phases to assess whether the intervention steps are being carried out as planned. Of course, there would then be no way to ensure that treatment integrity was intact during intervention sessions where an observer was not present. In such cases, observations of teacher behavior would be supplemented by checklists outlining the intervention steps. The teacher or treatment agent would be expected to complete the checklist every time the intervention was being implemented in an effort to promote compliance. Such checklists also may be completed by someone other than the treatment agent (e.g., classroom aide) on a regular basis. Without at least occasional treatment integrity checks, one cannot be sure that the intervention is being applied as designed.

Although it is important to demonstrate that an intervention has led to reliable changes in the student's behavior and performance, it is crucial to determine whether such changes are socially valid and clinically meaningful. For example, a mean increase in the percentage of on-task behavior from 50–65% during independent work may be statistically significant, but the end result is that the student still spends too much time off-task and is not any more productive academically. Interventions that lead to behavioral changes that do not meaningfully impact on the student's classroom performance are usually abandoned quite readily by the child's teacher.

The clinical significance and social validity of behavioral change can be assessed in a variety of ways (for details, see Kazdin, 1988; Schwartz & Baer, 1991). First, consumer satisfaction ratings could be completed by the student, teacher, and/or parents at the conclusion of treatment or at various points during the intervention. Each participant's views on specific components of the intervention could be obtained in this manner. A second, related technique is to have the teacher complete treatment acceptability ratings of various possible intervention strategies (Witt & Elliott, 1985). The acceptability of interventions may actually be assessed prior to treatment as an aid in the consultation and treatment design process (Bergan & Kratochwill, 1990).

A third way of determining the clinical significance of an intervention is to assess whether it has led to the normalization of behavior. Stated differently, does the intervention enhance the student's attention span, academic productivity, and social behaviors to the point where his or her performance is indistinguishable from his or her peers? This can be evaluated by collecting assessment data on one or more classmates during various points in the intervention. In this way, the treated child's performance can be compared directly to that of his or her normal counterparts. If ethical or practical considerations preclude the assessment of normal classmates, several statistical procedures can be used to determine whether clinically meaningful change has occurred. For example, if normative data are available for a specific measure, then a reliable change index (Jacobsen & Truax, 1991) can be calculated to evaluate whether the treatment has led to statistically reliable improvements in behavior. Further, Jacobsen and Truax (1991) have provided several formulas for determining whether an intervention has led to normalization of performance. For example, methylphenidate (Ritalin) has been found to normalize the task-related attention and academic productivity of a large percentage of children with ADHD who participated in a 6-week medication trial (DuPaul & Rapport, 1993; see Chapter 5 for details). Although normalization of classroom performance is not always possible, it is one of the more important ways to measure the actual value of obtained treatment effects.

DEVELOPMENTAL CONSIDERATIONS IN
THE ASSESSMENT OF ADHD

Developmental factors may alter the content and, to some degree, the process of conducting an ADHD evaluation, especially when the referred student is an adolescent (Shelton & Barkley, 1990). First, the overall functioning of the teenager with ADHD may be more impaired than during the childhood years, because of a higher risk for conduct disturbance or antisocial behavior (Barkley, Fischer et al., 1990; Gittelman et al., 1985; Satterfield, Hoppe, & Schell, 1982), academic underachievement (Hoy,

Weiss, Minde, & Cohen, 1978; Mendelson, Johnson, & Stewart, 1971), and low self-esteem (Ackerman, Dykman, & Peters, 1977; Feldman, Denhoff, & Denhoff, 1979). In addition, several empirical investigations have indicated a higher frequency of substance abuse (Gittelman et al., 1985) among adolescents with ADHD, especially when antisocial behavior problems (e.g., stealing, vandalism) are present. Thus, in addition to the core deficits of ADHD, teenagers with this disorder may exhibit a variety of behavioral and/or emotional disturbances, and procedures designed to screen for these associated difficulties must be incorporated into the evaluation of adolescents with ADHD (DuPaul, Guevremont, & Barkley, 1991a).

When evaluating an adolescent referred for ADHD-related difficulties, it is very important that a reliable history of the problem behaviors is obtained, because, by definition, ADHD symptoms should be evident prior to the age of 7 years old. Because the reliability of historical information provided by parents is often quite low, even for younger children, care should be taken to obtain "reliability checks" of parental verbal reports (Cantwell, 1986). A possible source of such information would be the student's school record including report cards, previous psychological evaluations, and disciplinary history.

A third factor to consider in the assessment of adolescents suspected of having ADHD is the input of the students themselves. The teenager's perception of current adjustment difficulties must be obtained in addition to parent and teacher reports. Adolescent self-report of ADHD symptoms has been found to correlate highly with parental report (Gittelman et al., 1985) and may provide further information (e.g., presence of depressive symptoms) not available from other sources. Moreover, adolescents are likely to agree more fully with the results of evaluations in which their opinions were given greater attention and, hence, may be more willing to participate with treatment recommendations (DuPaul, Guevremont, & Barkley, 1991a). Thus, the major change to the ADHD evaluation when assessing an adolescent is the inclusion of several self-report measures, such as a diagnostic interview with the student and the completion of behavior rating scales, in the multimethod assessment stage. The student may also play a more active role in the formulation, implementation, and assessment of the treatment plan. At the very least, self-report and consumer satisfaction data should be obtained from the student during the treatment evaluation stage on an ongoing basis.

The content of the ADHD evaluation is somewhat different when assessing an adolescent. As mentioned above, a diagnostic interview with the student should be conducted, which would incorporate DSM crite-

ria for the same disorders reviewed with the adolescent's parent and
teacher. Second, various self-report questionnaires are completed by the
student including the Youth Self-Report (YSR) version of the CBCL
(Achenbach, 1991) and possibly the ADD+H Adolescent Self-Report Scale
(Conners & Wells, 1985) or the Self-Evaluation (Teenager's) Self-Report
(Gittelman, 1985). Normative data are available only for the YSR. Given
the higher risk of affective or emotional disturbance among adolescents
with ADHD relative to their normal counterparts, it is often necessary to
include questionnaires that tap internalizing symptomatology such as the
Beck Depression Inventory (Beck, Ward, Mendelson, Mock, & Erbaugh,
1961), the Reynolds Adolescent Depression Scale (Reynolds, 1987), and
the Manifest Anxiety Scale (Taylor, 1951).

A final difference in the ADHD evaluation of adolescents is the
inclusion of behavior ratings from multiple teachers. The interpretation
of the resultant ratings can be problematic given the limited sample of
student behavior that each teacher observes. It is often helpful to obtain
ratings from several individuals, including nonteachers (e.g., guidance
counselor) with whom the teenager has the greatest amount of contact.
Rather than relying on the analysis of any single teacher rating (as with
younger children), consistencies among the resultant profiles (e.g., elevations on factors related to ADHD) are used to document the pervasiveness, or lack thereof, of behavioral control difficulties across settings.
Further details regarding the content of ADHD evaluations with adolescents are available in several recent reviews (Cantwell, 1986; DuPaul,
Guevremont, & Barkley, 1991a; Klorman, 1986).

CASE EXAMPLE

Arthur was a 7-year-old second grader referred to the school psychologist by his regular classroom teacher due to not completing independent
seatwork, talking without permission, and not complying with school
rules. The teacher indicated that the quality of his academic work was
similar to his classmates when she worked with him individually. However, due to his inconsistent completion of assigned work and frequent
inattention during tests, Arthur was reported to achieve below his presumed potential.

After briefly discussing the case, the school psychologist asked the
teacher to complete a screening instrument (i.e., the ADHD Rating Scale).
Arthur's ratings were beyond the 93rd percentile for the total score as
well as the Inattentive–Hyperactivity and Impulsivity–Hyperactivity factor
scores. Also, 10 of the 14 symptoms of ADHD (using DSM-III-R criteria)

were reported to be present at least "pretty much" of the time. Based on this screening information and the nature of the referral, a multimethod assessment of ADHD appeared warranted.

As a first step in the assessment process, an interview with Arthur's classroom teacher was conducted. In the course of the interview, it was reported that he displayed frequent problems with inattention, impulsivity, overactivity, and noncompliance across most school settings and classroom activities. These problems were most evident when independent seatwork was assigned and when the teacher was instructing the whole class or small groups. There did not appear to be any differences in this behavior across academic subject areas. Arthur was reported to evidence 11 of the 14 DSM-III-R symptoms of ADHD on a frequent basis. These symptoms had been exhibited on a daily basis over the past 6 months (i.e., since the beginning of the school year). Further, a significant number (i.e., 5 out of 9) of symptoms of ODD were reported to occur on a frequent basis. The latter included noncompliance with teacher commands, frequent losses of temper, and deliberate annoyance of others. Problems associated with other disorders (e.g., Conduct Disorder, Depression) were not reported to occur frequently.

As a result of his attention problems, Arthur was not achieving at a level commensurate with his classmates in either mathematics or reading skills. Nevertheless, his teacher did not feel that he had learning problems in either subject area. She reported that when she worked with him on an individual basis, he was able to demonstrate adequate knowledge in both skill areas (e.g., he was able to read high-interest material). When he was asked to complete independent work, particularly material that did not capture his interest, he was not able to demonstrate his abilities due to a lack of completion.

Arthur did not have many friends in the classroom and was rejected by many of his peers. He did not follow rules of games and frequently was verbally and physically aggressive in unstructured settings (e.g., playground). His teacher felt that many of his disruptive behaviors (e.g., talking out in the classroom) were an attempt to elicit attention from his peers. Unfortunately, these efforts toward peer interaction resulted in further ostracism by his classmates.

The teacher reported a great deal of frustration in trying to manage Arthur's behavior. Her interventions included ignoring his disruptive behavior, public reprimands to get back on task, sending notes to his parents following misbehavior, giving him a reward (e.g., access to classroom computer) for a week of appropriate behavior, as well as reducing the number of items he was expected to complete for seatwork. None of these strategies resulted in consistent behavioral improvement.

Arthur's report cards from previous school years were reviewed. The written comments of his kindergarten and first-grade teachers indicated that he displayed similar, albeit less severe, problems with behavior control. A pattern of attention and behavior control problems beginning at an early age and occurring across school years was evident.

Arthur's mother was interviewed briefly by telephone. She corroborated the teacher's report of significant problems with inattention, impulsivity, and overactivity. In fact, nearly all of the symptoms of ADHD were reported to occur on a frequent basis at home. These had been evident since he was 3 years old and attended a nursery school program. She reported that Arthur was very defiant and uncooperative at home, especially in reponse to maternal commands. He did not sustain his attention to most household chores, unless he was interested in completing them. A majority of the symptoms of ODD were indicated to be present. No further DSM-III-R symptomatology was reported. He did not have any history of significant medical difficulties or developmental delays. Arthur's father was reported to have had similar attention and behavior problems as a child, but he was now a successful businessman. No other significant problems were reported for immediate family members. Finally, she stated that she was very interested in receiving help in managing Arthur's behavior as the stress level in the household was directly related to the degree to which he behaved in an appropriate manner. Previous attempts at intervention, including family therapy, had failed.

Maternal responses on the CBCL resulted in significant elevations on three subscales: Attention Problems, Aggression, and Delinquent. *T*-scores on these scales were above 67, or the 95th percentile. All remaining subscales were below the 93rd percentile (i.e., in the normal range). Ratings on the ADHD Rating Scale were two standard deviations above the mean for the total score and both subscales. Arthur's attention problems were reported to occur in almost all home situations identified on the HSQ-R and their average severity was two standard deviations above the mean.

Teacher ratings were consistent with those provided by Arthur's mother. On the TRF-CBCL, significant elevations were obtained on the Attention Problems and Aggression subscales. *T*-scores were above 70, or the 98th percentile, for both dimensions. Remaining subscale scores were in the normal range. On the SSQ-R, Arthur was reported to exhibit attention problems in every school setting at a severity level that was 2 standard deviations above the mean. Teacher ratings on the Walker–McConnell Scale of Social Competence and School Adjustment resulted in below average scores for both peer-preferred and teacher-preferred behaviors. Finally, ratings on the Academic Performance Rating Scale were in the clinically significant range (i.e., 1.5 standard deviations below the mean) for the Academic Productivity factor only.

Arthur's behavior was observed on several occasions in both the classroom and on the playground. Classroom observations were conducted for 20 minutes on three occasions (once during math seatwork, twice while working on a phonics worksheet). Using the revised ADHD Behavior Coding system (see Appendix 2.1), he was noted to display high rates of off-task and fidgeting behaviors. Specifically, he was inattentive during an average of 45% of the observation intervals, while exhibiting repetitive motor movements approximately 20% of the time. In contrast, randomly selected classmates were observed to be off-task only 10% of the time and were fidgeting during less than 8% of the observation intervals. Arthur's playground behavior was observed on two occasions using the COSA. He was noted to be more verbally and physically aggressive than randomly selected classmates. Thus, direct observations were consistent with both parent and teacher report of significant behavior control difficulties.

Academic performance data were collected in conjunction with observations of Arthur's behavior during independent seatwork. He completed an average of 60% of the work assigned over these three occasions. This was in contrast to an average completion rate of 95% for his classmates. On a positive note, the accuracy of his work was uniformly high (i.e., $M = 93\%$ correct). This corroborates the teacher's contention that Arthur's abilities were commensurate with those of his classmates, but that he simply didn't finish the work that was assigned.

The next step in the evaluation process was to interpret the results. Arthur's teacher and mother independently reported that at least 8 of the 14 DSM-III-R symptoms of ADHD were evident on a frequent basis. According to his mother, he began exhibiting ADHD-related difficulties at the age of 3 with no diminishment of severity. Thus, these symptoms were evident at an early age and were chronic. Maternal and teacher ratings indicated that his problems with inattention, impulsivity, and overactivity were more frequent and severe than for the vast majority of boys his age. This was corroborated by direct observations of his classroom behavior. Further, attention problems were reported to be pervasive across numerous school and home situations. Finally, Arthur's ADHD-related behaviors had compromised his peer relationships and academic performance to a significant degree.

Although Arthur was also reported to display a signficant number of ODD symptoms, the presence of the latter could not fully account for his attention difficulties. It was particularly noteworthy that his symptoms of ADHD predated the onset of his problems with noncompliance and defiance. Specifically, the former were reported to occur as early as age 3, whereas the latter were not evident until Arthur was 6 years old. There were no indications of any emotional or learning difficulties that could account for his ADHD symptoms. Thus, he was determined to have both ADHD and ODD.

Several interventions were implemented based on this evaluation. First, the school psychologist and teacher designed a classroom intervention program that included token reinforcement, response cost, and a home–school communication program (see Chapter 4 for details of classroom programming). Second, referrals were made to a clinical child psychologist and Arthur's pediatrician for provision of parent training and a medication assessment, respectively. Parent training was necessary due to his high level of defiance and inattention at home. A medication assessment was recommended due to the severity of Arthur's ADHD and the high likelihood of continued impairment in functioning in a number of key areas. The chronicity and severity of his behavior problems might require special education programming in the future, which Arthur's family would like to avoid, if possible. The probability of special education placement might be reduced if Arthur was a positive responder to medication. Finally, a social skills intervention was designed to address Arthur's playground behavior. Specifically, a peer-mediated procedure was used wherein several of his classmates were trained to prompt and reinforce appropriate social behavior. It was felt that this combination of interventions would be necessary over the long term, given the chronicity and severity of Arthur's ADHD.

Continued assessment of Arthur's classroom performance was conducted by the school psychologist. This was done to evaluate his progress and determine if changes were necessary to his intervention program. Teacher ratings and classroom observations were obtained on at least a weekly basis during the initial stages of implementing the multicomponent behavioral intervention. Adjustments were made to the timing and frequency of reinforcement as a result. These same measures were used on a daily basis over several weeks of evaluating three different doses of Ritalin (i.e., 5 mg, 10 mg, and 15 mg). Over the course of the school year, these measures were periodically readministered to ascertain whether further adjustments in behavioral procedures or medication dosage were necessary.

SUMMARY

The school-based evaluation of ADHD is comprised of multiple assessment techniques utilized across a variety of settings and sources of information. Following a teacher referral for possible ADHD, five stages of assessment are conducted including screening for ADHD symptoms, multimethod assessment, interpretation of results to reach a classification decision, development of the treatment plan, and ongoing assessment of the intervention program. The goal of the evaluation is not simply to arrive at a diagnosis of ADHD, but to determine an intervention plan that is likely to succeed, based upon the information gathered. The use of a behavioral assessment approach incorporating parent and teacher interviews, parent and teacher rating scales, direct observations of behavior, and academic performance data is the optimal methodology for addressing both goals of the evaluation process. Assessment data should be collected on an ongoing basis throughout treatment to determine the efficacy and/or limitations of the intervention program.

APPENDIX 2.1
Criteria for the Revised
ADHD Behavior Coding System

1. **Off-Task Behavior:** This category is checked if the child interrupts his or her attention to the tasks to engage in some other behavior for 3 consecutive seconds or longer. Attention is defined as visually looking at the task materials or the child's hands if the child is using his or her fingers to count. Off-task is coded if the child breaks eye contact with the task materials or counting on fingers for at least 3 consecutive seconds.

2. **Fidgeting:** Any repetitive, purposeless motion of the legs, arms, hands, buttocks, or trunk. It must occur at least four times in succession to be considered repetitive, and it should serve no purpose. Examples include swaying back and forth, kicking one's legs back and forth, swinging arms at one's side, shuffling feet from side to side, shifting one's buttocks about in the chair, tapping a pencil or finger repeatedly on the table.

3. **Task-Relevant Vocalization:** Any vocal noise or verbalization made by the child that is relevant to the task. Examples include counting, making statements about the difficulty of the math problems or the child's performance on the task.

4. **Task-Irrelevant Vocalization:** Any vocal noise or verbalization made by the child that is not relevant to the academic task. Examples include singing, humming, making odd mouth noises, clicking one's teeth.

5. **Out of Seat:** Any time the child's buttocks break contact with the flat surface of the seat.

(See page 35 for the revised ADHD Behavior Coding System Sheet.)

APPENDIX 2.2
Criteria for the
Teacher–Student Behavior Coding System

The first observation categories pertain to who (teacher or student) initiated the interaction and how it was initiated (by teacher when student was on- or off-task, or by student in an appropriate or inappropriate manner).

TA/ON = Teacher Approaches Student Engaged in On-Task Behavior
Teacher verbally or physically initiates an interaction with student, who at moment of contact is engaged in on-task behavior (see Appendix 2.1). Not coded if student has raised hand or called out to get teacher's attention.

TA/OFF = Teacher Approaches Student Engaged in Off-Task Behavior
Teacher physically or verbally initiates an interaction with student who is off-task at that moment (see Appendix 2.1 for definition of off-task). TA/OFF is coded regardless of what happens after the interaction (e.g., a redirection back to work results in student going back on-task).

CA/APP = Child Approaches Teacher in an Appropriate Manner
Student physically or verbally initiates an interaction with the teacher in an appropriate manner including the following:
  · raising hand;
  · asking questions without raising hand when classroom rules are specifically relaxed (must be specified by the teacher, for example, during small-group instruction);
  · approaching teacher at desk during independent seatwork.

CA/INAPP = Child Approaches Teacher in an Inappropriate Manner
Student physically or verbally initiates an interaction with teacher in an inappropriate manner including the following:
  · Calling out without permission
  · Getting out of seat (unless during independent seatwork or similar activity when that is acceptable in the classroom)

The second category of teacher observation codes is a determination of whether the teacher–student interaction was positive, negative, or other.

Positive
Interaction includes any type of positive verbal comment regarding appropriate social or academic behavior. May also include physical contact (e.g., pat on shoulder) as long as it is not for discipline. Positive comments may be directed at the target student or the group if student is part of it.

Negative
Interaction includes verbal comments of disapproval such as criticism, negative reprimands, or if teacher threatens to punish the student. May include physical contact (e.g., leading student by hand to his or her desk) if it occurs

in response to inappropriate behavior on the part of the student. Student may be either directly targetted by the teacher or part of a group to whom the teacher makes a negative statement.

Other

Any other teacher–student interaction that is not coded as positive or negative, such as:

- Instructing the class;
- Answering questions (unless the teacher adds "good job" or other approval statement);
- Conversing with student;
- Giving directions to class (e.g., to change activities).

Phase _____
Day _____

CLASSROOM INTERACTIONS
OBSERVATION SHEET

Observer _____ Rel.? Y N

Date _____

Classroom _____

	1	2	3	4	5	6	7	8	9	10	11	12	Total A
TA/On	p n o	p n o	p n o	p n o	p n o	p n o	p n o	p n o	p n o	p n o	p n o	p n o	| |
TA/Off	p n o	p n o	p n o	p n o	p n o	p n o	p n o	p n o	p n o	p n o	p n o	p n o	| |
C/App	p n o	p n o	p n o	p n o	p n o	p n o	p n o	p n o	p n o	p n o	p n o	p n o	| |
C/Inapp	p n o	p n o	p n o	p n o	p n o	p n o	p n o	p n o	p n o	p n o	p n o	p n o	| |

	13	14	15	16	17	18	19	20	21	22	23	24	Total B
TA/On	p n o	p n o	p n o	p n o	p n o	p n o	p n o	p n o	p n o	p n o	p n o	p n o	| |
TA/Off	p n o	p n o	p n o	p n o	p n o	p n o	p n o	p n o	p n o	p n o	p n o	p n o	| |
C/App	p n o	p n o	p n o	p n o	p n o	p n o	p n o	p n o	p n o	p n o	p n o	p n o	| |
C/Inapp	p n o	p n o	p n o	p n o	p n o	p n o	p n o	p n o	p n o	p n o	p n o	p n o	| |

	25	26	27	28	29	30	31	32	33	34	35	36	Total C
TA/On	p n o	p n o	p n o	p n o	p n o	p n o	p n o	p n o	p n o	p n o	p n o	p n o	| |
TA/Off	p n o	p n o	p n o	p n o	p n o	p n o	p n o	p n o	p n o	p n o	p n o	p n o	| |
C/App	p n o	p n o	p n o	p n o	p n o	p n o	p n o	p n o	p n o	p n o	p n o	p n o	| |
C/Inapp	p n o	p n o	p n o	p n o	p n o	p n o	p n o	p n o	p n o	p n o	p n o	p n o	| |

(continued)

	37	38	39	40	41	42	43	44	45	46	47	48	Total D
TA/On	p n o	p n o	p n o	p n o	p n o	p n o	p n o	p n o	p n o	p n o	p n o	p n o	| |
TA/Off	p n o	p n o	p n o	p n o	p n o	p n o	p n o	p n o	p n o	p n o	p n o	p n o	| |
C/App	p n o	p n o	p n o	p n o	p n o	p n o	p n o	p n o	p n o	p n o	p n o	p n o	| |
C/Inapp	p n o	p n o	p n o	p n o	p n o	p n o	p n o	p n o	p n o	p n o	p n o	p n o	| |

	49	50	51	52	53	54	55	56	57	58	59	60	Total E
TA/On	p n o	p n o	p n o	p n o	p n o	p n o	p n o	p n o	p n o	p n o	p n o	p n o	| |
TA/Off	p n o	p n o	p n o	p n o	p n o	p n o	p n o	p n o	p n o	p n o	p n o	p n o	| |
C/App	p n o	p n o	p n o	p n o	p n o	p n o	p n o	p n o	p n o	p n o	p n o	p n o	| |
C/Inapp	p n o	p n o	p n o	p n o	p n o	p n o	p n o	p n o	p n o	p n o	p n o	p n o	| |

	61	62	63	64	65	66	67	68	69	70	71	72	Total F
TA/On	p n o	p n o	p n o	p n o	p n o	p n o	p n o	p n o	p n o	p n o	p n o	p n o	| |
TA/Off	p n o	p n o	p n o	p n o	p n o	p n o	p n o	p n o	p n o	p n o	p n o	p n o	| |
C/App	p n o	p n o	p n o	p n o	p n o	p n o	p n o	p n o	p n o	p n o	p n o	p n o	| |
C/Inapp	p n o	p n o	p n o	p n o	p n o	p n o	p n o	p n o	p n o	p n o	p n o	p n o	| |

	73	74	75	76	77	78	79	80	Total G
TA/On	p n o	p n o	p n o	p n o	p n o	p n o	p n o	p n o	| |
TA/Off	p n o	p n o	p n o	p n o	p n o	p n o	p n o	p n o	| |
C/App	p n o	p n o	p n o	p n o	p n o	p n o	p n o	p n o	| |
C/Inapp	p n o	p n o	p n o	p n o	p n o	p n o	p n o	p n o	

Data Summary Chart

Total # of Intervals Observed: _____

	A	B	C	D	E	F	G	Total	% Int.
TA/On	| |	| |	| |	| |	| |	| |	| |	| |	| |
TA/Off	| |	| |	| |	| |	| |	| |	| |	| |	| |
C/App	| |	| |	| |	| |	| |	| |	| |	| |	| |
C/Inapp	| |	| |	| |	| |	| |	| |	| |	| |	| |

APPENDIX 2.3
Criteria for the
Social Behavior Coding System

Four categories are used to code peer interactions including positive, negative/nonaggressive, aggressive, and noninteractive. In addition, the person with whom the target student is interacting is coded in one of two categories, including teacher or peer. Scoring rules are as follows:

> *Positive*: Cooperative play or work, on-task behavior, compliance, smiling or laughing, affection, conversation, help-giving, and so forth.
> *Negative/nonaggressive*: Violation of rules, noncompliance, off-task behavior, disruption, or other behaviors not involving acts of physical or verbal aggression or property infringements.
> *Aggressive:* Verbal or physical aggressive acts or property infringement.
> *Noninteractive:* Not interacting with a peer or adult.

The components of each of these categories and decision rules are described below.

POSITIVE

1. On-task: visual orientation towards assigned task materials for entire interval (no more than 2 consecutive seconds of diverting visual attention away from work).

2. Cooperative work: actively engaging in an academic task with other students. Examples include painting the same picture together, working on math problems, quizzing each other on spelling words, and so forth. Students must have the teacher's permission to engage in this behavior.

3. Help-giving: showing, assisting, or telling another how to do something or expressing a desire to do so. Differentiate from bossiness by facial expressions, tone of voice, and reactions of others.

4. Compliance: doing something someone else has requested or asks the child to do, or not doing something that someone has asked the child not to do. Only code as positive if it is compliance with a request that is not for a negative or aggressive action.

5. Cooperative play: actively engaging in a sport, game, or play activity. Examples include playing catch with a ball, jumping rope, playing checkers or a board game, playing tag, and so forth.

6. Conversation: talking to or listening to another or others in a pleasant manner (must have teacher permission for this to be coded as positive in the classroom setting otherwise it is coded as negative/nonaggressive). Examples include

Adapted from "Impact of social problem-solving training on aggressive boys: Skill acquisition, behavior change, and generalization" by D. C. Guevremont and S. L. Foster, 1993, *Journal of Abnormal Child Psychology*, *21*, 13–28. Adapted by permission of the authors.

talking about a TV show, talking about school, listening to someone else talk about something. (The child must be actively involved in the conversation rather than just standing by.)

7. Affection: may be verbal such as praising or complimenting another, or physical such as putting an arm around another's shoulder, patting, holding hands, and so forth. Differentiate from negative or aggressive by facial expressions, tone of voice, reactions of others, and whether students have permission to talk or interact in the classroom.

8. Smiling or laughing: an upward turn in the mouth (smile) with or without audible laughter. Only code as positive when it does not occur in the context of negative (e.g., off-task, disruptive) or aggressive (e.g., teasing) actions.

9. Other: any positive behavior when the child is engaged in an appropriate action (e.g., paying attention to the teacher during a class lecture) or pleasant interaction (e.g., invites another person to play a game).

NEGATIVE/NONAGGRESSIVE

1. Violation of rules: breaking a rule either implicitly or explicitly operating in a particular context (e.g., leaving the desk without permission of the teacher, cheating on a test, cutting someone in line). Use the responses of others to code when the operating rules are not clear.

2. Noncompliance: refusing to do what another person has asked by either ignoring the request (passive) or saying "No" and/or engaging in an alternative behavior (active). Not coded as negative if noncompliance is in response to a request to engage in a negative or aggressive behavior or if the request is made by another child and appears unreasonable (e.g., another child asks the child for all of his or her cookies at lunch).

3. Off-task: visual nonattention to one's task or assigned behavior for longer than 2 consecutive seconds. For example, looking out the window during independent seatwork or conversing with another child without permission during a class activity.

4. Disruption: any behavior that interferes with an ongoing activity (e.g., it causes at least a temporary halt in the activity). For example, throwing an object into the air in class, interrupting someone's conversation, talking out loud in class without permission, drumming on the desk loudly in class.

5. Other: any negative behavior where the child is engaged in an inappropriate action (e.g., throwing trash on floor) or unpleasant interaction (e.g., bragging or showing off) not including aggressive acts.

AGGRESSIVE

1. Verbal or physical:

   a. Bossiness—telling another child what to do when the other child did not ask for help or is not trying to do it.

   b. Teasing—calling another person a name, making fun of someone, tempting someone with a toy or food but then not sharing, making faces, and so forth. Differentiate from games and playing by facial expressions, tone of voice, and responses of others.

    c. Threat—verbal threat to do another person physical harm or to tell something negative about the person to others. Also includes physical gestures such as raising a fist or getting ready to tear up another's paper.

    d. Rejection—rebuffing another child verbally (e.g., not allowing someone else to play the game).

    e. Insult—swearing or using obscene gestures.

    f. Yelling—yelling, screaming, or using a loud, unpleasant tone of voice at another person (e.g., the teacher tells the child to sit down and the child says, "I WILL," loudly).

    g. Physical aggression—hitting, tripping, tackling, pushing, biting, kicking, throwing an object at someone, spitting at someone, and so forth done in a negative manner or with enough force to hurt the other person. Use facial expressions, tone of voice, and responses of others to code.

    h. Quarreling—disagreeing or arguing with another in a loud and unpleasant tone of voice.

    2. Property infringement: grabbing or stealing another's property, breaking or damaging property (e.g., tearing another person's paper, throwing someone's ball into the woods, knocking over a chair on purpose).

    3. Other: any aggressive behavior that involves physical force used on another person (e.g., dragging someone, pulling their hair) or the destruction or damage of property (including the child's own property).

NONINTERACTIVE

Coded when the child is not interacting with another person (adult or peer). For example, this category would be coded if the child is playing alone and is not smiling at, looking at, or talking to another person. This category would not be coded if the child is participating appropriately in a game with other children (e.g., standing silently at first base in a baseball game).

DECISION RULES FOR SCORING

    1. If you can hear the child, use verbal and nonverbal cues to code.

    2. If you cannot hear, use nonverbal cues such as (a) facial expressions; (b) tone or volume of voice; (c) laughter/crying.

    3. When the behavior is ambiguous, pay attention to the context in which it occurs and use responses of peers and teachers as cues.

    4. If a behavior can be scored as either positive or negative, or positive and aggressive (e.g., the child grabs toy away from one child and gives it to another child) always score as negative or aggressive. Negatives or aggressives always override a positive when they occur together. If they occur in a sequence in the same interval both behavior categories are coded.

3

ADHD and Learning Difficulties:
What Is the Connection?

Children with ADHD frequently are reported to underachieve academically (Barkley, 1990). Within classroom settings, these children often exhibit significantly lower rates of on-task behavior during instruction and independent work periods than those displayed by their classmates (Abikoff et al., 1977). As a result, children with ADHD have fewer opportunities to respond during academic instruction and complete less independent work than their peers (Pfiffner & Barkley, 1990). This problem may, at least partially, account for the association of ADHD with academic underachievement, as up to 80% of children with this disorder have been found to exhibit learning and/or achievement problems (e.g., Cantwell & Baker, 1991; Frick et al., 1991; Lambert & Sandoval, 1980). Further, the results of prospective follow-up studies of children with ADHD into adolescence (e.g., Barkley, Fischer, et al., 1990) indicate that the greatest risk for this population is chronic academic underachievement along with higher rates of dropping out of school.

Given the association between ADHD and academic underachievement, it is important for school psychologists and other education professionals to be aware of the potential for learning difficulties among these children. In addition, it is incumbent upon these professionals to design and implement effective interventions to enhance academic functioning. The purpose of this chapter is to provide an overview of the research literature examining the connection between ADHD and academic problems. Specific learning problems found to be associated with ADHD will be reviewed. In addition, empirical studies examining possible causal connnections between learning difficulties and ADHD will be reviewed in some detail. The possibility of treating ADHD plus learning disabilites as a subtype of ADHD is discussed in this context. Next, suggestions for assessment and intervention to address academic performance difficulties among students with ADHD will be delineated. Finally, recent changes to federal guidelines regarding the possible eligibility of children with ADHD for special education services will be reviewed. Suggestions are offered for determining whether a specific child with ADHD may be eligible for special education in keeping with these new regulations.

ASSOCIATION OF ADHD WITH COGNITIVE DEFICITS

Differences between children with ADHD and their normal counterparts have been found in several areas of cognitive functioning. First, they often display difficulties on tasks that require complex problem-solving strategies and organizational skills (Barkley, 1990; Tant & Douglas, 1982). Interestingly, these problems are not necessarily due to a lack of problem-solving abilities per se, but rather appear to reflect either insufficient effort or inefficient use of proper strategies during the task itself (Barkley, 1990; Voelker, Carter, Sprague, Gdowski, & Lachar, 1989). A second area of deficit relative to normal peers is frequently observed on neuropsychological measures of "executive" functioning (Barkley, 1990; Barkley, Grodzinsky, & DuPaul, 1992). Tests that purportedly assess problem solving, response inhibition, and sustained effort have been found to reliably discriminate between children with and without ADHD (Barkley, Grodzinsky, & DuPaul, 1992; Chelune, Ferguson, Koon, & Dickey, 1986). Again, the strategies that children with ADHD employ on these tasks are inefficient, frequently impulsive, and poorly organized (Zentall, 1988). Thus, it is no wonder that teachers of these students frequently report difficulties with note taking, completion of long-term assignments, desk organization, and study skills.

Another area of functioning where children with ADHD may be more likely that nondisordered children to evidence difficulties is speech and language development. Although empirical investigations have provided equivocal results regarding possible delays in the onset of speech, there is relatively consistent evidence of expressive language difficulties among many children with ADHD (Barkley, 1990). Specifically, 10–54% of children with ADHD may exhibit expressive language problems relative to 2–25% of the normal population (Barkley, DuPaul, & McMurray, 1990; Hartsough & Lambert, 1985). Further, children with ADHD evidence a higher rate of dysfluent (e.g., misarticulations) and/or disorganized speech on tasks that require verbal explanation (e.g., responding to reading comprehension questions) (Hamlett, Pelligrini, & Conners, 1987; Zentall, 1985). Deficits in verbal functioning may be chronic, especially when an adolescent's ADHD symptoms are associated with severe aggressive or antisocial behavior (Moffitt & Silva, 1988).

Problems with fine and gross motor coordination may be associated with ADHD. Group studies have found that approximately 52% of children with ADHD are reported to display poor fine motor coordination as compared to a maximum of 35% of normal children (Barkley, DuPaul, & McMurray, 1990; Hartsough & Lambert, 1985; Szatmari et al., 1989). Such findings have been obtained rather consistently on tasks such as maze drawings or pegboard tests (e.g., Ullman, Barkley, & Brown, 1978). These results are not surprising as teachers of students with ADHD frequently report them to have significant problems with handwriting and penmanship (Barkley, 1990). Several studies have documented a greater frequency of neurological "soft" signs, including gross motor coordination difficulties and motor overflow movements, among children with ADHD relative to their normal and/or learning disabled counterparts (Denckla, Rudel, Chapman, & Krieger, 1985). For example, when asked to perform specific muscle group movements (e.g., toe tapping), children with ADHD may display unnecessary associated movements perhaps indicative of poor motor inhibition (Denckla & Rudel, 1978).

There is some controversy as to whether ADHD is associated with delays in general intellectual functioning. At a group level of analysis, children with this disorder consistently score an average of 7–15 points below their own siblings or typical children on standardized tests of intelligence (Barkley, 1990). Although these differences could represent an actual discrepancy in cognitive functioning between groups, there are at least two alternative explanations for these results. First, differential IQ test performance may be due to differences in test-taking behavior such as greater levels of inattention among the ADHD group relative to their normally functioning peers (Barkley, 1990). A second possible factor accounting for these findings is the greater number of children with learning disabilities in the ADHD group. Thus, lower IQ test scores for the ADHD group, as a whole, may be due to the scores of a subset of children who also have learning disabilities. Supporting this contention are the results of two studies that found no differences in IQ between ADHD and normal samples when the influence of learning disabilities was partialled out (August & Garfinkel, 1989; Dykman & Ackerman, 1991). Regardless of obtained differences in IQ between normal and ADHD samples, it is clear that the range of intellectual functioning in groups of children with ADHD is similar to that obtained in the normal population (i.e., represented by a normal distribution from significantly below average to significantly above average functioning).

Summary

Children with ADHD are at higher risk for a number of weaknesses in areas of performance related to cognitive functioning relative to their peers. Specifically, a signficant percentage of children with this disorder display problems with problem-solving and organizational skills, expressive language abilities, and/or fine and gross motor control. When any one of these difficulties or their combination is exhibited by a child with ADHD, the risk for scholastic underachievement is compounded. In contrast to these concerns, there are at least two positive findings from this research literature. First, on the average, children with ADHD do not differ from the rest of the school population in intellectual functioning. That is, this disorder does not appear to affect their general cognitive abilities. Second, many children with ADHD do not evidence the specific cognitive deficits listed above. Although as a group children with ADHD are at a greater than average risk for language, motor control, and problem-solving difficulties, many children with this disorder do not exhibit these problems.

ASSOCIATION OF ADHD WITH ACADEMIC UNDERACHIEVEMENT

One of the most common and potentially debilitating difficulties exhibited by children with ADHD is chronic academic underachievement relative to their intellectual abilities (Barkley, 1990). The clear majority of students with this disorder obtain lower academic grades than expected across one or more subject areas. Further, they typically obtain significantly lower standardized achievement test scores than comparable groups of typical children (Barkley, DuPaul, & McMurray, 1990; Cantwell & Satterfield, 1978). Problems with academic performance are differentially associated with ADHD even among groups of children with other psychological disorders. For example, children with ADHD have been found to receive the poorest teacher ratings of academic competence on the CBCL among clinic-referred groups of children (McConaughy, Achenbach, & Gent, 1988). Their academic underachievement is presumably due to the exhibition of the core symptoms (i.e., inattention, impulsivity, and motor restlessness) of ADHD in classroom settings, although this is a matter of some debate, as discussed in the next section.

The chronic achievement difficulties encountered by many children with ADHD increase their risk for poor scholastic outcome, as measured by a number of variables. Approximately 40% or more of children with

ADHD are placed in special education programs for students with learn-ing disabilities or behavior disorders (Barkley, 1990). Further, about one-third of children with ADHD in research samples have been retained in at least one grade before reaching high school (Barkley, DuPaul, & McMurray, 1990; Brown & Borden, 1986). School suspensions and expulsions occur at a higher than average frequency for students with ADHD, although this may be due, at least partially, to the higher rate of Conduct Disorder among children with attention deficits (Barkley, DuPaul, & McMurray, 1990). In addition, the high school dropout rate is higher (i.e., about 10%) among students with this disorder relative to the general population (Barkley, DuPaul, & McMurray, 1990). The academic performance difficulties asso-ciated with ADHD may even persist into adulthood; follow-up studies indi-cate that only about 20% of adults with a childhood history of the disorder are continuing their education at age 21 as opposed to about 50% of nor-mal samples (Weiss & Hechtman, 1993). The educational problems and outcomes associated with this disorder thereby increase the risk of experi-encing significant vocational and social difficulties in adulthood (Barkley, DuPaul, & McMurray, 1990; Weiss & Hechtman, 1993).

POSSIBLE CAUSAL CONNECTIONS BETWEEN ADHD AND ACADEMIC PROBLEMS

Hypothesized Relationships between ADHD and Academic Problems

Given the chronic academic underachievement and related learning dif-ficulties that children with ADHD may experience, several possible con-nections between academic skills deficits (i.e., learning disabilities) and ADHD have been proposed in the research literature. At least three hy-pothesized causal connections have been delineated: (1) academic skills problems lead to the exhibition of ADHD-related behaviors, (2) the be-havioral symptoms of ADHD (inattention, impulsivity, and overactivity) disrupt academic skill acquisition and performance, and (3) both ADHD and learning difficulties are caused by one or more third variables (e.g., neurological deficits). Each of these hypotheses is detailed below followed by a section summarizing the results of empirical studies designed to investigate them.

Hypothesized Relationship #1: Academic Skills Problems Cause ADHD

One possible connection between learning difficulties and ADHD is that academic skills deficits eventually lead to the display of inattention, impulsivity, and related behavior problems. This hypothesis has been articulated most clearly by McGee and Share (1988). These authors posit that learning disabilities lead to chronic academic failure that, over time, causes a child to develop a poor academic self-concept (i.e., low self-esteem). As a result of a lack of confidence in their own academic abilities, these children are less motivated to attend to instruction and follow classroom rules. These apparent behavioral symptoms of ADHD then lead to further academic underachievement, thus completing the vicious circle. Given this scenario, McGee and Share (1988) argue that the learning difficulties of children with apparent ADHD should be the primary focus of treatment rather than the behavioral symptoms of ADHD per se.

McGee and Share (1988) cite several lines of evidence as support for this hypothesis. First, low scholastic achievement is a signficant characteristic of children with ADHD. Second, children with ADHD, as a group, exhibit deficient peformance on cognitive tests that also are correlated with reading disabilities (e.g., naming tasks, tests of perceptual processing speed). Third, the attentional deficits of children with ADHD may reflect poor motivation rather than an intrinsic deficit in concentration abilities. Fourth, McGee and Share (1988) state, albeit erroneously, that there is no evidence that the primary treatments for ADHD (e.g., stimulant medication) lead to improvements in academic performance concomitant with reductions in ADHD symptomatology. Although their arguments in support of those hypotheses are quite convincing, there are important limitations to each of these, which will be delineated in the next section.

Hypothesized Relationship #2: ADHD Leads to Academic Problems

It is possible that the primary behaviors comprising ADHD (i.e., inattention, impulsivity, and overactivity) disrupt the child's ability to acquire academic skills and/or to demonstrate their knowledge in a consistent fashion (Silver, 1990). One of the earliest versions of this hypothesis was proposed by Keogh (1971). She stated that behaviors related to ADHD may interfere with learning in at least two ways. First, the child's high activity level could divert his or her attention from instruction and thereby minimize the *acquisition* of academic information. Alternatively, because children with ADHD are impulsive, they may make decisions on academic tasks in too rapid a fashion, thus debilitating their *performance* on independent tasks.

In support of this hypothesis is the growing evidence that stimulant medication (e.g., methylphenidate) not only ameliorates ADHD symptomatology, but leads to enhancement of academic performance as well

(DuPaul & Barkley, 1990; Rapport & Kelly, 1991). Thus, a treatment that directly affects a child's attention span and behavior control often leads to concomitant, albeit indirect, enhancement of productivity and accuracy on school tasks, thereby implicating ADHD symptoms as the primary cause of a child's academic difficulties. Nevertheless, there have been few direct studies of the causal relationship between ADHD and learning difficulties, and thus conclusions about causality are premature. Further, although a minority of children with ADHD have been found to evidence learning disabilities (see below), most do not have specific learning deficits (Cantwell & Baker, 1991). Therefore, this hypothesis does not explain why some children with ADHD evidence learning disabilities while others do not.

Hypothesized Relationship #3: Unspecified Third Variable Leads to Both ADHD and Academic Problems

The two hypotheses described above have proposed direct causal relationships between ADHD and learning difficulties. It also is possible that both problems are caused by a separate and distinct third variable. The most common hypothesis is that some nonspecific neurological impairment may lead to both ADHD and learning difficulties, at least in some children (Keogh, 1971). A variety of other organismic (e.g., temperament, language difficulties) and environmental (e.g., discordant homes) variables also have been posited as causal factors for both ADHD and academic difficulties (Hinshaw, 1992a).

Research investigating this hypothesis has been plagued by the fact that groups of children identified with ADHD and/or learning deficits are typically heterogeneous. Rather than searching for a single causal factor, multiple variables may need to be investigated, thus complicating verification of this hypothesis (Cantwell & Satterfield, 1978; Hinshaw, 1992a). In fact, it may be that distinct causal mechanisms are involved for different subgroups of children (Hinshaw, 1992a). Longitudinal investigations that assess hypothesized developmental trajectories for varying subgroups of children with ADHD, learning problems, or both will be necessary to delineate the multiple variables involved.

Association between ADHD and Academic Problems: Empirical Evidence

One factor that has obfuscated conclusions about the association between ADHD and learning problems is the confusion between academic skills deficits (i.e., learning disabilities) and academic performance deficits. The former presumes a lack of *ability* to learn a specific subject matter, at least as the material is currently taught. As such, the student may show deficiencies in the actual skills being taught even under conditions of individual instruction. Alternatively, a deficit in academic performance would be defined as an instance where a student possesses the necessary skills but does not demonstrate this knowledge on a consistent basis under typical classroom conditions (e.g., by producing accurate independent seatwork). In the case of the child with ADHD, a lack of attention to academic materials may lead to poor performance on assigned tasks even though the child may possess the requisite skills to complete the assignment correctly. Further, inattention and behavioral control difficulties could compromise the student's *availability* for learning (e.g., missing important teacher lecture points due to inattention) and thus lead to greater levels of academic underachievement (Silver, 1990). The academic performance of children with ADHD also may be deficient due to their inefficient and inconsistent problem-solving abilities (Douglas, 1980). Unfortunately, much of the work that has investigated the relationship between ADHD and academic problems has not clearly delineated between academic skills deficits and performance decrements.

Empirical investigations of the association between ADHD and academic problems primarily have employed correlational designs. Very few studies have been conducted that have used research designs allowing for attributions of causality and specific examination of the hypotheses listed above. In contrast, much research has examined the prevalence of academic problems in populations of children with ADHD. Most of these studies defined academic problems as "learning disabilities," although there have been great inconsistencies in the definition of this construct across studies, as was discussed above. Nevertheless, the term learning disabilities will be used herein when discussing this literature because of the preference for this label by the authors of the studies reviewed. Although substantial numbers of children with ADHD have been found to evidence learning disabilities relative to the normal population, the prevalence rates vary greatly between studies and the association between the two disorders is decidedly less than perfect. In the next two sections, a brief overview of this research literature will be provided. Several recent papers provide more comprehensive reviews of this area of research (Cantwell & Baker, 1991; Hinshaw, 1992a; Semrud-Clikeman et al., 1992).

Prevalence of Learning Disabilities in ADHD Samples

At least 17 separate studies have been conducted over the past 15 years that have determined the percentage of children with ADHD who also had learning disabilities in one or more subject areas (see Table 3.1 for a listing of these studies). The obtained prevalence rates for learning disabilities have varied widely across studies, ranging from a low of 7% (August & Holmes, 1984) to a high of 92% (Silver, 1981). Averaging across studies, approximately one out of every three children with ADHD was found to have a learning disability (M = 31.1%; median = 27%). The association between ADHD and learning disabilities was even stronger for those children identified with both ADHD and a conduct disorder (see Table 3.1).

As expected, the prevalence of learning disabilities among normal controls is much lower than among their ADHD counterparts, ranging from 0% (Barkley, 1990) to 22% (Semrud-Clikeman et al., 1992). The mean percentage of learning disabilities in the control groups across studies was 8.9% (median = 3%), which corresponds to estimates of the prevalence of this disorder in the general population. Based on these studies, it appears that children with ADHD are roughly three to four times more likely to exhibit learning disabilities than their peers are.

The studies summarized above have led to several important conclusions about the association of ADHD and learning disabilities. First, investigations employing epidemiological samples are consistent in establishing a signficant correlation between academic underachievement and the display of inattention and hyperactivity (see Hinshaw, 1992a; Semrud-Clikeman et al., 1992 for reviews). This association is strongest among children of elementary school age (i.e., 6–11 years old). Second, although learning disabilities also is highly correlated with other disruptive behavior disorders (e.g., Conduct Disorder), the relationship with academic difficulties is strongest for ADHD (Frick et al., 1991; Hinshaw, 1992a). In fact, the coexistence of ADHD with other behavior disorders may account for the association of the latter with learning disabilities. Third, the relationship between ADHD and learning disabilities is highly dependent upon the criteria used to define learning disabilities. Recent studies employing stringent criteria for learning disabilities (e.g., Frick et al., 1991; Semrud-Clikeman et al., 1992) are consistent in identifying the overlap between ADHD and learning disabilities to be less than 20%. Although this represents a signficant number of children, the extent of learning disabilities among students with ADHD is not as high as was once believed. Finally, the academic problems of children with ADHD are not limited to learning disabilites, as they are also at higher risk for grade retentions, failing grades, and dropping out of high school (Hinshaw, 1992a).

Prevalence of ADHD in Samples of Children with Learning Disabilities

Several studies have examined the incidence of ADHD among students initially identified as having learning disabilities. Table 3.2 includes seven studies that have been conducted in this area. Prevalence rates for ADHD

TABLE 3.1. Studies Examining the Prevalence of Learning Disabilities in Children with ADHD

Study	Sample description	Diagnostic groups	N	Rates of LD (%)
August & Garfinkel (1989)	School-based epidemiologic	ADHD	50	22
		Control	47	8
Holborow & Berry (1986)	School-based epidemiologic	ADHD	188	27
		Control	1,405	5
Lambert & Sandoval (1980)	School-based epidemiologic	ADHD	100	14.8–42.6
		BD	44	0.0–14.6
		Control	108	2.8–11.3
McGee et al. (1984)	School-based epidemiologic	ADHD	18	19
		CD	21	19
		ADHD+CD	24	37
		Control	426	7
Schachar et al. (1981)	School-based epidemiologic	ADHD	31	23
		Control	1,285	2
August & Garfinkel (1990)	Clinic-referred	ADHD	115	39
		Control	50	8
August & Holmes (1984)	Clinic-referred	ADHD	14	7
		ADHD+CD	24	8
Barkley (1990)	Clinic-referred	ADHD	42	19.0–26.2
		Control	36	0.0–2.9
Cantwell & Satterfield (1978)	Clinic-referred	ADHD	93	27.6
		Control	54	5.5
Dykman & Ackerman (1991)	Clinic-referred	ADHD	182	45
		Control	52	0
Frick et al. (1991)	Clinic-referred	ADHD	111	18
		ADD+H	97	17
		ADDnoH	15	20
		CD	68	16
		Clinic control	42	2
Halperin et al. (1984)	Clinic-referred	ADHD	241	9
Levine et al. (1982)	Clinic-referred	ADHD	220	66
Livingston (1990)	Clinic-referred	ADHD	147	>50
		Control	52	Not reported
Nussbaum et al. (1990)	Clinic-referred	Young ADHD	38	29
		Old ADHD	36	53
Semrud-Clikeman et al. (1992)	Clinic-referred	ADHD	60	23–30
		Academic Problems	30	10–33
		Control	36	2–22
Silver (1981)	Clinic-referred	ADHD	95	92
		Clinic control	100	4

Note. LD = Learning Disability; BD = Behavior Disorder; CD = Conduct Disorder; ADD+H = Attention Deficit Disorder with Hyperactivity; ADDnoH = Attention Deficit Disorder without Hyperactivity.

ranged from 18% to nearly 60% with a mean percentage of 37.2% (median = 38.2%) across studies (see Table 3.2). As with the studies reviewed in the previous section, the percentage of children identified as having ADHD was partially a function of the criteria used to define this disorder. For instance, Fuerst, Fisk, and Rourke (1989) used cluster analyses of Personality Inventory for Children (Wirt, Lachar, Klinedinst, & Seat, 1977) scores to obtain a relatively low prevalence rate of 18% for ADHD in their learning disability sample. Alternatively, Holborow and Berry (1986) used a more liberal criterion of exceeding a cutoff score for Hyperactivity on the Abbreviated Conners Teacher Rating Scale. As a result, they found that over 41% of the children with learning problems in their sample also met their criteria for ADHD. Interestingly, the latter result is commensurate with the prevalence rate obtained by Vatz (1990) who, relative to this group of studies, used the most comprehensive assessment battery (i.e., structured diagnostic interview with parents and two teacher rating scales) to define ADHD (see Table 3.2).

It is clear that a substantial proportion of students with learning disabilities also exhibit significant symptoms of ADHD. In fact, students with learning disabilities are at least seven times more likely to have ADHD

TABLE 3.2. Studies Examining the Prevalence of ADHD in Children with Learning Disabilities

Study	Sample description	Diagnostic groups	N	Rates of ADHD (%)
Cantwell & Baker (1991)	Speech and language impaired	Total sample LD	600 42	19 40
Felton et al. (1987)	School-based sample	RD Non-RD	45 53	57.7 24.5
Fuerst et al. (1989)	Referred for learning difficulties	LD	132	18
Holborow & Berry (1986)	School-based epidemiologic	LD Non-LD	123 1,470	41.1 7.9
Levine et al. (1982)	Referred for learning difficulties	LD	646	34
McConaughy et al. (in press)	School-based epidemiologic	LD	503	28.1–36.3
Vatz (1990)	School-based epidemiologic	LD Random controls	84 87	42 Not reported

Note. LD = learning disabled; RD = reading disabled.

than their normal counterparts. Further, the prevalence of ADHD in the learning disabled population is higher than the incidence of learning disabilities among ADHD samples. The strength of this association has led to the question of whether ADHD and learning disabilities are one and the same disorder (Silver, 1990). The empirical evidence suggests, however, that learning disabilities and ADHD are separate but overlapping dimensions as depicted in Figure 3.1. Although they share considerable variance, their association is not nearly as complete as would be expected if they were identical disorders. As discussed below, it may be that ADHD is associated with certain subtypes of learning disabilities (e.g., nonverbal learning disabilities; Rourke, 1988). In similar fashion, learning disabilities may be more prominent among specific subtypes of ADHD (e.g., ADDnoH), although empirical investigations have cast doubt on the latter assumption (Lahey & Carlson, 1992). Thus, the association between ADHD and learning disabilities is probably a function of specific characteristics exhibited by certain individuals with either disorder rather than a unitary phenomenon for all children with either disorder.

Studies of Causal Relations between ADHD and Learning Disabilities

To date, no controlled, longitudinal investigations have been conducted that allow for a direct assessment of causal connections between ADHD and learning disabilities. However, the results of two recent studies employing structural equation modeling partially address this issue. The results of these studies imply that the predominant direction of causality

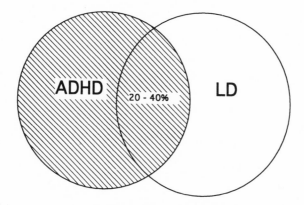

FIGURE 3.1. Venn diagram depicting the overlap between learning disabilities and ADHD.

is for attention deficits to influence academic achievement rather than the converse.

Fergusson and Horwood (1992) investigated possible reciprocal relationships between ADHD and reading achievement in a sample of 777 children from New Zealand. Measures of reading achievement and ADHD-related behavior were collected at two points of time, when the subjects were 10 and 12 years of age. Possible causal connections between ADHD and academic functioning were analyzed using structural equation modeling procedures. These statistical techniques are designed to test the "fit" of obtained data to a theoretical model of causal relationships among specific variables. In this case, a model of reciprocal, causal connections between ADHD and reading achievement was proposed and tested. The results of this study indicated that a child's level of attention deficit at 12 years old negatively influences reading achievement, although there was no evidence indicating that reading ability at this age exerted any effect on attention deficits. Thus, ADHD symptoms appeared to be, at least in part, causally related to reading achievement levels in this sample. The authors of this study are quick to point out, however, that it is possible that different relationships between attention deficits and reading achievement exist among younger or older age groups.

Similar findings were obtained by Rowe and Rowe (1992) who employed structural equation modeling to test two possible models for the relationship between reading achievement and inattentiveness in the classroom. The first model hypothesized that, although several factors (e.g., family socioeconomic status, attitudes towards reading, and reading activity at home) may impact on reading achievement, inattentiveness has a direct, negative influence on achievement. The second model proposed a reciprocal, causal relationship between inattentiveness and reading achievement, while allowing for the effects of home background factors on these two variables. Subjects included 5,092 students from Australia who were grouped into four age groups: 5–6 years, 7–8 years, 9–11 years, and 12–14 years. Teacher ratings, self-report ratings, and achievement tests were used to measure classroom inattentiveness, home background factors (e.g., socioeconomic status), and reading achievement.

The results of this study supported both proposed models of influence between reading achievement and inattentiveness. As posited in the first model identified above, classroom inattentiveness was found to directly influence reading achievement, student attitudes towards reading, and reading activity in the home in a negative fashion. Therefore, greater levels of inattentiveness were associated with lower reading achievement scores. In fact, of the variables studied, classroom inattentiveness accounted for the most variance in reading achievement, as depicted in Figure 3.2. The amount of variance accounted for ranged from 13.4%

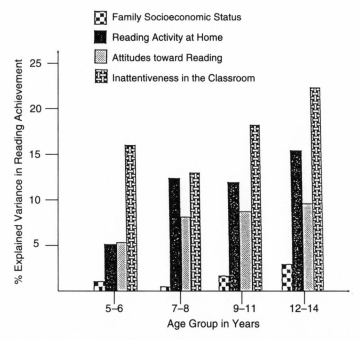

FIGURE 3.2. Histogram showing proportions of explained variance in reading achievement as a function of family socioeconomic status, reading activity at home, attitudes toward reading, and inattentiveness in the classroom, for four age groups of students. From "The relationship between inattentiveness in the classroom and reading achievement (Part B): An explanatory study" by K. J. Rowe and K. S. Rowe, 1992, *Journal of the American Academy of Child and Adolescent Psychiatry, 31,* 357–368. Copyright 1992 by the American Academy of Child and Adolescent Psychiatry. Reprinted by permission.

(7- to 8-year group) to 22.9% (12- to 14-year group). The proposed reciprocal influence model also was supported as higher levels of reading achievement were found to have a significant, positive impact on classroom attention.

Although structural equation modeling techniques do not allow direct tests of causality, they do provide measures of relative influence among variables. It is clear from the two studies reviewed above, that ADHD-related behavior (e.g., inattentiveness) directly influences reading achievement in a negative fashion with higher levels of inattention associated with inferior reading performance. The results of the Rowe and Rowe (1992) study, in particular, indicate that inattentiveness may play an even stronger role in influencing reading achievement than do other factors (e.g., family socioeconomic status) purported to have an effect on reading. It is important to note, however, that the relationship between achievement and ADHD is most likely bidirectional, although this notion was not supported by Fergusson and Horwood's (1992) study.

Limitations to Results of Empirical Investigations

In addition to the fact that no study has been conducted that has directly evaluated the causal relationship between ADHD and learning disabilities, there are several other factors that limit conclusions about the association between the two disorders based on the extant literature. One of the most ubiquitous difficulties with previous investigations in this area has been the inconsistency in definitions of learning disabilities utilized across studies (Barkley, 1990; Frick et al., 1991; Hinshaw, 1992a). Depending on the study, a learning disability has been defined in a variety of ways, including below average performance on an achievement test, a discrepancy of more than 1 standard deviation between IQ and achievement test scores, or teacher ratings of significant learning problems. Not surprisingly, this lack of consensus on the definition of learning disabilities has led to a wide range of prevalence rates for learning disabilities in samples of children with ADHD (see Table 3.1) and has, in some cases, overinflated the incidence of learning disablities (see Semrud-Clikeman et al., 1992, for a discussion of this issue).

Another limitation of the available research literature has been the use of a single measure to define learning disabilities and/or ADHD within a given study. For example, Holborow and Berry (1986) used cutoff scores on a teacher rating scale to determine ADHD and learning disabilities status. Even when such measures are reliable and valid, the use of a single measurement technique to diagnose either disorder may lead to erroneous classification decisions, and this practice is not recommended for either research or clinical purposes.

Most of the studies conducted to date have used clinic-referred samples to investigate the degree to which learning disabilities and ADHD are associated. This may lead to an inflation in the prevalence rate of learning disabilities in ADHD samples, and vice versa, because children with multiple problems are more likely to be referred for clinic-based services (Semrud-Clikeman et al., 1992). Thus, the average prevalence rate of learning disabilities in ADHD samples reported above (i.e., 31.1%) should probably be viewed as an upper bound estimate as is the same figure for the incidence of ADHD in samples of children with learning disabilities.

Conclusions

Despite the above limitations, the available, empirical evidence indicates a consistent relationship between ADHD and academic skills deficits (i.e., learning disabilities). Approximately one out of every three or four children with ADHD is likely to have a specific learning disability. Further, the majority of children with ADHD will be underachieving academically, presumably due to inconsistent completion of assignments and/or low levels of accuracy on seatwork and tests. Nearly 40% of students with learning disabilities will display significant symptoms of ADHD as well. Thus, there is a great deal of overlap between the two disorders as depicted in Figure 3.1. It is important to note, however, that the association between ADHD and learning disabilities is not perfect and they are not one and the same disorder as has been asserted by some investigators (McGee & Share, 1988). In fact, most children with ADHD do *not* have a learning disability and most students with learning disabilities do *not* meet diagnostic criteria for ADHD. Nevertheless, the fact that a significant minority of children in each group can be identified with both disorders must be considered when planning school-based assessment and intervention procedures, as discussed below.

It is unclear whether ADHD "causes" or leads to learning disabilities in some children or vice versa. No study has been conducted that can adequately address this issue. However, investigations employing structural equation modeling have shed some light on this question. These indicate that ADHD-related behaviors, specifically inattentiveness, exert a strong, negative influence on reading achievement. This relationship may be reciprocal (i.e., level of reading achievement may influence classroom inattentiveness), however the effect of ADHD on achievement appears to be more clear-cut. In fact, the results of one study (Rowe & Rowe, 1992) indicate that inattentiveness is one of the most prominent factors determining reading achievement.

Although the direction of causality is presently unknown, it is clear that many children with ADHD have academic skills deficits that must be addressed. It has been speculated that certain subtypes of ADHD may be more likely than others to exhibit learning problems. For instance, some studies have investigated whether children with ADDnoH are at higher risk for learning deficits than children who are hyperactive. In general, these studies have not found significant differences in the prevalence of learning disabilities between ADHD subtypes (Lahey & Carlson, 1992). Conversely, certain subtypes of children with learning disabilities may be at higher risk for behavior control problems including ADHD. Specifically, Rourke (1988) has identified children with nonverbal learning deficits to be at higher risk for such difficulties. In fact, future research into the association between ADHD and learning disabilities should divide samples into known subtypes of each disorder rather than grouping children into two heterogeneous samples. The former procedure may provide the best opportunity to identify which children with ADHD are at greatest risk for learning deficits and vice versa.

SUBTYPING OF ADHD
BASED ON ACADEMIC SKILLS DEFICITS

Given the heterogeneity in functioning among children with ADHD, efforts have been made to identify possible subtypes of the disorder that may be more homogeneous within important dimensions (e.g., hyperactivity, aggression, internalizing symptoms). Because almost one-third of children with ADHD exhibit significant learning deficits, it is worth considering whether the presence of learning disabilities could represent a viable subtype of the disorder. To be practically useful, children with both ADHD and learning disabilities should differ from those with ADHD alone, with respect to etiology, developmental course, long-term outcome, and/or response to treatment (Barkley, 1990). In other words, they must differ in clinically meaningful ways beyond discrepancies that are specific to the measures on which the subtyping classification was made (i.e., academic achievement). In this section, we briefly review the arguments and evidence for and against a learning disabilities subtype of ADHD.

Beyond the increased risk for learning disabilities associated with ADHD, there are at least two additional reasons for exploring the value of an ADHD + learning disabilities subtype. First, subdividing children on the basis of learning deficits could be helpful in determining the causal mechanisms underlying both their behavioral and cognitive difficulties. Rather than searching for unitary causes for all children with either disorder, it may be more productive to explore the possibility of different etiologies for subtypes of both learning disabilities and ADHD (Hinshaw, 1992a; Rourke, 1988). For example, the attention deficits of children with reading disabilities may be caused by or related to a different factor or set of factors than those leading to attention deficits without reading difficulties (Felton, Wood, Brown, Campbell, & Harter, 1987).

A second factor used to argue in favor of a learning disabilities subtype for ADHD relates to possible differences in long-term outcome. It is possible that children with both ADHD and some form of learning disability are at greater risk for chronic difficulties than are students who have either ADHD or a learning disability in isolation. For example, Beitchman, Wekerle, and Hood (1987) found significant expressive and receptive language deficits and visual-motor difficulties among a small group of preschoolers with both ADHD and language delays. Based on these findings, they proposed that such youngsters are at greater risk for exhibiting ADHD and reading disabilities later in life. In similar fashion, Felton et al. (1987) discovered differential patterns of performance on various tests of verbal skills among children with ADHD who were subdivided on the basis of the presence of reading disabilities. The fact that children with both ADHD and reading disabilities exhibited weaknesses in all areas of verbal functioning led these investigators to hypothesize that these children were at greatest risk for chronic deficits. It should be pointed out, however, that a more problematic outcome for children with both ADHD and learning disabilities remains a hypothesis, as no well-controlled longitudinal investigations specifically examining this issue have been conducted.

Children with both ADHD and learning disabilities have been found to differ from youngsters with only ADHD or learning disabilities along several dimensions. The most prominent finding is that children identified with both ADHD and learning disabilities are "doubly handicapped" (August & Garfinkel, 1990). In addition to displaying behaviors associated with ADHD, children who have both disorders display deficiencies on cognitive tests that are associated with both ADHD and learning disabilities. August and Garfinkel (1990) found children with reading disabilities alone to have difficulties on tasks requiring "automatic processing" skills (e.g., rapid letter identification, naming objects). Alternatively, children with ADHD alone were found to display normal automatic processing skills but to be deficient on tests that required sustained and effortful processing (e.g., memorizing rote material). Children with both ADHD and reading disabilities displayed weaknesses on tasks in both the automatic and effortful processing domains. Further, children with both ADHD and learning disabilities have been found to be at a higher risk for separation anxiety (Dykman & Ackerman, 1991) and social rejection (Flicek, 1992) than those with either disorder in isolation. These and other findings have been used to support the differentiation of ADHD into behavioral (i.e., ADHD without learning disabilities) and cognitive (i.e., ADHD with learning disabilities) subtypes (August & Garfinkel, 1989).

Despite the above findings, it is premature to conclude that subtyping ADHD on the basis of learning deficits is a practical procedure. Most of the studies examining the subtyping issue have obtained differences between subtypes on measures related to academic functioning (e.g., IQ, learning tasks, academic achievement tests). These differences would be expected as they measure the same dimension that was used to define the subtypes. Other than the isolated cases (e.g., Flicek, 1992) cited above, most studies have not obtained qualitative or quantitative differences in behavioral functioning between subtypes (August & Garfinkel, 1989, 1990; Dykman & Ackerman, 1991; Halperin et al., 1984). Further, children with ADHD and learning disabilities do not differ from those with ADHD alone in response to treatment with stimulant medication (Dykman & Ackerman, 1991; Halperin et al., 1984). Thus, reliable evidence establishing differences between subtypes with respect to etiology, developmental course, long-term outcome, and response to treatment has not been gathered. Until further research is conducted on this issue, subtyping ADHD along different dimensions (e.g., with and without hyperactivity) will be more useful for practitioners.

ASSESSMENT GUIDELINES: ADHD AND ACADEMIC PERFORMANCE DEFICITS

As previously noted, the academic achievement difficulties of children with ADHD can be divided into two categories: academic performance deficits and academic skills deficits. Thus, the school-based assessment of students referred for attention problems must include measures of academic achievement that tap potential performance and skills deficits. Although the assessment of ADHD is detailed in Chapter 2, the following section will delineate evaluation procedures relevant to the academic functioning of referred children. First, methods to screen for academic skills deficits among children who might have ADHD will be discussed. In similar fashion, procedures to screen students with academic skills difficulties (i.e., learning disabilities) for ADHD are covered. Next, because the most frequent achievement problem that children with ADHD exhibit is with respect to inconsistent academic performance (e.g., work completion), techniques to assess possible performance deficits will be detailed. Finally, methods to determine whether a child's attention problems are due to a lack of academic skills, ADHD, or both will be delineated. A case study will be presented to further explicate this often difficult discrimination.

Screening Procedures

Whenever a child is referred for attention and behavior control problems that may be related to ADHD, several procedures should be incorporated into the evaluation to screen for academic skills deficits. First, questions related to academic difficulties should be incorporated into the parent and teacher interviews (see Chapter 2; Barkley, 1990). In particular, the child's teacher should be asked to provide information regarding possible difficulties in each subject area. Second, teacher ratings of academic achievement difficulties should be obtained through use of the APRS (DuPaul, Rapport, & Perriello, 1991). Scores that are greater than or equal to 1.5 standard deviations below the mean for the child's age and gender for the APRS Total Score and Academic Success subscale are considered significant for screening purposes. The child's teacher should be queried about responses to specific APRS items to clarify the specific nature of possible academic difficulties.

In most cases, children with ADHD will be reported to be at or near grade level across all subject areas with no question of academic skills deficits. Ratings on the Academic Success subscale of the APRS would be expected to be within 1.5 standard deviations of the mean. These same children are typically reported to evidence problems with academic performance (e.g., poor completion and/or accuracy on independent seatwork) with below average ratings for the APRS Total and Academic Productivity scales. Further assessment of academic performance difficulties should be conducted, as discussed below.

If interview and rating scale data indicate potential academic skills deficits, further assessment of learning abilities will be necessary. Although a psychoeducational evaluation incorporating IQ and achievement measures typically is conducted, a behavioral assessment of academic skills deficits is preferred for a number of reasons (e.g., greater relevance to teaching strategies, stronger ecological validity). A behavioral assessment usually will include curriculum-based measurement probes (Shinn, 1989), direct observations, review of written products, and problem-focused interviews with the teacher (for details, see Shapiro, 1989; Shapiro & Kratochwill, 1988). The assessment of academic functioning should be conducted contemporaneously with further evaluation of ADHD, as discussed in Chapter 2.

Children referred for an evaluation of possible learning disabilities should be screened for possible ADHD, given that they are at higher risk for the latter disorder relative to their peers. This screening should be done even if the referral agent did not specify attention and/or behavior problems as part of the reason for the evaluation request. Screening procedures for ADHD are discussed in detail in Chapter 2 (pp. 27–28). These include questioning the teacher(s) about the presence of possible ADHD-related behaviors. This is most easily accomplished by having the teacher complete the ADHD Rating Scale (DuPaul, 1991a). Using DSM-III-R criteria, if eight or more symptoms of ADHD are reported to occur on a frequent basis, further assessment of this disorder is warranted. If all or most of the six ADHD symptoms related to inattention are endorsed as occurring frequently, further assessment of Undifferentiated ADD (i.e., ADDnoH) should be conducted. Finally, if a lesser number of symptoms is reported, this does not rule out further assessment of ADHD, however, the latter becomes less of a priority for evaluation.

Assessing Academic Performance Deficits

Even when children with ADHD do not demonstrate significant weaknesses in specific academic skills, they often have difficulty completing independent work in a timely fashion, obtaining accurate scores on classroom tests, studying for exams, taking notes on classroom lectures, and following through on homework assignments. In fact, behaviors related to academic performance are among the most important targets for change in any intervention program devised to address ADHD (see Chapters 4 and 5). Therefore, assessment of academic behaviors is a standard component of an evaluation of ADHD.

Some of the more important academic behaviors to assess include the completion and accuracy of independent classwork, completion and accuracy of homework, and organizational skills (e.g., neatness of desk, accuracy of lecture notes). Methods for obtaining these data include direct observations of classroom behavior, teacher ratings, and collection of products (e.g., homework assignments, seatwork) completed by the student. These are discussed in greater detail in Chapter 2 (pp. 37). It is expected that children with ADHD will complete significantly less work and/or complete tasks in a less accurate fashion than their classmates due to problems with inattention and impulsivity.

Differentiating between ADHD and Academic Skills Deficits

As reviewed above, there is a great deal of overlap between ADHD and academic skills deficits or learning disabilities. Thus, many youngsters referred for an ADHD evaluation will be found to exhibit both ADHD and academic skills deficits. The vast majority of children with ADHD, however, do not have problems with academic skills per se. Rather, their problems with inattention and impulsivity lead to difficulties following directions; completing tasks in a consistent, accurate fashion; and obtaining high test scores. Thus, one of the goals of an ADHD evaluation is to determine whether a student's academic problems are due to ADHD, learning disabilities, or both. What makes this discrimination particularly difficult is the ambiguity of the many definitions of learning disabilities, as well as the inconsistencies in learning disability definitions across school districts. Regardless of the definition of learning disability employed, the goal relative to an evaluation of ADHD is to assess whether a child's apparent symptoms meet criteria for ADHD and to what extent the student's academic problems are accounted for by difficulties with inattention, impulsivity, and overactivity.

There are several factors to consider in determining whether a child's problems with attention span, impulse control, and activity level are due to ADHD or are secondary to academic skills deficits. These considerations are listed in the context of three possible scenarios:

1. If the data collected in the course of the ADHD evaluation, as described in Chapter 2, indicate clinically significant levels of ADHD symptoms to be evidenced across settings on a chronic basis, it is highly

likely that the child's academic problems are secondary to ADHD. In this case, parent and teacher interview data, parent and teacher ratings, and the results of direct observations are consistent in placing the child's ADHD-related behavior in the extreme range for his or her gender and age. Further assessment of possible learning disabilities is warranted only if there is some question of below average *ability* in one or more academic areas.

2. Alternatively, the assessment data may be relatively consistent in indicating that few symptoms of ADHD are present, and those symptoms observed are exhibited primarily in academic situations (e.g., classroom instruction, independent seatwork). In such cases, parent and teacher interview data, parent and teacher ratings, and direct observation data will be in the normal range for ADHD symptoms. If academic problems are present, then hypotheses other than ADHD must be explored, including the possibility of academic skills deficits.

3. Conclusions based on the above two scenarios are relatively straightforward. More difficult interpretation decisions must be made in cases where assessment data are inconsistent relative to the frequency, severity, and cross-situational pervasiveness of possible ADHD symptomatology. For instance, a child's teachers may report significant ADHD symptoms, while his or her parents report few, if any, attention and behavior control problems. Although the general problem of interpreting inconsistent assessment data is discussed in Chapter 2, the specific discrimination between ADHD and academic skills deficits will be aided by considering the following:

a. Children with ADHD typically obtain clinically significant ratings on parent and teacher ratings of disruptive behavior problems in addition to ADHD (e.g., Aggression subscale on the CBCL). Children with learning disabilities in the absence of ADHD usually do not obtain high scores in these dimensions (Barkley, DuPaul, & McMurray, 1990). Further, children with learning disabilities rarely are impulsive, disinhibited, and aggressive, while children with ADHD are more likely to display such difficulties (Barkley, 1990).

b. Children with learning disabilities obtain average range scores on measures that tap the situational pervasiveness of behavior (e.g., HSQ, SSQ) and attention (e.g., HSQ-R, SSQ-R) problems, while those with ADHD usually receive high scores for the number of problem situations and the mean severity of behavior problems on these measures (Barkley, DuPaul, & McMurray, 1990).

c. Children with learning disabilities who do not have ADHD usually are observed to exhibit rates of on-task behavior and work completion that are no different from their normal counterparts when observations of independent seatwork are conducted (Barkley et al., 1990).

d. Students with learning disabilities also differ from those with ADHD with respect to the onset and pervasiveness of apparent ADHD symptoms. Usually, children who are exhibiting problems with attention and behavior control due to academic skills deficits lack an early childhood history of hyperactivity and problem behavior. The latter is a hallmark of ADHD, as it is typically a disorder of early onset. In contrast, the attention problems of students with learning disabilities usually arise in middle childhood (i.e., third or fourth grade) and are exhibited only in specific situations. Usually, attention problems are reported to occur only when children are receiving academic instruction and/or completing work in their most problematic subject areas. Alternatively, children with ADHD are likely to exhibit ADHD symptoms across most, if not all, school and home situations.

e. Children with ADHD alone are likely to obtain scores on individual academic achievement tests that are similar to their peers, in contrast to the below average scores usually obtained by students with learning deficits.

Overall, children with academic skills deficits can be differentiated from those with ADHD on the basis of the onset, severity, and situational pervasiveness of observed ADHD symptoms. In particular, the more specific the attention and behavior problems are to academic situations and tasks, the more likely it is that these difficulties are secondary to academic skills deficits rather than ADHD.

CASE EXAMPLE

David was an 8-year-old boy referred by his second grade teacher. Concerns were raised regarding problems with inattention and difficulties of an academic nature. David was reported to exhibit significant difficulties completing assigned work within a reasonable time period and to daydream frequently during classroom instruction. He displayed these problems on an inconsistent basis across school days. The teacher was particularly concerned that David was making very slow progress with reading skills and had difficulties comprehending material he had just finished reading.

An interview with David's mother indicated that his birth, early development, and medical histories were unremarkable. His activity level as a toddler and preschooler was described as "normal for a boy." His father was reported to have evidenced learning problems and possible ADHD as a child, but no other signficant problems were reported for family members. His mother did not report any significant problems handling David's behavior at home and described his peer relationships as "excellent." David was not receiving any form of psychotherapy at the time of the evaluation, although his mother did report recently placing him on a modified Feingold diet with resultant mild changes in behavior control. No formal behavior modification strategies were being used in either home or school settings.

A psychoeducational evaluation was conducted by the school psychologist including intelligence testing and several individual achievement tests. The results of these suggested that David was of average intelligence with a relative weakness in verbal abilities. Achievement testing indicated a number of deficits in language and reading functioning. Based on these results, the school team suggested that David receive academic support in reading and language arts skills several times per week with a resource room teacher.

Several measures were employed to evaluate whether David might have ADHD. A diagnostic interview with David's mother was conducted wherein only 2 of the 14 symptoms of ADHD were reported as present on a frequent basis. These included distractibility and often shifting from one uncompleted activity to another. Notably, David was reported to evidence inattention only on tasks that were school-related (e.g., reading), but was able to complete assigned household chores in a reliable fashion. No problems with impulsivity or overactivity were reported. David was not reported to evidence behaviors related to any other behavior disorder including Conduct Disorder, Depression, or Anxiety Disorder.

David's mother completed several rating scales to document the severity of his behavior control problems relative to other boys his age. Her responses on the CBCL resulted in a normal range profile (i.e., T-scores < 65) across all clinical scales including those related to ADHD. On the ADHD Rating Scale, only 5 of the 14 symptoms of ADHD were reported to occur on a frequent basis. Ratings on the HSQ-R indicated that mild attention problems were present only in selected home settings (e.g., when asked to complete homework). Scores on the Social Skills Rating System (Gresham & Elliott, 1990) were in the normal range. Thus, parent ratings did not indicate ADHD symptoms to be problematic nor were these seen as pervasive across settings.

David's second-grade teacher completed similar questionnaires. Her responses on the TRF-CBCL resulted in borderline significant ratings (i.e., T-score = 66, or greater than the 93rd percentile) on the Attention Problems subscale. Remaining scales including those related to other disruptive behavior disorders were in the normal range. Scores on the Social Skills Rating System did not indicate clinically significant levels of peer relationship difficulties. On the ADHD Rating Scale, 5 of the 14 symptoms of ADHD were reported to occur on a frequent basis. On the SSQ-R, mild attention problems were reported to occur across most structured classroom settings. The most significant problems related to ADHD that were reported were with respect to concentration and completion of tasks, not with impulse control or hyperactivity. Thus, the symptoms reported by David's teacher were more consistent with ADHD–Predominantly Inattentive Type (i.e., ADDnoH).

David was observed in his regular classroom on several occasions using the Restricted Academic Situation Coding System (Barkley, 1990). Each observation took place during a time when David was assigned independent seatwork related to reading and language arts. Averaged over three 20-minute observations, David was observed to be on-task approximately 80% of the time, although these percentages ranged from a low of 53% to a high of 90%. Thus, his task-related attention was quite variable across days. David exhibited fidgety, restless behavior during an average of only 28% of the observation intervals. David completed an average of 80% of the work assigned to him at a relatively low accuracy level (i.e., 74%). Although he did evidence some behaviors related to ADHD, his main problems were related to his understanding and accurate completion of assigned tasks.

In summary, most of the data collected in the course of this evaluation were not consistent with the conclusion that David had ADHD. In fact, only one measure, teacher ratings on the CBCL, was in the clinically significant range for this disorder. The remaining measures were in the normal range including parent interview data, parent and teacher ratings on the ADHD Rating Scale, parent ratings on the CBCL, and behavioral observation data. Behaviors related to ADHD were strictly in the realm of inattention and, more specifically, inattention during academic tasks only. According to his parents, David was quite attentive to household chores and other nonacademic tasks assigned to him. Thus, David's problems with inattention were seen to be a reflection of his frustration in attempting tasks that were quite difficult for him rather than representing ADHD. Recommendations included further behavioral assessment of possible academic skills deficits to determine appropriate goals and procedures to increase his scholastic competencies. Although it was assumed that improving his academic skills would enhance his on-task behavior, the latter was directly targeted for change utilizing a classroom-based contingency management program combined with a daily report card system (see Chapter 4).

IMPLICATIONS FOR INTERVENTION

The determination of whether a student's academic difficulties are due to ADHD, an academic skills deficit, or both has direct implications for classroom intervention (Cantwell & Baker, 1991). The behaviors targeted for change, the treatment settings, and the specific interventions employed will vary as a function of assessment decisions. As discussed in Chapter 4, the usual treatment targets for a student with ADHD are behaviors related to classroom deportment, such as paying attention to instruction, staying seated, and following classroom rules. To the extent that academic performance difficulties are present, certain scholastic behaviors will be targeted as well, including timely completion of seatwork and/or accuracy of written work. For those children with academic skills deficits, achievement-related behaviors and academic skill development are the primary targets for intervention. These would include not only behaviors related to independent seatwork, but other academic survival skills as well, such as correct responding during reading group, accurate note taking during lectures, and providing correct answers to written test items. When a child is found to have both ADHD and an academic skills deficit, scholastic behaviors typically serve as the primary targets for intervention. This is due to the frequent finding that when academic performance is enhanced, classroom deportment often improves as well (Hinshaw, 1992b; McGee & Share, 1988). It is not unusual, however, to find circumstances where both academic and deportment behaviors must be targeted for change to obtain consistent and durable effects. Further, for those youngsters who have both ADHD and learning deficits, extrinsic motivational programming must be combined with academic interventions regardless of the specific behaviors targeted for change (Hinshaw, 1992b).

Intervention programs designed to treat children with ADHD commonly are applied across a variety of settings, given the cross-situational pervasiveness of symptoms of this disorder (Barkley, 1990). For instance, token reinforcement systems may be applied across a variety of situations (e.g., playground, classroom, cafeteria) in both school and home settings in an attempt to enhance compliance with rules and attention to assigned tasks. In contrast, the primary intervention setting for children with academic skills deficits is the classroom. Although a number of classroom settings may be involved, treatment of academic difficulties rarely takes place outside of the classroom, yet strong arguments for adjunctive, home–school interventions have been made in recent years (Kelley, 1990). Those children with both ADHD and academic skills deficits will require treatment in multiple settings implemented by a number of professionals. In such cases, the need for effective communication and collaboration among the individuals involved in the child's treatment is obvious (see Chapters 4–8).

As discussed in subsequent chapters, the two most effective interventions for ADHD are stimulant medication (e.g., methylphenidate) and behavior modification procedures. Although the latter may involve changes to both antecedent conditions (e.g., more frequent prompts to pay attention) and consequences (e.g., positive reinforcement for task completion), motivational programming has received most of the emphasis in the ADHD treatment literature (Pfiffner & Barkley, 1990). Thus, behaviorally based classroom interventions for ADHD usually include token reinforcement systems combined with response cost wherein contingencies are available at school, at home, or in both settings in order to motivate the child to attend to assigned tasks and classroom rules (see Chapter 4 for details).

In contrast, academic skills deficits are not directly enhanced by pharmacotherapy and are usually treated with psychoeducational programming designed to ameliorate presumed "processing deficits" that underlie the child's learning problems (Semrud-Clikeman et al., 1992). This treatment approach remains quite prevalent in this country despite a lack of evidence for its efficacy (e.g., Kavale & Mattson, 1983). Behaviorally based and instructionally based interventions for academic skills deficits that have received empirical support include modifications to both antecedent and consequent conditions (see Stoner, Shinn, & Walker, 1991). Although motivational programming similar to that employed for ADHD has been found helpful in addressing academic skills deficits, there is an equivalent emphasis in the literature on changing antecedent stimulus conditions (e.g., rate of presentation of academic material). Thus, even though both ADHD and academic skills deficits can be treated behaviorally, the specific parameters of the intervention program will vary as a function of diagnostic status.

ADHD AS A SPECIAL EDUCATION CATEGORY

Prior to 1991, students with ADHD were not eligible to receive special education services unless they qualified for such services on the basis of existing classification categories (e.g., specific learning disability, seriously emotionally disturbed). Thus, the vast majority of children with ADHD were placed in regular education classrooms with minimal alterations made to their instruction. Due to the intense lobbying efforts of a variety of professional and parent groups, a change in the interpretation of federal guidelines was issued by the U.S. Department of Education in 1991 (see Hakola, 1992). In this section, we will provide a synopsis of these changes in federal regulations as well as offer suggestions to school psychologists on how to determine whether a specific child with ADHD requires special education services.

In a memorandum to chief state school officers issued on September 16, 1991, officials from the U.S. Department of Education provided clarification of the department's policy to address the educational needs of children with ADHD (Davila, Williams, & MacDonald, 1991). The gist of their memo was that students classified as having an ADHD may qualify for special education services in one of three ways. First, a child with both ADHD and another disability (e.g., learning disability) could qualify for special education services under one of the existing disability categories defined in Part B of the Individuals with Disabilities Education Act (IDEA) of 1990 (i.e., reauthorization of the Education of the Handicapped Act [EHA]). This was the only way a child with ADHD could qualify for special education prior to the issuance of this memo.

A second possibility for special education eligibility was identified under the "Other Health Impaired" category of Part B. The memo defined this eligibility as follows:

> The term "other health impaired" includes chronic or acute impairments that result in limited alertness, which adversely affects educational performance. Thus, children with ADD should be classified as eligible for services under the "other health impaired" category in instances where the ADD is a chronic or acute health problem that results in limited alertness, which adversely affects educational performance. *In other words, children with ADD, where the ADD is a chronic or acute health problem resulting in limited alertness, may be considered disabled under Part B solely on the basis of this disorder within the "other health impaired" category in situations where special education and related services are needed because of the ADD.* (Davila et al., 1991, p. 3; italics added)

This is likely to be the most commonly applied criterion to judge a student's eligibility for special education services on the basis of having ADHD. It clearly states that if the child's alertness is limited by chronic ADHD to the extent that his or her educational performance suffers, then the child may require special education services. The previous sentence describes most, if not all, children diagnosed with ADHD, as, by definition, it is a chronic disorder wherein they exhibit limited alertness and their academic performance is deleteriously affected. The difficult decision, therefore, is whether the child actually *needs* special education programming to address these difficulties and/or academic competencies or whether interventions in the general education classroom will be sufficient.

A final criterion that could be used to determine a child's eligibility for instructional modifications on the basis of having ADHD is contained in Section 504 of the Rehabilitation Act of 1973. Such modifications may or may not require the provision of special education services. This is a civil rights law that states that schools must address the needs of children considered to be handicapped as competently as the needs of nonhandicapped students are met. A "handicapped person" is defined as, "any person who has a physical or mental impairment which substantially limits a major life activity" (Davila et al., 1991, p. 6). Certainly, academic performance and school functioning can be considered a "major life activity." Thus, even children with ADHD who are not eligible for special services under Part B could be considered in need of individualized intervention on the basis of being handicapped in accordance with Section 504.

If the above regulations are interpreted loosely, one could make a case for most children with ADHD to be eligible to receive some degree of special education services. Given the high percentage of children already receiving such services and the limited database supporting the overall efficacy of special education, however, this may not be a prudent course of action. Rather, as is the case for children with other behavior disorders, one of the main criteria for receipt of special education services should be the child's response to interventions in the general education classroom (Gresham, 1991). Thus, the diagnosis of ADHD does not necessarily warrant the receipt of special education services, unless the child's behavior has not changed as a function of regular classroom interventions (National Association of School Psychologists, 1992a; Silver, 1990).

Zirkel (1992) has designed a checklist for determining the legal eligibility for special education services in accordance with the regulations enumerated above (see Appendix 3.1). Figure 3.3 presents a decision-making flow chart that has been adapted from Zirkel's checklist. Using this checklist and flow chart as guides, the following steps should be followed in determining whether a specific child will require special education services for ADHD:

1. Conduct an evaluation of ADHD and related difficulties, as discussed in Chapter 2. If the child is found to meet the criteria for ADHD, then, by definition, he or she has a chronic condition that significantly limits alertness, thus satisfying two components of the eligibility criteria for special education services under the "other health impaired" category of Part B, as discussed above.

2. If the child is found to exhibit behaviors related to one of the existing classification categories of the EHA/IDEA (e.g., learning disability), then special education services may be warranted.

3. If the child does not qualify for special education services under one of the existing categories, then two more determinations must be made. First, does the child's ADHD-related behavior in the classroom significantly limit his or her educational performance? This can be de-

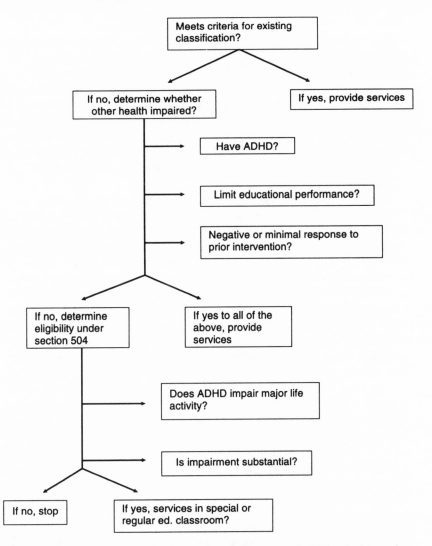

FIGURE 3.3. Flow chart for making special education eligibility decisions for students with ADHD. From "A checklist for determining legal eligibility of ADD/ADHD students" by P. A. Zirkel, 1992, *Special Educator, 8*(7), 93–97. Copyright 1992 by LRP Publications. Reprinted by permission.

termined using academic performance data, as discussed in Chapter 2. Usually, some aspect of a child's academic achievement is deleteriously affected by his or her ADHD symptomatology. Thus, some form of intervention will be necessary given that section 504 stipulates such action given that the handicap substantially impairs a major life activity (i.e., education). The typical, initial step is to design and implement an intervention program in the general education classroom (see Chapter 4). Such programs will include modifications to the child's instructional program based on behavioral principles. The child also may be referred to his or her physician for consideration of a trial of stimulant medication, as discussed in Chapter 5.

4. The last, and most critical, criterion for special education eligibility is whether the child *needs* such services because of his or her ADHD. This criterion could be interpreted in a variety of ambiguous ways. Therefore, the most objective way to reach a decision regarding this criterion is through evaluating the efficacy of regular classroom interventions (Gresham, 1991). Baseline data should be collected on a number of target behaviors prior to implementing a specific intervention (including medication). After implementing the recommended treatment(s), data are collected again on the same variables to assess behavioral change. If the child does not exhibit significant improvement following a trial of regular classroom intervention(s), one of three possible courses of action is followed. First, changes could be made to the intervention program in the regular classroom. Alternatively, the child could receive some form of special education programming. An additional alternative would be to both make changes in regular education interventions and provide special education programming.

5. Whether special education services are provided or not, interventions addressing the child's ADHD will be necessary. The efficacy of both regular and special education interventions should be evaluated on a continuous basis to determine when changes in programming and/or placement are necessary.

SUMMARY

Most children with ADHD will exhibit significant problems with academic performance, such as slow work completion, inconsistent accuracy on seatwork and homework, and poor study skills. Further, about one-third of these children will display academic skills that are significantly below average, and therefore they may be characterized as having a learning disability. The fact that academic problems are consistently associated with ADHD has direct implications for the assessment and treatment of these students. The evaluation of ADHD must not only be directed towards behavior control difficulties, but should include measures of academic performance as well. Further, such children should routinely be screened for academic skills deficits, with additional assessment of academic functioning conducted as necessary. In similar fashion, intervention programs designed to treat ADHD must include target behaviors related to academic performance. In the case of children who have both ADHD and academic skills deficits, treatment must be directed toward ameliorating both conditions simultaneously. Finally, recent changes to federal guidelines have allowed for the provision of special education services to children with ADHD solely on the basis that this disorder limits their educational performance. Special education eligibility decisions should be made on the basis of a reliable assessment of ADHD, the degree to which the child's ADHD impacts academic and social functioning, and the success of regular classroom interventions in ameliorating academic and behavioral difficulties related to ADHD.

APPENDIX 3.1

Zirkel's Checklist for Determining Legal Eligibility of ADD/ADHD Students

PART I

1. Does the student evidence, to a prepondent extent, all the qualifications of "other health impaired" under the IDEA:

• a chronic or acute health problem?	YES	NO
• if YES, does this problem result in limited strength, vitality, or alertness?	YES	NO
• if YES, does the limited strength, vitality, or alertness adversely affect the child's educational performance to the extent of necessitating special education?	YES	NO

2. If the student does not qualify under "other health impaired," does the student evidence, to a preponderant extent, all the qualifications for "specific learning disability" under the IDEA:

• a basic psychological processing disorder in understanding or using language that is manifested in a severe discrepancy between achievement and intellectual ability in (a) oral comprehension, (b) listening comprehension, (c) written expression, (d) basic reading skill, (e) reading comprehension, (f) mathematics calculation, or (g) mathematics reasoning?	YES	NO
• if YES, is the severe discrepancy not correctable without special education and related services?	YES	NO
• if YES, is the problem only secondarily or not at all attributable to (a) environmental, cultural, or economic disadvantage, (b) visual, hearing, or motor disabilities, (c) mental retardation, or (d) emotional disturbance?	YES	NO

3. If the student does not qualify under "other health impaired" or "specific learning disability," does the student evidence, to a preponderant extent, all the qualifications for any other disability under the IDEA:

• severe emotional disturbance?	YES	NO
• mental retardation?	YES	NO
• autism or traumatic brain injury?	YES	NO

PART II

4. If the student does not qualify under *Part I*, does the child's ADD/ADHD condition meet all the qualifications under Section 504:

• is the condition mental or physical?	YES	NO
• if YES, does it impair a major life activity, such as education?	YES	NO
• if YES, is the degree of this impairment substantial?	YES	NO

PART III

5. If the student does not qualify under *Part I* or *Part II*, is the child eligible under a state law that supplements the IDEA or Sec. 504?   YES   NO

4

Classroom-Based
Intervention Strategies

School-aged children spend 6–8 hours per day, 5 days per week in school and classroom settings. These environments are typified by requirements for children to follow rules, interact appropriately with other children and adults, participate in adult-directed instructional activities, learn what is being taught, and refrain from disrupting or disturbing the learning and activities of others. For teachers, imparting the knowledge and skills comprising the curriculum and teaching children to behave in a manner consistent with social, cultural, and organizational requirements are demanding tasks. This work is even more demanding when it involves children diagnosed with ADHD, as the behaviors characteristic of these children frequently interfere with classroom learning and socially acceptable behavior. The purpose of this chapter is to present and discuss classroom-based strategies for managing the behavior of children diagnosed with ADHD and for facilitating the critical classroom functions of teaching and learning where these children are involved.

Before discussing strategies, however, we examine briefly some of our assumptions regarding children identified with ADHD and interventions intended to support these children in their school experiences. Our first assumption is that ADHD should be considered a serious concern that will endure over time and be associated with difficult-to-manage behavior in classroom settings. As such, children diagnosed with ADHD likely will experience academic and social learning difficulties across many, but not all, classroom situations, and throughout their school-age years. For those children experiencing school-based problems, involved professionals will need to take a systematic and ongoing approach to designing, implementing, and evaluating classroom-based interventions and accommodations to prevent, ameliorate, or manage presenting problems. To facilitate such an approach, throughout this chapter the strategies presented are reviewed based on empirical support for them in the research literature of education and psychology. In addition, some promising strategies for instructional and behavioral management are discussed, including strategies with demonstrated effectiveness with children experiencing a variety of school-based problems (e.g., reading and other academic skills problems). We also discuss the issue of support for teachers in carrying out behavioral and educational interventions and accommodations.

To date, researchers in the area of interventions for children with ADHD have focused on issues and strategies pertaining to managing social behavior and deportment in the classroom, primarily via medication and contingency management. Although this work has been quite productive, its focus on optimizing social behavior, avoiding behavioral maladjustment, and preventing antisocial behavior represents only one aspect of school and classroom concerns regarding ADHD. The other side of this coin is optimizing the academic achievement and performance of identified children. Social and academic problems can be seen as related and viewing them as such leads to our second assumption. Specifically, we assume that both the social and the achievement problems of childhood can be approached productively as instructional problems (Colvin & Sugai, 1988). That is, we as educators and psychologists have a critical role to play in arranging for and conducting instruction to promote both academic and social skill development so as to prevent and solve problems in these areas.

This chapter presents prevention and intervention strategies related to core areas of academic and social functioning likely to be of concern where children identified with ADHD are concerned. These strategies involve instructional activities that range from adult-directed (e.g., contingency management), to peer-directed (e.g., peer tutoring procedures), and self-directed (e.g., self-management). They have in common the goal of preparing children to become self-directed learners whose classroom deportment and achievement are similar to that of their typical peers.

Our third assumption is related to viewing social and achievement concerns as problems requiring systematic instruction. Specifically, professionals involved with children with ADHD should take an educative approach to behavior problems (Evans & Meyer, 1985; Meyer & Evans, 1989). From this perspective, interventions for behavior problems have the explicit goal of teaching identified children the skills and knowledge necessary to replace problem behaviors with acceptable ones. An educative approach represents an alternative to interventions that are solely child-focused and primarily concerned with the elimination or reduction of problem behaviors.

Taking an educative approach to behavior problems leads us to our fourth assumption: Dealing effectively and in an educative manner with behavior problems will require the development and implementation of programmatic behavior and teacher support plans (Horner, Albin, & O'Neill, 1991). These support programs go beyond the more prevalent emphasis on the manipulation of consequences that have come to typify behavior management interventions in schools. These plans include the identification and allocation of resources and support needed by teachers to carry out interventions and to make instructional accommodations in support of students with special needs. Teacher support plans will be discussed in more detail in the latter portion of this chapter.

Finally, it is assumed that persons endeavoring to manage or alter the problematic behavior of children in a systematic fashion will have completed appropriate professional training and/or will be practicing under the supervision of an appropriately trained and credentialed professional (see Jenson, Clark, Walker, & Kehle, 1991; McConnell, & Hecht, 1991, for discussions of professional training needs for behavioral and instructional interventions, respectively). Further, more intrusive behaviorally based programs likely should be reviewed and approved by a panel of professionals and lay persons from the school community. For example, programs warranting review might include those involving the systematic sanctioning of penalties (e.g., loss of instructional or recess time) contingent on inappropriate or undesired behavior.

Given the previous assumptions, classroom-based intervention strategies for ADHD should be grounded in the guidelines for interventions presented in Table 4.1. First and foremost, the development and evaluation of interventions for ADHD are empirically based. Treatment strategies are chosen based, in part, on their demonstrated efficacy in the research literature. Further, the relative success of an intervention program is assessed by using appropriate evaluation measures (see Chapter 2). Second, the child's needs are paramount in the selection of intervention strategies. Treatment goals are delineated relative to socially valid outcomes for the child with ADHD. Third, given that a team of professionals typically is involved in the treatment of ADHD, the responsibilities of each team member must be delineated clearly to ensure that intervention strategies are implemented with integrity. Fourth, the focus of treatment is primarily on *increasing* the frequency and/or duration of appropriate behaviors (e.g., academic productivity and accuracy) rather than simply *decreasing* disruptive classroom activities. Finally, each child's response to intervention is presumed to be unique, and therefore the effects and side effects of a particular treatment are unknown prior to its implementation. This implies the need for ongoing and comprehensive evaluation of all intervention strategies.

TABLE 4.1. Guidelines for the Design, Implementation, and Evaluation of Interventions for Learning and Behavior Problems

1. Intervention development, evaluation, and revision are *data-based* activities.
2. Intervention development, evaluation, and revision are driven by *child advocacy* and focus on attainment of clearly identified, socially valid *child outcomes*.
3. Intervention procedures must be thoroughly identified and defined, as well as implemented with integrity by persons with clearly delineated responsibilities.
4. Effective interventions produce or lead to increased rates of appropriate behavior and/or improved rates of learning, not solely decreases in undesirable or disturbing behavior.
5. Prior to its implementation, an intervention's effects on the behaviors of the identified child, the teacher, and on the classroom are unknown.

GENERAL CONSIDERATIONS FOR CLASSROOM-BASED INTERVENTIONS

As mentioned previously, classroom-based interventions tend to consist of manipulations of consequent events (i.e., reinforcers and punishers), particularly where behavior management is concerned. This tendency to focus on the manipulation of consequences also is apparent in the research literature on classroom interventions for children identified with ADHD (see for reviews Pfiffner & O'Leary, 1993; Rapport, 1987a). Here, intervention research has emphasized the use of positive reinforcement, sometimes coupled with mild forms of punishment (e.g., response cost and time out from positive reinforcement). In the field of applied behavior analysis in general, a shift in emphasis is well underway toward preventing and managing behavior and achievement problems through antecedent manipulations and environmental arrangements (Sulzer-Azaroff & Mayer, 1991). There is a need for similar emphases in the area of classroom-based management of children with ADHD. Examples of potential directions for such work are discussed later in this chapter.

Intervention procedures based on principles of human behavior have a long and well-documented history of effectiveness in ameliorating children's learning and behavior problems in school settings, including children with ADHD (Sulzer-Azaroff & Mayer, 1977, 1986, 1991). For example, these behavior change strategies have been successful in reducing the disruptive, off-task behavior of children identified with ADHD and increasing their academic productivity (e.g., Rapport, Murphy, & Bailey, 1980, 1982). Given the difficulties hypothesized to underlie the problems exhibited by children with ADHD (e.g., problems with delayed responding, motivation deficits, lack of internalized rules), this finding is not surprising. It may be that behavioral interventions increase the overall level of appropriate classroom behavior by capturing the child's attention through enhancement of the stimulation or motivational value of the task at hand. Well-documented specific intervention strategies are discussed in the following sections, under the broad rubrics of school-based contingency management procedures (e.g., positive reinforcement) and systems that involve home-based delivery of contingencies. In designing behaviorally based interventions for classroom problems related to ADHD, the following issues will require careful professional attention:

1. A careful and thorough assessment of the specific presenting problems should be conducted to guide the design and selection of intervention components (e.g., target behaviors, instructional strategy, motivational program).

2. Children diagnosed with ADHD typically require more frequent and specific feedback than their classmates to optimize their performance. As such, initial phases of interventions aimed at ADHD-related problems should incorporate contingencies that can be delivered in a relatively continuous manner. Leaner schedules of reinforcement should be introduced cautiously and gradually, as some laboratory-based evidence indicates that children with ADHD have more difficulty maintaining their behavior under intermittent reinforcement schedules than do their peers (Douglas, 1984). Related to the issue of timing of reinforcement, in one study (Rapport, Tucker, DuPaul, Merlo, & Stone, 1986) children with ADHD tended to choose smaller, more immediate rewards over larger, delayed rewards contingent upon completion of academic work. These results serve to emphasize the need to attend to the general notion that to be effective, positive reinforcement of target behaviors should occur immediately following those behaviors.

3. Although contingent positive reinforcement should be the primary component of a behaviorally based intervention program for problems related to ADHD, some evidence exists to suggest that exclusive reliance on reinforcement may distract the child from the task at hand. Alternatively, this concern may be ameliorated by the use of positive reinforcement coupled with the use of mild negative consequences, such as prudent reprimands (Abramowitz, O'Leary, & Rosen, 1987; Rosen, O'Leary, Joyce, Conway, & Pfiffner, 1984) and redirection of the child toward appropriate task behavior. When utilized, verbal reprimands and redirection activities need to be *specific* regarding the teacher's concerns and wishes, and *consistently delivered immediately* following the occurrence of problem behavior(s) (Abramowitz & O'Leary, 1991; Pfiffner & O'Leary, 1993). Further, treating children with dignity and respect requires that reprimands and redirective statements be made in a *brief, calm, and quiet*

manner. As much as possible, reprimands should be delivered *privately* while making eye contact with the child.

4. If student behavior during independent work periods is targetted for change, initial task instructions should involve no more than a few steps. The child should then repeat the directions back to the teacher to demonstrate understanding. Similarly, student homework and tasks to be completed should be assigned one at a time, with lengthier tasks broken into smaller units. In some cases, the overall amount of assigned work would be reduced for the child with ADHD. The length and complexity of the workload would be increased gradually as the child demonstrates successful independent completion of increasingly larger units. Repetitive material (e.g., reassigning erroneously completed worksheets) should be avoided. Alternatively, an assignment that taps the same skill or concept area could be substituted to avoid boredom and potential exacerbation of attention problems.

5. Academic products and performance (e.g., work completion and accuracy) are preferred as targets of intervention, as compared with specific task-related behaviors (e.g., attention to task or staying in one's seat), for several reasons. First, this preference promotes teacher monitoring of important student outcomes. Second, this preference promotes attention to the organizational and academic skills (e.g., working with the appropriate materials for an assignment, soliciting formative feedback on initial task performance) necessary for independent learning and for generating the academic products. Third, a focus on active academic responding does not violate the "Dead-man test for behavior" articulated by Lindsley (1991). This "rule" states that "if a dead boy could do it, it wasn't behavior" (Lindsley, 1991, p. 457). Employing treatment targets such as "sitting still" and "not calling out" violate the Dead-man test. Finally, this preference for academic responding as a treatment target promotes a focus on behavior that is incompatible with inattentive and disruptive behavior and as such may lead to multiple desired outcomes (Pfiffner & O'Leary, 1993).

6. In general, preferred activities (e.g., free-choice activity time, access to a classroom computer) should be used as reinforcers rather than concrete rewards (e.g., candy). Such arrangements may include contingencies such as making access to a preferred classroom activity contingent upon completion of an assignment in a less-preferred subject area (e.g., completion of math worksheet leads to access to reading activities). Further, the specific rewards or reinforcers employed should be varied or rotated frequently to prevent disinterest with them and thus with the program (i.e., reinforcer satiation). Finally, rather than assuming that specific activities will be motivating for the child, develop reward "menus"

by directly asking the child what he or she wants to earn or by observing his or her preferred activities.

7. Employ a "priming" procedure with the child prior to academic assignment periods (Rapport, 1987b) to enhance the positive incentive value of classroom privileges. This procedure involves the teacher and student reviewing a list of possible classroom privileges *prior* to beginning an academic work period wherein the student chooses which activity he or she would like to participate in following the work period.

8. The integrity or fidelity with which an intervention program is implemented must be monitored and evaluated (Gresham, 1989). Such monitoring can serve as the basis for making changes in program components, justifying additional resource needs, and/or developing and providing additional training materials or sessions with those carrying out the procedures. An intervention integrity checklist (Gresham, 1989) is provided in Figure 4.1 as an example of one method for monitoring program integ-

Components	Monday	Tuesday	Wednesday	Thursday	Friday	% Component Integrity
1. Describes system	XI	XI	XI	XI	XI	100%
2. Displays/Describes reinforcers	XI	IO	IO	XI	XI	60%
3. 3 X 5 card placed on desks	XI	XI	XI	XI	XI	100%
4. Card taped on 3 sides	XI	XI	XI	XI	XI	100%
5. 4 slips of colored paper placed in cards	XI	XI	XI	XI	XI	100%
6. Lottery in effect ½ hour	XI	IO	IO	IO	XI	40%
7. Slips removed contingent on rule violation	XI	IO	XI	IO	IO	40%
8. Restates rule contingently	IO	IO	IO	XI	XI	20%
9. Tickets placed in box	XI	XI	XI	XI	XI	100%
10. Drawing on Friday	NA I	NA I	NA I	NA I	XI	100%
11. Winner selects reinforcer	NA I	NA I	NA I	NA I	XI	100%
Daily Integrity =	91%	64%	73%	82%	82%	

X = Occurrence $\bar{X}$ Integrity = 78%
O = Nonoccurrence

FIGURE 4.1. Direct observation form for recording treatment integrity of the response cost lottery. From "Assessment of treatment integrity in school consultation and prereferral intervention" by F. M. Gresham, 1989, *School Psychology Review, 18,* 37–50. Copyright 1989 by the National Association of School Psychologists. Reprinted by permission.

rity. Gresham (1989) employed this checklist to assess the accuracy of implementation of a classroom response-cost lottery system. An independent observer evaluated the degree to which the classroom teacher completed the 11 main steps of this intervention on a daily basis. Thus, integrity of intervention could be evaluated by component across days or by days across components. Such information is invaluable in determining the need for additional teacher training and support in implementing classroom interventions. This type of checklist could be altered to reflect the specific components of any particular intervention procedure.

CONTINGENCY MANAGEMENT PROCEDURES

The use of positive reinforcement of appropriate academic and social behavior should be viewed as the cornerstone in the design of classroom-based behavior management strategies. By definition, a positive reinforcer is an event, condition, or stimulus that increases the future likelihood of an action or behavior that it immediately follows (Sulzer-Azaroff & Mayer, 1991). For children with ADHD, the research literature indicates that several different behavior management strategies based on positive reinforcement can favorably enhance classroom behavior. A representative range of such strategies includes the use of contingency contracting, the use of positive reinforcement coupled with penalties or redirection contingent upon problematic behavior, and the use of home-based contingencies to influence in-school behavior. Although most of these procedures involve contingent social praise from the teacher (e.g., O'Leary, Pelham, Rosenbaum, & Price, 1976), research indicates that children with ADHD may not exhibit consistent behavioral change in the absence of more powerful contingencies (Barkley, 1990). Thus, formal classroom behavior change programs are likely to require one or more of the following components: token reinforcement, contingency contracting, response cost, and time-out from positive reinforcement. Each of these techniques is described below, along with additional discussion of factors to consider when preparing for their use in classrooms.

Token Reinforcement Programs

Contingent social praise and attention can be effective in producing positive behavioral change with many children. However, typically it is insufficient to bring about consistent improvement in the classroom behavior and academic performance of children with ADHD (Pfiffner & Barkley, 1990). Behavioral strategies that incorporate secondary generalized reinforcers (e.g., token economies) can provide the reward immediacy, specificity, and potency that often are required for children diagnosed with ADHD. Behavior management systems incorporating these components have been shown to be highly successful in enhancing the academic productivity and appropriate behavior of inattentive children (e.g., Ayllon, Layman, & Kandel, 1975; Robinson, Newby, & Ganzell, 1981).

Designing a school-based token reinforcement system involves the following steps:

1. One or more classroom situations are identified as problematic for the child and are targetted for intervention. These situations may be determined through a teacher interview and/or use of an objective rating scale such as the SSQ-R (DuPaul & Barkley, 1992). Direct observations in the classroom should be used to validate the selection of these problematic situations and behaviors (see Chapter 2). Typically, classroom work periods requiring independent completion of tasks present the greatest difficulty in terms of behavior control for children with ADHD.

2. Target behaviors are selected and typically include academic products (e.g., number of math problems completed in a given amount of time) or specific actions (e.g., appropriate interactions with peers during recess). In general, products are preferred due to the relative ease of their collection and monitoring. In addition, academic productivity typically involves behaviors that are incompatible with inattentive and disruptive behavior (see Robinson, Newby, & Ganzell, 1981).

3. Types of secondary reinforcers (i.e., tokens) to be used are identified, and may include multicolored poker chips, check marks or stickers on a card, or points on a card stand. Younger children (e.g., up to 9 years old) generally prefer tangible rewards (e.g., poker chips), whereas older children and adolescents respond more positively to points or check marks. Token economy systems typically are considered too complicated for children under 5 years of age. With preschool-age children, the use of primary reinforcers (e.g., parental or teacher praise, hugs, or other social attention) contingent upon the occurrence of appropriate behavior is recommended.

4. The values of target or goal behaviors must be determined. That is, the number of tokens earned by completing each target behavior or its subcomponents should be determined by task difficulty, with completion of more difficult or time-consuming tasks worth more tokens than less involved assignments. Where necessary, targetted behaviors are broken down into their component parts (e.g., "successful work completion" may be defined as completing a certain number of items within a specified time period, attaining a certain level of accuracy, and reviewing the work before requesting the teacher's feedback) to allow children to earn tokens for partial completion of a task or reaching a certain performance

criterion. In these instances, a task analysis may be necessary to explicitly delineate the components of expected behaviors.

5. The teacher and student should jointly develop a list of privileges or activities within the school for which tokens may be exchanged, ranging from inexpensive to costly ones. It may be beneficial to ask parents to collaborate on the development of this list and, in addition, to make privileges available at home in exchange for tokens. The number of tokens or points necessary to purchase each privilege can be determined collaboratively among those individuals involved in the program. As a rough guide, estimate the maximum number of tokens that could be earned on a daily basis and divide this sum evenly among available reinforcers, then add or delete tokens to the cost of each item in accordance with the value of the privilege or activity to the child.

6. The value of the tokens should be taught or demonstrated to involved children (i.e., via exchanges for backup reinforcers [e.g., privileges] accompanied by discussion), and initial criteria should be set so as to ensure early success in earning tokens. Take, for example, a child for whom the percentage of assigned math problems completed is chosen as a target behavior. The child typically completes somewhere between 50–60% of math problems. An initial completion rate of 50% might be the criterion selected for the first few days of the program.

7. Tokens are exchanged for classroom privileges on at least a daily basis. However, as a rule, shorter delays between receiving tokens and exchanging them for backup reinforcers will result in a more effective program. Although tokens can serve as immediate rewards of an interim nature, they may lose their value as reinforcers if they cannot be "cashed in" until after a long period of time has elapsed.

8. The effectiveness of the intervention program should be evaluated in an ongoing fashion, utilizing multiple outcome measures. Based on the results of this ongoing evaluation, new behavioral targets may be added, old ones deleted or modified, and privileges rotated or varied. Also, the delivery of tokens and the timing of token exchanges may be altered. Response cost procedures (as discussed below) also may be incorporated into the system when some improvement in appropriate behavior has been achieved, yet disruptive or inattentive behaviors remain problematic.

9. Following initial implementation and behavioral improvement, several additional procedures may be necessary to ensure the generalization of obtained effects across time and settings. First, any additional problematic situations must be identified and targetted for change by implementing the above strategies (i.e., steps 2–8). It is erroneous to assume that one need only obtain performance in one situation for such behavior to spontaneously generalize to other settings (Stokes & Baer,

1977). Second, the use of tokens and backup reinforcers should be faded gradually. For example, rather than continuing to provide tokens following successful completion of each step in an academic task, reinforcement would be provided contingent upon completion of several steps first, and then following completion of the entire assignment. Eventually, the system would evolve into a contingency contract as discussed below. Numerous other strategies are available in the professional literature for enhancing both generalization and maintenance of treatment gains (see Horner, Dunlap, & Koegel, 1988; Stokes & Osnes, 1989).

Contingency Contracting

Contingency contracting is a behavior management technique that involves the negotiation of a contractual agreement between a student and teacher (see DeRisi & Butz, 1975). Typically, the contract stipulates the desired classroom behaviors and consequences available contingent upon their performance. As with a token economy program, specific academic and behavioral goals are identified for the child to meet in order to gain access to preferred activities or other rewards. Contracting typically involves a direct connection between target behaviors and primary contingencies, rather than the use of secondary reinforcers such as tokens. As such, there may be a longer time delay between behavior completion and reinforcement than with a token economy program. A sample contract appears in Figure 4.2.

Although contingency contracting is a relatively straightforward procedure, a number of factors may directly influence its efficacy with the ADHD population. First, the age of the child is an important consideration. Contracting procedures typically are unsuccessful with children under the age of 6, perhaps due to a lack of sufficiently developed rule-following skills and inability to defer reinforcement for longer time periods in young children. A second consideration is the length of the time delay between the required behavior and reinforcement. For example, failure is inevitable for a procedure requiring an 8-year-old child with ADHD to accurately complete math problems at a rate of 80% of assigned problems each day for a 1-week time period before earning a reward. Timing of reinforcement is a crucial issue in implementing behavior management programs with children, especially those with ADHD. To increase the probability of improved outcomes in the example given, access to preferred activities should be provided at the conclusion of the successful work period or school day.

The choice of target behaviors and the manner of incorporating them into an intervention program are important determinants of a behavioral contract's success. For example, during the initial stages of a contracting

I, _____ , agree to do the following:
   [insert student's name]

1. Complete all of my written math and language arts assignments, with at least 80% accuracy, before lunch time.
2. Give [insert teacher's name] my full attention when he or she is speaking to the class or to my reading group.
3. Remain quiet, and follow directions when lining up for recess, lunch, and music class.
4. Follow all playground rules (e.g., no fighting) during recess.

Each day that I do these things, I will be allowed to choose **one** of the following:

1. 15 minutes' time at the end of the school day to play a game with a classmate.
2. Use the classroom computer for work or play for 15 minutes.
3. Assist my teacher by completing some errands (take attendance forms to the office) or in class jobs (collect student math assignments).

If I have a successful week, I will have earned one of the special weekend activities with my parents, such as: [e.g., a trip to the park, a bicycle ride, having a friend visit for lunch or dinner]. If I do not complete these classroom responsibilities, then I will lose the opportunity to participate in daily free time activities.

I agree to fulfill this contract to the best of my abilities.

   Signed,

_____   _____
      Student's signature   *Teacher's signature*

   Date _____

FIGURE 4.2. Sample behavior contract.

procedure the following features should be avoided: large numbers of goals, extremely high standards of quality, and completion of complex (e.g., multistep) tasks. For the child with ADHD, such requirements likely will initially lead to failure. A preferable approach would be to target a few simple behaviors or products so that the child can achieve success right from the start. More difficult or complex goals could be incorporated gradually into later iterations of the contract such that terminal objectives are reached with minimal failure along the way.

A final important consideration in designing a behavioral contract is the identification of appropriate reinforcers. All too often, identified reinforcers take the form of activities or items that are assumed by school

personnel to motivate children. Assumptions about the reinforcer preferences of the children we work with are a good starting point for designing contracts and contingency management procedures. However,
reinforcer preferences can be very idiosyncratic, and, as such, it is suggested that individual reward menus be derived. Two alternatives for
doing so are suggested. First, it is advisable, especially with older children, to negotiate directly with the student regarding possible privileges.
Direct negotiation not only assures identification of potent reinforcers,
but also enlists the student's cooperation and investment in the contractual process. Second, naturalistic observations can be conducted to identify a child's preferred activities for use as reinforcers. Such observations
might include identifying those "off-task" behaviors (e.g., drawing, playing with objects at seat) that the child frequently engages in while assigned
to do independent work. This strategy would be helpful especially when
a child is unable to provide suggestions for rewards.

Response Cost

Contingency management strategies consisting solely of positive reinforcement procedures are rarely effective in maintaining appropriate
levels of academic and social behavior among children with ADHD
(Abramowitz & O'Leary, 1991; Pfiffner & O'Leary, 1993). In fact, several
studies have documented that levying mild penalties following inappropriate (i.e., off-task) behavior is effective in promoting consistent behavioral change (Pfiffner & O'Leary, 1987; Pfiffner, O'Leary, Rosen, &
Sanderson, 1985; Rosen et al., 1984). For example, in addition to prudent reprimands and verbal redirection, penalties involving the loss or
removal of privileges, points, or tokens (i.e., response cost) contingent
upon inattentive, disruptive behavior has proven beneficial when used
in combination with reinforcement-based procedures.

The concurrent use of token reinforcement and response cost has
been demonstrated to increase the levels of on-task behavior, seatwork
productivity, and academic accuracy of children with ADHD (DuPaul,
Guevremont, & Barkley, 1992; Rapport, Murphy, & Bailey, 1980, 1982).
In several cases, classroom improvement was equivalent to that obtained
with stimulant medication (Rapport et al., 1982). For example, Rapport
(1987a, 1987b) describes a token delivery system that incorporates response cost. The student and teacher are each supplied with a card stand
or electronic apparatus that serve to display point totals earned by the
child.[1] Points are earned for in-seat, academically engaged behavior on a

1. The most recent electronic version of this contingency management system, known as the
Attention Training System, currently is available from Gordon Systems, Inc., 301 Ambergate
Rd., DeWitt, NY 13214.

fixed-interval schedule and are deducted following incidents of off-task behavior. Points are awarded or deducted by the teacher changing the card displayed on his or her card stand (or by pressing a button on a remote control device). With this system, students change their own cards to match the teacher's or receive/lose points on the electronic apparatus via the remote mechanism controlled by the teacher. Thus, token delivery and deduction are accomplished on a remote basis by the teacher, allowing for simultaneous teaching of and/or involvement in activities with other students. As with other token systems, at the conclusion of an academic work period a child's accumulated points are traded for various back-up reinforcers (e.g., a choice activity).

The efficacy of response-cost programming can be illustrated by examining Figures 4.3 and 4.4 from Rapport (1987a). These data represent the response of an 8-year-old boy with ADHD to varying doses of

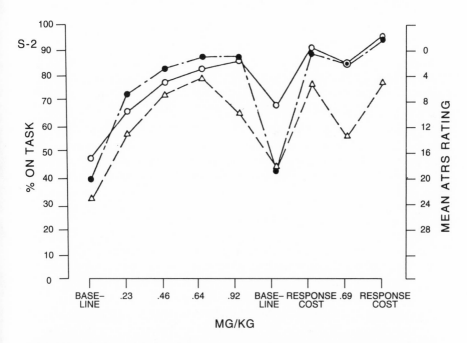

FIGURE 4.3. The mean percentage of intervals of daily on-task behavior across academic areas (closed circles = math; open circles = phonics) and experimental conditions. The right-hand ordinate represents teacher-rated social behavior (open triangle = Abbreviated Conners Teacher Rating Scale [ATRS]) whereby the numbers become smaller as the child improves. From "Attention deficit disorder with hyperactivity" by M. D. Rapport, 1987a, in *Behavior therapy with children and adolescents: A clinical approach* (p. 338), M. Hersen and V. B. Van Hasselt (Eds.), New York: Wiley. Copyright 1987 by John Wiley & Sons. Reprinted by permission.

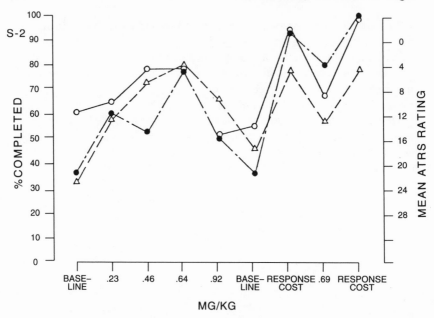

FIGURE 4.4. The mean percentage of daily problems completed across academic areas (closed circles = math; open circles = phonics) and experimental conditions. The right-hand ordinate represents teacher-rated social behavior (open triangle = Abbreviated Conners Teacher Rating Scale [ATRS]) whereby the numbers become smaller as the child improves. From "Attention deficit disorder with hyperactivity" by M. D. Rapport, 1987a, in *Behavior therapy with children and adolescents: A clinical approach* (p. 339), M. Hersen and V. B. Van Hasselt (Eds.), New York: Wiley. Copyright 1987a by John Wiley & Sons. Reprinted by permission.

methylphenidate (Ritalin) and to a response cost system implemented in his regular classroom. Figure 4.3 shows treatment-related changes in this boy's on-task behavior and teacher ratings of classroom deportment over the course of the school year. Response cost procedures were implemented in a staggered fashion (i.e., using a multiple baseline design) across math and phonics class periods. During baseline conditions, this boy was observed to attend to task materials during an average of 40–50% of observation intervals. The implementation of response cost procedures led to an increase in the frequency of on-task behavior to approximately 90% of observation intervals. This improvement in attentiveness was similar to or, in the case of some doses, superior to that obtained with methylphenidate. Response cost also enhanced this boy's completion of academic problems relative to baseline conditions (see Figure 4.4). In fact, improvements in academic productivity were superior to those obtained with methylphenidate. Thus, response cost procedures can be used to not only affect task-related attention but could elicit changes in academic performance as well.

Several issues should be considered when deciding to use response cost procedures. For example, response cost is a form of punishment, and its use could result in the child taking a negative view of the entire token system. Thus, in introducing the program and its components to the student and teacher, emphasis should be placed on the program's positive aspects (e.g., emphasize that the student will have a chance to earn points and rewards for completing work accurately). In addition, initial and ongoing efforts should be made to adjust and arrange contingencies such that the child is earning more points than he/she is losing. For example, many children with ADHD will initially test the system by deliberately engaging in off-task behavior to see if they will lose points. To prevent teachers from being caught up in a "point reduction game" of this sort, it is recommended that point reductions not occur more than once per minute regardless of the frequency of off-task behavior. Also, the teacher should be instructed to look away from the child immediately following point reductions (Rapport, 1987b). Finally, a child's point total should never fall below zero and when a point total is zero, all disruptive, off-task behavior should be ignored. If zero point totals are a common occurrence, the contingencies may need to be revised (e.g., increased in potency) so that point reductions do not occur for minor infractions. Once the child begins to experience success and is invested in the system, the criteria for point reductions can become more stringent in efforts to further improve classroom behavior and performance.

Time-Out from Positive Reinforcement

Another type of mild punishment that may be appropriate for classroom use consists of various forms of time-out from positive reinforcement. Time-out from positive reinforcement, as its name implies, involves restricting the child's access to positive reinforcement (e.g., teacher and peer attention). An adaptation of Barkley's (1987) procedures designed for use within the home may be most applicable. To be effective, time-out procedures should be (1) implemented only when there is a reinforcing environment to be removed from, (2) implemented swiftly following a rule infraction, (3) applied with consistency, and (4) employed for the smallest amount of time (e.g., 1–5 minutes) that proves effective. Removal from a reinforcing environment is the most salient variable for determining the effectiveness of this procedure, *not* the amount of time spent in the time-out area. If the child is to be moved to a time-out area, this area should be located in a relatively dull location within the classroom (*not* a separate room, closet, cloakroom, or hallway) to allow for monitoring of the child's activities. Criteria for terminating the time-out period should include (1) a time-out period sufficiently long enough to be effective (i.e., 1 minute for every 2 years of age of the child), (2) a short period of calm, nondisruptive behavior required prior to its termination, and (3) the child's expressed willingness to correct, amend, or compensate for the misbehavior that led to the time-out contingency. Finally, children who leave the time-out area without permission should have their time interval lengthened by a fixed amount for each violation, or lose points or tokens if a token economy system is being used.

As with response cost, it is imperative that restrictive procedures such as time-out be employed only in the context of ongoing positive reinforcement programming. Further, time-out contingencies should be an intervention of last resort following implementation of a hierarchy of both positive and less restrictive aversive behavior management procedures. For example, inappropriate behavior would lead initially to brief, prudent reprimands, followed by response cost, followed by time-out with head down at desk, followed by time-out in a corner of the room. More severe disruptive behaviors (e.g., physical aggression) should lead to immediate application of the more restrictive, time-out procedures. When used, time-out procedures need to be monitored very carefully, as they are not considered viable ongoing management strategies, but rather short-term behavior reduction techniques.

Home-Based Contingencies

Home-based contingency management procedures, based on the child's behavior and/or academic performance at school, can be used as an effective supplement to classroom-based behavior change systems (see Atkeson & Forehand, 1979, for a review). These procedures have several beneficial features. First, on a daily basis the child receives direct feedback from his or her teachers about performance in several areas of classroom functioning. Second, parents receive daily information about the child's classroom performance, thus providing an ongoing forum for teacher–parent communication. For children experiencing classroom difficulties, this schedule of communication is preferable to waiting for a parent–teacher conference or an end-of-the-term report card. Finally, the system circumvents some of the practical limitations (e.g., restricted range of possible reinforcing activities) of classroom-based contingency management systems because it involves the parents in providing reinforcement for in-school behavior.

An example of a home-based reinforcement program for a student with ADHD has been proposed (DuPaul, Guevremont, & Barkley, 1991b) and employs a daily report card similar to the one displayed in Figure 4.5.

For each child, several behavioral goals are identified such as: paying attention to class activities, completion of assigned work, accuracy of work, and following rules. The specific goals should vary with respect to the presenting problems of the individual student (e.g., interactions with classmates may be targetted if the child is prone to arguing and fighting with peers). The columns of the card can be used to convey information across different subject areas or periods of the school day. Thus, if the child has more than one teacher, they all may participate. The teacher enters ratings (on a 5-point scale from "excellent" to "terrible") of the child's performance in the appropriate area of the card, initials the card, and provides comments where necessary. Ratings and comments are made in ink to prevent their alteration by the child. The student is responsible for giving the card to each teacher and bringing it home on a daily basis.

DAILY STUDENT RATING CARD

NAME _____ DATE _____

Please rate this child in each of the areas listed below as to how he performed in school today using ratings of I to 5. I = excellent, 2 = good, 3 = fair, 4 = poor, 5 = terrible or did not work.

AREA	CLASS PERIODS / SUBJECTS					
	I	2	3	4	5	6
participation						
class work						
handed in homework						
interaction with other children						
teacher's initials						

Place comments on back if needed :

FIGURE 4.5. Daily report card for use in a home-based reinforcement program for ADHD. From *Attention-Deficit Hyperactivity Disorder: A handbook for diagnosis and treatment* (p. 522) by R. A. Barkley, 1990, New York: Guilford Press. Copyright 1990 by The Guilford Press. Reprinted by permission.

Given the use of quantitative ratings, school–home notes can be used within a token economy system based at home. For example, the teacher provides quantitative ratings of performance in each goal area, as discussed above. When the card is brought home, the parent(s) briefly discusses the positive and negative ratings with the child. Then, specified point values are assigned to the numbers on the card and summed to yield the net total points earned for the day. For example, each teacher rating of "1" could be converted to 25 points, each "2" worth 15 points, each "3" equal to 5 points. Ratings of "4" or "5" would result in the deduction of 15 and 25 points, respectively. To produce positive behavior change, a home token reinforcement program must be arranged such that these points can lead to the purchase of backup reinforcers (e.g., household privileges, television time, spending a night at a friend's home). As with other token programs, this system's effectiveness is dependent upon its motivational value and the availability of a variety of backup reinforcers.

Kelley (1990) has recently written a text that provides thorough coverage of this topic and focuses on developing and using what she calls "school–home notes" as a means of communication among parents, teachers, and children. A variety of school–home notes are presented in her text, all of which could be adapted for use with students who are exhibiting ADHD-related behaviors. For example, Figure 4.6 shows a school–home note that could be used in treating a student with ADHD at the secondary school level. There is an increased emphasis on homework completion and test grades at this level. The teacher is able to alert parents as to upcoming homework assignments on a regular basis, as well. At the secondary level, teachers typically prefer to complete school–home notes on a weekly rather than a daily basis.

Several factors may limit the effectiveness of home-based reinforcement programs (Rapport, 1987a). One of the primary drawbacks of such a system is that, by definition, it involves a delay in the provision of reinforcement. Given that children with ADHD have difficulty delaying reinforcement (Barkley, in press; Rapport, Tucker, DuPaul, Merlo, & Stoner, 1986), home-based reinforcers may be less powerful relative to classroom-based contingencies that are more immediately linked to the behaviors of interest. This issue is particularly important in working with children younger than the age of 6. Second, school personnel have limited means for assessing parental implementation of the procedures. Finally, when home-based reinforcers are used, parents should be discouraged from relying solely on material rewards, which can lose some of their potency over long periods of time. Instead, parents should be provided with assistance in developing an array of potential reinforcers of an activity, social, or material nature. These reinforcers should be salient to the child, readily available in the home or community, inex-

SCHOOL–HOME NOTE

Name ___Richard_____ **Date** ___10/20_____

SUBJECT___Math_____

Was prepared for class	(Yes) No NA		Homework assignment:
Used class time well	(Yes) No NA		Test Friday on
Handed in homework	(Yes) No NA		Chapter 3

Homework/(Test)Grade   F D (C) B A NA   Teacher's Initials_WJ_

Comments: Seems to be paying attention better and using his time well.

SUBJECT___Social Studies___

Was prepared for class	Yes (No) NA		Homework assignment:
Used class time well	(Yes) No NA		Answer questions
Handed in homework	Yes (No) NA		1–10, page 113

(Homework)Test Grade   F (D) C B A NA   Teacher's Initials_MS_

Comments: Did not bring notebook; he talked a good bit during class.

SUBJECT___English_____

Was prepared for class	(Yes) No NA		Homework assignment:
Used class time well	(Yes) No NA		None
Handed in homework	Yes No (NA)		

Homework(Test)Grade   F D (C) B A NA   Teacher's Initials_H_

Comments: Participated nicely in class.

Parent Comments: ___Ms. Sessions, Richard says he handed in his___

___homework. Would you mind checking with him?___

FIGURE 4.6. Abbreviated school–home note used with middle and high school students. (This note was completed by Richard, his teachers, and his parents.) From *School–home notes: Promoting children's classroom success* (p. 74) by M. L. Kelley, 1990, New York: Guilford Press. Copyright 1990 by The Guilford Press. Reprinted by permission.

pensive if they involve a monetary cost, and rotated on a regular basis to prevent boredom with the "same old rewards." It is particularly important to use reinforcers that are viewed as "necessities" by the child (e.g., watching television, playing video games, riding bicycle) rather than an exclusive reliance on "luxury" items that the child could live without (e.g., going to favorite restaurant, trip to amusement park).

In view of the limitations to home–school communcation systems enumerated above, it is worthwhile to delineate the factors that will enhance the efficacy of home-based contingencies. These factors are listed in Table 4.2. First, daily and weekly goals are specified in a positive manner. To pass the Dead-man test, target behaviors involve the active performance of classroom responsibilities (e.g., work completion) rather than an absence of inappropriate behavior. Second, both academic and behavioral goals are included. In an effort to increase the chances of initial success, one or two goals should be readily attainable by the child. This will serve to "hook" the child into cooperating with the system before increasing standards or expectations for performance. Third, it is important to employ only a few goals at a time so that the student and teacher are not overwhelmed by the system. Fourth, teacher feedback about the child's performance should be quantitative. Although qualitative statements can be informative, they are ofttimes vague and nonspecific (e.g., "Johnny had a good day today"). Next, feedback is provided by subject or class period. This provides the student with specific information about performance, allows for more frequent feedback, and circumvents a loss of motivation if the child experiences difficulties in the early part of the day. In the latter situation, if ratings on the daily report card were based on the entire day's performance, it is likely that the child would still obtain low ratings even if his or her behavior improved over the course of the day. Sixth, home–school communication occurs on a daily or weekly basis to facilitate the provision of frequent reinforcement. Seventh, a hierarchy of short- and long-term privileges at home are tied directly to teacher ratings on the daily report card. It is unlikely that a child with ADHD will exhibit improvement in the absence of external reinforcement. Next, parents should be involved in planning the home–school com-

**TABLE 4.2. Components of Effective Home–School
Communication Programs**

1. Daily and/or weekly goals are stated in a positive manner.
2. Both academic and behavioral goals are included.
3. A small number of goals are targetted at a time.
4. The teacher provides quantitative feedback about student performance.
5. Feedback is provided by subject or class periods.
6. Communication is made on a regular basis (either daily or weekly).
7. Home-based contingencies are tied to school performance. Both short- and long-term consequences are employed.
8. Parental cooperation and involvement are solicited prior to implementation.
9. Student input into goals and contingencies is solicited, particularly with older children and adolescents.
10. Goals and procedures are modified, as necessary.

munication program from the onset to ensure understanding of and cooperation with the procedures. Older children and adolescents should also be included in planning the program for the same reasons. Finally, goals and procedures are modified on an ongoing basis in accordance with student progress or lack thereof.

In summary, home-based contingency systems can be effective in enhancing school performance, especially when used to supplement class-room-based behavior change procedures (e.g., cover periods of the school day when the latter procedures are not in effect). Students who display ADHD-related behaviors that are considered milder in severity should be particularly responsive to home–school programming. As with other contingency management strategies, attention to the details of identifying target behaviors and reinforcers, linking the two, and monitoring and managing the system to ensure its integrity will be critical to successful outcomes.

SELF-MANAGEMENT INTERVENTIONS

One of the primary goals of treatment for ADHD is to enable a student to develop adequate levels of self-control. The latter term implies that a child will exhibit age-appropriate social and academic behaviors on an independent basis (i.e., with a minimum of accomodation on the part of the environment). Although this is an admirable treatment goal, it is quite difficult to obtain in practice, given the chronic and multifaceted nature of ADHD. Self-management interventions for ADHD are comprised of strategies incorporating self-monitoring, self-reinforcement, and/or self-instruction (Barkley, 1989). These strategies, especially those incorporating self-instruction, have sometimes been referred to as cognitive-behavioral interventions because of their emphasis on changing within-child variables. In recent years, self-management interventions have become increasingly popular as treatments for a variety of classroom difficulties including ADHD (see Shapiro & Cole, 1994). In general, despite their apparent potential in ameliorating ADHD symptoms, these interventions have not been uniformly successful (Abikoff, 1985). Nevertheless, we will review findings relevant to each of the three self-management approaches enumerated above while highlighting procedures that may have greater applicability for practitioners.

Self-Monitoring

Children can be taught to observe and record the occurrence of their own behaviors. For instance, a child with ADHD might be trained to recognize and record instances of on-task behavior during academic work.

Typically, an auditory or visual stimulus (e.g., beep from a tape recorder, hand signal from the teacher) is used periodically throughout a specific time period to signal the child to observe his or her current behavior.[2] The child then records whether he or she was on-task on a grid or chart taped to his or her desk. Self-monitoring can be used in isolation or, more typically, in combination with other self-management procedures. Although this intervention has not been studied extensively with children who have received a clinical diagnosis of ADHD, attentive behaviors have been found to increase as a function of self-monitoring especially when combined with self-reinforcement or external reinforcement (e.g., Barkley, Copeland, & Sivage, 1980).

Self-Reinforcement

The most promising self-management intervention for ADHD requires students to not only monitor their behavior but also to evaluate and reinforce their own performance (Barkley, 1989). In fact, the combination of self-monitoring and self-reinforcement has been found effective in improving on-task behavior, academic accuracy, and peer interactions for students with ADHD (Barkley et al., 1980; Hinshaw, Henker, & Whalen, 1984). These effects are enhanced further when stimulant medication is used in combination with these procedures (Barkley, 1989).

Self-reinforcement strategies may be particularly helpful for addressing ADHD-related problems in two situations. First, a student can be trained to monitor and reinforce his or her own behavior while fading the use of an externally based, contingency management program (Barkley, 1989). The premise is that positive behavioral change will be maintained despite the reduction in teacher feedback or other forms of reinforcement. Of course, backup reinforcers (e.g., classroom or home privileges) *must* be used as teacher monitoring and feedback is faded. The fading of backup reinforcement must take place over an extended time period. A second situation in which self-reinforcement is an appropriate treatment for ADHD is at the secondary level where teachers and students are reluctant to employ contingency management procedures. Thus, self-management may be a more acceptable intervention at the secondary level and therefore will be more likely to be implemented on a consistent basis.

An example of the use of self-monitoring and self-reinforcement procedures for ameliorating ADHD symptoms is based on the work of

---

2. A less intrusive method for signalling self-monitoring is available through the use of a vibrating device that is attached to the child's clothing. This device can be programmed to signal the child at various intervals. One such device is called the MotivAider and is marketed by CMI, Inc., 46 Dow Highway, Suite 3, Eliot, ME 03903.

Rhode, Morgan, and Young (1983) who used these strategies to facilitate the mainstreaming of six elementary students with "behavioral handicaps." The initial stages of the program involve the use of a token reinforcement program and verbal feedback from the teacher based on teacher ratings of student behavior during specific intervals in the classroom. Ratings are provided using a 6-point criterion hierarchy as displayed in Table 4.3. Separate evaluations of behavioral and academic performance can be made using this system. Teacher-provided points are exchanged for backup reinforcers in school or at home as in a standard token economy.

Once behavioral and/or academic gains are exhibited by the student, the latter is trained in evaluating his or her own behavior using the criteria displayed in Table 4.3. At this stage, the teacher's ratings continue to be used to determine how many points that the student has earned. In addition, the student can earn one bonus point for matching teacher ratings exactly. If the student's ratings deviate by more than one point

TABLE 4.3. Criteria for Teacher and Student Ratings in a Self-Reinforcement Program

Rating	Criterion performance
5 = Excellent	Followed all classroom rules for entire interval. Work 100% correct.
4 = Very good	Minor infraction of rules (e.g., a talk-out or out-of-seat) but followed rules rest of interval. Work at least 90% correct.
3 = Average	Did not follow all rules for entire time but no serious offenses. Work at least 80% correct.
2 = Below average	Broke one or more rules to the extent that behavior was not acceptable (e.g., aggressive, noisy, talking) but followed rules part of the time. Work approximately 60–80% correct.
1 = Poor	Broke one or more rules almost entire period or engaged in higher degree of inappropriate behavior most of the time. Work between 0–60% correct.
0 = Unacceptable	Broke one or more rules entire interval. Did not work at all or work all incorrect.

Note. Adapted from "Generalization and maintenance of treatment gains of behaviorally handicapped students from resource rooms to regular classrooms using self-evaluation procedures" by G. Rhode, D. P. Morgan, and K. R. Young, 1983, *Journal of Applied Behavior Analysis, 16,* 171–188. Copyright 1983 by the Society for the Experimental Analysis of Behavior. Adapted by permission.

from the teacher ratings, the student does not earn any points for that interval. Thus, contingencies are associated with both behavioral improvement *and* rating one's performance similar to the teacher.

Over the course of time, the teacher ratings are gradually faded such that the student ratings are the primary arbiter for earning backup reinforcement. This is facilitated by (1) the use of random "matching challenges" that occur on a periodic basis and (2) the gradual reduction in frequency of these matching challenges. For example, the initial cutback in teacher ratings may involve a matching challenge that occurs every other day, on the average. Then, the teacher matches are faded to every 3rd day, once weekly, and once biweekly, on the average. If, at any point in time, the student's performance deteriorates and/or the teacher suspects inflation of student ratings, then matching challenges are conducted more frequently.

In the program described by Rhode, Morgan, and Young (1983), the students eventually employed self-ratings only with no backup reinforcers. This led to maintenance of significant behavioral improvements across resource and regular classroom settings (see Figure 4.7). These results have been replicated using a similar program with high school students who were exhibiting learning and behavior problems (Smith, Young, Nelson, & West, 1992). Thus, it would seem that the use of variations of this program could have applicability for the treatment of ADHD-related behaviors across a wide age span. Nevertheless, it is important to note that a key variable influencing the success of these procedures is the continued use of external reinforcers contingent on student ratings. It is unlikely that the effectiveness of this intervention would be maintained if backup reinforcement was reduced or eliminated earlier in the sequence of program steps.

Self-Instruction

Self-instruction training has been minimally successful, when used in isolation, in the treatment of ADHD (Abikoff, 1985; Barkley, 1989). There is some evidence that when combined with other interventions (e.g., contingency management, stimulant medication), self-instruction training may be helpful (Barkley, 1989), however, the empirical evidence is not uniform in this regard (e.g., Abikoff & Gittelman, 1985a). These procedures were originally employed with hyperactive children by Meichenbaum and Goodman (1971) and, more recently, several textbooks have been published on the subject (Braswell & Bloomquist, 1991; Kendall & Braswell, 1985).

Self-instruction training usually involves a series of steps designed to help the child to "stop, look, and listen." First, the trainer models a

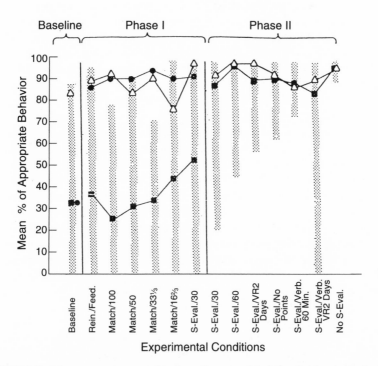

● =Resource room (Subjects)
■ =Regular classroom (Subjects)
△ =Regular classroom (Peers)
▓ =Range/Regular classroom (Subjects)

FIGURE 4.7. Mean percentages and ranges of appropriate behavior for six students with behavioral handicaps as a function of self-evaluation procedures. Normative data in the form of mean percentages of appropriate behavior for randomly selected peers are also included. During Phase I, intervention was implemented in the resource room only. During Phase II, intervention was implemented in the regular classroom only. Rein/Feed. = teacher ratings only. Match/100 = student and teacher ratings compared 100% of the time. Match/50 = student and teacher ratings compared 50% of time. Match/33 1/3 = student and teacher ratings compared 33.3% of time. Match/16 2/3 = student and teacher ratings compared 16.67% of time. S-Eval./30 = student ratings only every 30 minutes. S-Eval./60 = student ratings only every 60 minutes. S-Eval./VR 2 Days = student ratings only every other day. S-Eval./No Points = student ratings only with no reinforcement. S-Eval./Verb. 60 min. = student verbal report every 60 minutes. S-Eval/Verb. VR2 days = student verbal report every other day. No S-Eval. = no student or teacher ratings. From "Generalization and maintenance of treatment gains of behaviorally handicapped students from resource rooms to regular classrooms using self-evaluation procedures" by G. Rhode, D. P. Morgan, and K. R. Young, 1983, *Journal of Applied Behavior Analysis, 16,* 171–188. Copyright 1983 by the Society for the Experimental Analysis of Behavior. Reprinted by permission.

systematic approach to completing a task in the presence of the child by stating these steps aloud while performing the actions. Usually, a task that requires effortful thought and reflective responding will be used (e.g., a maze). Next, the child is asked to imitate the trainer's completion of the same or a closely similar task while stating the steps aloud. The third level of training is where the student completes the task while whispering the steps aloud. Fourth, the child covertly reviews the steps (i.e., thinks through the task) while completing the problem. Initially, the trainer provides reinforcement (e.g., praise and backup contingencies) for successful completion of the task. Over the course of training, this reinforcement gradually becomes self-initiated as the child learns to praise his or her efforts in a covert manner.

Although self-instruction programming has a great deal of intuitive appeal in fostering self-control, there is some question as to its efficacy when used in isolation (Abikoff, 1985). There appear to be two issues that are pertinent to this discussion. First, one of the major limitations of self-instruction training has been a lack of generalization of success from the training setting to other situations (e.g., classroom). In fact, the original premise underlying this treatment modality was that it would lead to greater generalization across settings than is obtained with contingency management procedures due to its altering of within-child variables (Meichenbaum & Goodman, 1971). Unfortunately, this premise has not been borne out in the research literature (Barkley, 1989). Second, there is some question as to the active components of this treatment. Specifically, are the gains associated with self-instruction techniques a function of the cognitive training or are these a result of motivational components? In other words, is the training in self-instruction effective beyond what would be obtained by using reinforcement procedures alone? If not, then it would appear that the self-instruction training is a superfluous intervention. It is encumbent upon researchers interested in these strategies to address these two issues before widespread adoption of self-instruction in the treatment of ADHD can be advocated.

EFFECTIVE EDUCATIONAL STRATEGIES

In addition to the proven benefits of reinforcement-based contingency management strategies, students identified with ADHD are likely to benefit from prevention-oriented behavior and classroom-management strategies. In addition, children with this disorder may require remedial or supplemental instruction aimed at improving basic academic skills, learning and study skills, and self-management of one's own learning. In general, ameliorating the classroom difficulties experienced by target students should involve multiple prevention and intervention approaches including (1) active and ongoing teaching of classroom rules, routines, and expectations for appropriate classroom behavior, (2) grading practices and contingencies to support the rules, routines, and expectations, (3) changes in instructional routines and curricula to improve rates of learning, (4) ongoing monitoring of progress in basic skill areas (i.e., reading, writing, math, and spelling), and (5) teaching students to be competent at organizing and studying academic materials.

In considering the classroom learning and performance of children with ADHD, a number of variables will need to be analyzed, ranging from the child's basic academic skills to the observable classroom behaviors that are potentially interfering with the child's classroom performance. A nonexhaustive list of such variables is provided in Table 4.4. For many children experiencing achievement and/or behavior problems in the classroom, a first step in pursuing problem resolution is to determine whether the problem is a skills (e.g., academic competencies) or a conditions (e.g., instructional design) problem so that an appropriate intervention might be designed. One of the difficulties facing professionals serving children with ADHD however, is that classroom difficulties are likely to be a combination of *both* skills and conditions problems. Because of this likely interaction, decisions must be made with respect to a starting point for assessment (see Chapter 2) and in determining whether the various components of an intervention plan will be delivered in isolation, sequentially, or in combination. In most cases, multiple interventions will be implemented across settings and professionals to address the skills and conditions factors listed in Table 4.4.

The prevention and intervention strategies discussed in this section are those with empirical support for their effectiveness in ameliorating some of the skills difficulties listed in Table 4.4. However, it must be noted that these routines, strategies, and approaches to teaching have only recently begun to be researched specifically with respect to their effects on the learning and behavior of children with ADHD. We begin our discussion here with a focus on antecedent teacher behaviors (i.e., proactive strategies occurring prior to the display of problem behaviors).

Teaching Classroom Rules and Expectations (Prevention)

Teacher-provided cues, prompts (including performance feedback), or signals to do or not do something can be quite effective in managing problem behaviors and promoting active engagement in academic work, task completion, and performance accuracy (Paine, Radicchi, Rosellini, Deutchman, & Darch, 1983; Sulzer-Azaroff & Meyer, 1991). Simply put, if one person wants something to be done by another, the easiest way to pro-

TABLE 4.4. Skills and Conditions to Consider in Evaluating and Treating Classroom-Based Problems Associated with ADHD

Skills	Conditions
Reading skills	Severity of ADHD symptomatology
Writing skills	Classroom management and motivational strategies
Spelling skills	Instructional routines
Math skills	Curricula
Study skills, organizational skills, and self-management skills	Home–school communication
Social and interpersonal skills	Community-based interventions (e.g., medication)

mote its occurrence is by communicating those expectations in an unambiguous fashion. This line of discussion is not intended to suggest or imply that teachers have been remiss in what they have asked or required of children with ADHD. The point is, however, that at times all of us forget to do the "simple things" in carrying out our educational responsibilities. At other times, we firmly believe that we already have communicated our expectations clearly and no further explanation is necessary.

Take, for example, the issue of classroom rules. It seems safe to assume that all children, including those identified with ADHD, who understand and follow classroom rules will experience greater success in school than children who do not understand and follow these rules (Madsen, Becker, & Thomas, 1968; Paine et al., 1983). However, the clarity with which classroom rules are taught to and understood by students, in general, is not fully understood. In a recent pilot study investigating children's understanding of classroom rules, Stoner and Green (1992a) found that fewer than 10% of first, second, and third graders interviewed could accurately state or identify the rules pertaining to their own classrooms. Of further interest and importance here is that each of the involved teachers firmly believed that their classroom rules had been taught clearly and unequivocally. Further clarification of this initial finding is warranted, as well as investigation into how best to foster effective teaching, understanding, and following of classroom rules. Such studies are needed both at the level of carefully controlled research, and at the level of solving the problems experienced by individual children and teachers in our caseloads.

Initial directions for variables to include in such work have been identified by educational researchers such as Martens and Kelly (1993), Ysseldyke and Christenson (1987, 1988), and others (e.g., Elliott, Witt, & Kratochwill, 1991; Paine et al., 1983; Sprick & Nolet, 1991; Witt &

Martens, 1988). These professionals have suggested that the following proactive teacher behaviors can be effective in promoting appropriate classroom behavior:

1. Teachers remind students of the classroom rules, and they actively teach these rules by discussion and by pointing out examples of students following them (i.e., "catch" students following the rules).

2. Teachers maintain eye contact with students as appropriate to the particular lesson or activity in progress.

3. Teachers remind students about expected behaviors that are critical to an activity *before* the start of the activity.

4. Teachers circulate throughout the classroom, monitoring student behavior and providing feedback in an unobtrusive fashion.

5. Teachers use nonverbal cues and signals to redirect a student while teaching others.

6. The pace of instructional lessons is brisk and directed by the teacher.

7. Teachers ensure that academic and nonacademic activities and routines are understood by students (e.g., when a project is considered complete, what expectations and activities are involved in today's math class). Teachers manage transitions from one activity to another in a brief and well-organized manner (e.g., state the expectations and activities involved in a transition from math period to recess).

8. Teachers frequently communicate their expectations about the use of class time in a clear manner. For example, Sprick and Nolet (1991) suggest posting (e.g., written on the blackboard) class schedules broken down into blocks of time with clear expectations for student behavior noted for each time block. In addition, they recommend providing students with "challenge problems" at the beginning of a given class period. These challenges provide students with an activity related to the lesson to get them involved in the subject matter while the transition is completed and to pique their interest in and attention to the lesson.

Incorporating these strategies into daily classroom routines can be useful in preventing and managing challenging classroom behavior. In addition, many of these procedures have been shown to be correlated with improvements in student achievement (Martens & Kelly, 1993).

In addition to careful consideration of classroom and instructional routines, in working with children identified with ADHD teachers should consider environmental arrangement strategies that will allow for more careful monitoring of the activities of identified students. For example, placing the child's desk near the teacher's may promote monitoring of student behavior, as well as decrease the likelihood of misunderstanding of directions for an assignment. Teachers also should consider arrangements that will ensure student participation in class activities and not restrict opportunities to learn and benefit from instruction, while limiting proximity to potential distractions inherent in any given classroom. For example, a child identified with ADHD probably will not do well when seated beside a frequently used classroom activity center.

Instructional Management and Remediation in Basic Skill Areas

Classroom-based research efforts involving children with ADHD have tended to focus on the issues of behavior management discussed in the previous sections of this chapter. Relatively little research has been conducted regarding instructional, curricular, or classroom environment manipulations aimed at enhancing the learning and academic performance of these children. Our speculation is that this phenomenon is a result of a combination of two variables. First, disruptive behaviors frequently are of paramount concern to teachers and lead them to refer children to specialists. Second, historically, research knowledge and practices regarding ADHD and related problems have emerged from within the domains of medical and clinical professionals rather than from the educational arena. However, given that children with ADHD are at risk for developing achievement problems, we would be remiss in not including some mention of basic issues in instruction, as well as strategies for remediation in basic skill areas such as reading, writing, and spelling.

There is a pressing need for research into the effects of various curricular, instructional, and environmental interventions on the learning, academic performance, and classroom behavior of children with ADHD. Until that research is accumulated, however, a good place to glean direction is in the literature on interventions for achievement problems that has developed under the general rubric of instructional strategies for use in special education. There is no logical reason why these interventions could not be successful with children with ADHD. A complete treatment of the topic of instruction is well beyond our scope, and numerous books are available on the topic (see Berliner & Rosenshine, 1987, for a thorough, readable treatment of critical issues in classroom teaching). However, it is our hope that these ideas will spark the development of sorely needed classroom-based research and practices linking ADHD and instructional strategies.

Basic Instructional Processes

As reviewed and discussed by Rosenshine (1987), effective teaching involves the sequential arrangement of six primary instructional functions: review, presentation, guided practice, corrections and feedback, independent practice, and weekly/monthly reviews. For example, *review* involves checking for prerequisite skills and knowledge and discussion of previously taught material and information relevant to the current lesson. Next, new information or material (i.e., facts, discriminations, basic concepts and relations) is *presented* in manageable steps or units, using clear positive and negative examples. Once the new material and examples have been presented, students are provided with numerous opportunities for *guided practice* with high rates of success. Then, based on student performance during the practice exercises, teachers provide students with *corrections and feedback*, and reteaching of material as needed to strengthen the new learning. When students are able to respond correctly a high percentage of the time to questions and problems involving the new material, they are ready for independent practice. *Independent practice* is intended to build fluency and autonomy with newly learned material, so that students can apply the new learning to various problems and understand it within a variety of contexts. Finally, *weekly and/or monthly reviews* are provided, again in the interest of building fluency and independent application of the learned material.

In a discussion of what he calls "simple views of effective teaching (p. 93)," Berliner (1987) suggests that these teaching functions promote student learning for two primary reasons. First, the strategies ensure that students are provided with the opportunities to learn what they are supposed to learn. Second, by working through cycles of review, practice, feedback, corrections, and more practice, teachers ensure that students are performing accurately and becoming more fluent. Doing so helps to avoid situations in which students repeatedly practice or perform their school work inaccurately, thereby strengthening "mis-rules" (e.g., add when I see a "–" sign and subtract when I see a "+" sign). Further, these factors can be manipulated and individualized with respect to difficult-to-teach material or students. For example, more opportunities to practice and a greater frequency of feedback might be provided around material broken down into smaller units, when teaching a student who is experiencing difficulty in a particular subject area.

The instructional support and remediation strategies discussed below incorporate factors that have been associated with improved performance among children with ADHD. These include opportunities to learn via active responses to teacher directions and instruction, coupled with opportunities for the provision of frequent feedback and corrections. These strategies are presented only briefly here, with the intent of providing the interested reader with direction for further reading or study.

Reading Skills

Research findings suggest that success in reading in the early school years is related to later school achievement and adjustment (Chall, 1983). As such, skill in reading is a critical building block for a child's successful school experience (Anderson, Hiebert, Scott, & Wilkinson, 1985). Reading instruction and remediation can be construed broadly as divisible into the two related areas of decoding and comprehension.

Gaining meaning from written information involves the decoding of text. The importance of children learning to decode text is such that the Commission on Reading of The National Academy of Education (Anderson et al., 1985) has recommended that *all children* receive instruction in phonics as part of early reading instruction. Similarly, other leading researchers in the field of reading instruction (Carnine, Kameenui, & Silbert, 1990; Grossen & Carnine, 1991) suggest that systematic phonics-based training should be a part of a student's first 2 years of reading instruction. Grossen and Carnine (1991) discuss four primary components of such instruction: (1) teaching letter–sound correspondence in isolation, (2) teaching the blending of sounds, (3) providing immediate feedback and corrections on oral reading errors, and (4) providing for extensive practice using sounds in isolation, word lists, and words in the context of reading passages. Students who come to possess fluent decoding skills thus are well prepared to become skilled readers who obtain meaning from text, as decoding skills are complemented with other forms of reading instruction.

Comprehensive reading instruction includes a great deal more than teaching phonics skills. For example, Sindelar and Stoddard (1991) have suggested that students experiencing difficulty with reading may benefit from a variety of other strategies within three primary areas: (1) building fluency in reading/decoding, (2) building vocabulary, and (3) strengthening comprehension skills. A few of these strategies are noted here. Instruction for building reading and decoding fluency includes such strategies as repeated readings wherein passages are read several times (Samuels, 1979; O'Shea, Sindelar, & O'Shea, 1987) and previewing of new readings (Rose & Sherry, 1984). Both interventions have been shown to enhance the reading fluency and comprehension of students with LD. Sindelar and Stoddard (1991) also suggest that systematic instruction in vocabulary is warranted as part of comprehensive reading instruction. These authors go on to note several research studies documenting the effectiveness of vocabulary- building strategies such as teaching synonyms via matching of printed words (Pany, Jenkins, & Shreck, 1982), teaching sets of words that belong within categories (Beck, Perfetti, & McKeown, 1982), and preteaching vocabulary words contained in a new reading assignment (Wixon, 1986).

Last, but certainly not least, we note some instructional strategies to promote reading comprehension. First, as noted by Grossen and Carnine (1991), reading for comprehension assumes skill in decoding. Given fluent decoding skills, a number of instructional activities may be utilized to enhance reading comprehension (see Grossen & Carnine, 1991; Sindelar & Stoddard, 1991, for reviews). For example, prereading discussions of the assignment can help to put the reading into a context that the student can understand and relate to. Background knowledge or information related to the reading may be checked for and supplemented, as may necessary vocabulary. In addition to these prereading activities, several strategies to enhance comprehension may be used either during reading, or following the completion of a passage. Students can be taught to understand readings and their structure by learning to ask a series of questions, known as story grammar or story patterns (Carnine & Kinder, 1985). Students also can be taught to draw diagrams or maps of the text that they are reading to help support their comprehension of material (Grossen & Carnine, (1991). Reading comprehension also can be facilitated by the development of writing and spelling skills (Anderson et al., 1985).

Writing and Spelling Skills

In addition to instruction in reading, language arts instruction typically focuses on the development of writing and spelling skills. Skills in both of these areas are critical to the development of functional communication abilities. In other words, writing and spelling skills allow writers to have their intended effect on their reader(s). With respect to writing and spelling strategies, we remain focused on strategies intended to increase student opportunities to learn and practice specific skills, and to receive feedback and corrections on that practice. Specifically, we draw on the work of William Heward, Timothy Heron, and their colleagues at Ohio State University, who have begun to investigate the effects of various instructional strategies to improve student writing and spelling (see Heward, Heron, Gardner, & Prayzer, 1991; Okyere & Heron, 1991).

A primary concern of Heward et al. (1991) is that, in general, students experience too few opportunities to write in their classrooms, and as such they receive minimal feedback in the interest of developing writing skills. To address these issues these researchers have developed two school-based strategies (i.e., selective grading and telephone managed, home-based writing) to promote daily student writing accompanied by frequent feedback. Selective grading is a strategy developed specifically to ease the potentially overwhelming burden on teachers of having to grade and provide feedback on daily writing assignments for every child in a class. The primary components of selective grading involve (1) daily writing assignments based on story starters and topics for all students, (2) teacher evaluation of 20–25% of student papers, (3) teacher presentation to the whole class based on evaluation of the selected papers, (4) additional student writing with contingencies for specific amounts of writing, and (5) available bonus points for individual writing that meets certain criteria related to the skills being taught.

The telephone managed writing program prepares and involves parents as monitors and reporters of their children's home-based writing. With this system, teachers leave a daily message containing a new writing assignment. Children or parents call in to get the message. Next, the child writes for 10 minutes on the given topic. Parents then evaluate, score, and reinforce the child's writing. Overall evaluation of each child's progress is based on the amount of written material produced and the number of specific target skills utilized. Both of these instructional strategies have been documented to promote increases in written output and improvement in student writing skills (Heward et al., 1991).

The range of available remedial spelling approaches has been reviewed by Okyere and Heron (1991) and includes approaches to teaching spelling that integrate reading and spelling instruction, others that stress whole word learning, and strategies that involve both visual and phonological skills. Available strategies also include an effective, easy-to-use, self-correction strategy that has been documented to improve deficient student spelling skills (Okyere & Heron, 1991). As such, self-correction is suggested as one starting point for remedial spelling instruction. Essentially, this involves daily spelling practice consisting of a four-step process: (1) comparing misspelled words to a correctly spelled model, (2) identifying types of spelling mistakes made (e.g., omitted letters), (3) correction of misspellings using four basic proofreading marks, and (4) correctly writing the word. Utilization of the strategy requires teaching students to use proofreading marks and self-correction forms, in addition to arranging for monitoring of individual student progress on an identified pool of words using a series of pretests and posttests. Okyere and Heron (1991) note several positive features of self-correction including its ease of use, its provision of immediate feedback to students, and its ability to support individualized instruction.

Clearly, this discussion of academic skills instructional strategies is far from comprehensive. However, teachers and school psychologists with thorough knowledge of these and other procedures can utilize instructional interventions to build comprehensive and effective educational programs for students with ADHD who exhibit academic skills deficits.

Peer Tutoring

Another instructional strategy that can be used to support the development and remediation of basic skills is peer tutoring. Peer tutoring is a good example of an effective instructional strategy and is now gathering empirical support for its efficacy with students identified with ADHD. Classwide peer tutoring materials and procedures, as developed at the University of Kansas by Charles Greenwood and his colleagues (Greenwood, Carta, & Hall, 1988; Greenwood, Maheady, & Carta, 1991), were designed as a set of strategies aimed at increasing student opportunities to practice and develop fluency with newly developing basic academic skills such as math, spelling, and reading. The strategies are not intended to supplant regular instruction in the basic skill areas. Recently, DuPaul and Henningson (1993) reported the results of a case study involving classwide peer tutoring as an intervention for a second-grade boy with ADHD. The research findings indicated that, as a function of classwide peer tutoring, significant improvement was achieved in the student's on-task behavior, activity level, and academic performance (see Chapter 6 for details of peer tutoring).

Study and Organizational Skills

Children diagnosed with ADHD often present with a variety of academic performance problems in the areas of work completion, organization of desks and other materials, following directions, and studying for tests (Barkley, 1990). Children experiencing such difficulties may benefit from direct instruction in study and organizational skills. However, the effects of such instruction in these skill areas on the academic performance of children with ADHD remains to be documented empirically.

An organized and thorough set of field-tested materials for teaching study and organizational skills to students in Grades 3 through 6, has been published as *Skills for School Success (Grades 3-6)* by Archer and Gleason (1989). The goal of these authors was to prepare a curriculum to teach study skills for gaining, responding to, and organizing information. In this fashion, students would be encouraged to become more actively engaged in the classroom learning process. Similar work has been conducted at the University of Kansas, by Donald Deshler, Jean Schumaker, and their colleagues, with a focus on strategies for use by secondary-level students (Deshler & Schumaker, 1988; Ellis, Deshler, & Schumaker, 1989).

As reviewed by Gleason, Colvin, and Archer (1991), students can be taught several strategies related to gaining information from written materials. These strategies involve previewing readings to identify main ideas and topics, reading text and concomitantly answering prepared questions about the reading, and utilizing strategies for taking careful and complete notes about the reading. In gaining meaning from text, children also must learn to read and understand the maps, graphs, pictures, and other visual aides that frequently accompany text. A second study-skills area involves utilizing information gleaned from texts to respond to questions or other assignments based on the material. In this domain, the *Skills for School Success* curriculum contains lessons on carefully reading and answering end-of-unit questions, organizing and preparing written summaries of material that has been read, and taking quizzes and tests. For example, in learning to take quizzes and tests, students are taught how to anticipate the content of a forthcoming test, how to study and prepare for tests, and how to respond to particular types of questions such as multiple-choice items.

Finally, Archer and Gleason (1989) have developed lessons for elementary-aged children on how to manage time and materials in school. Three main topics are covered including the organization of a school materials notebook, preparation and use of an assignment calendar, and the setup and completion of a neat, well-organized paper. For example, in setting up assignment papers, students are taught what is referred to as the *HOW strategy*. Here, the components and organization of a paper *Heading* are learned, including name, date, and subject. Next, children are taught the components of a paper's *Organization*, including the use of margins and blank lines. Finally, instruction focuses on what it means to produce a paper that is *Written* neatly, including writing on lines and erasing neatly when necessary. Across each of these study-skills areas, it is suggested that teachers first must provide appropriate models, then supply regular opportunities for the study and organizational skills to be practiced by students, and finally give positive feedback and corrections as necessary. Few would disagree that these study and organizational skills are invaluable to all students, including those with ADHD. What is suggested here is that the effects of direct instruction in these skills on children with ADHD begin to be investigated (see Chapter 8 for additional discussion of this topic).

SUPPORT FOR TEACHERS

Given evidence that a student is not meeting the expectations of his or her current classroom, reasonable interventions and accommodations should be made in attempts to allow the student to meet those expectations and achieve academic success. Such accommodations might include matching instructional materials with current academic skills, providing more frequent positive and corrective feedback, enhancing motivation to engage in academic work, and increasing opportunities to learn and practice newly acquired skills. It also must be recognized, however, that teachers who are expected to make such accommodations should themselves be able to expect systematic assistance by way of consultation and support services for the design, implementation and evaluation of classroom-based interventions.

"Teacher support systems" have been identified by Horner et al. (1991) as being critical to the successful education of students with challenging behaviors. These researchers have noted that teacher support systems rely on instructional and behavioral programs that are grounded in three important commitments: (1) teaching students in those classrooms or schools in which they would be educated were they not exhibiting challenging behaviors, (2) providing support in an ongoing fashion, and (3) producing positive and broad lifestyle outcomes, including preparing the student to participate successfully in the community and society.

Given these commitments, teacher support systems for providing services to students identified with ADHD should consist of the following components, as identified by and adapted from Horner et al. (1991):

1. A systematic screening and identification process to ensure identification of all students in need of the behavioral or instructional support. For example, the Systematic Screening for Behavior Disorders (Walker & Severson, 1988) approach may be a viable choice for this purpose.

2. Comprehensive procedures linking assessment and program development to address achievement and behavior problems.

3. Procedures to ensure the design, implementation, and evaluation of interventions and accommodations to address student learning and behavior problems.

4. Procedures to ensure the transfer of responsibility for intervention program continuance to regular classroom staff.

5. Provision of ongoing supervision and monitoring across classrooms and other school settings, with a focus on structuring educational environments that are purposeful, organized, and supportive, while producing positive student outcomes.

6. Provision for evaluations of and revisions to the support system.

Mechanisms for providing teacher support are considered necessary components in the treatment of children with ADHD. Given the frequency and severity of the disruptive behaviors that these students exhibit, it is not uncommon for teachers to express feelings of frustration and helplessness when attempting to manage their classrooms. These feelings should be expected and validated by professionals and parents who are interacting with classroom teachers. Further, efforts should be made to help teachers deal with these feelings productively (e.g., by providing instructional materials related to stress management). A second, related factor to consider is that making teaching accommodations often requires time, patience, resources, and training beyond that which is currently available to the teacher. For instance, the implementation of an individualized token reinforcement program in the context of a classroom of 25–30 children is often a prohibitive enterprise for the teacher. Thus, the selection of treatment strategies should be made in view of constraints placed on the teacher. The characteristics of the teacher support system enumerated above are designed to address these practical issues in a proactive fashion rather than waiting for teacher complaints to occur.

Implementation of teacher support systems will require professionals with assessment and program development expertise, educators with supervisory or administrative rank and responsibilities for monitoring ongoing educational programs, and personnel to provide intervention assistance as needed in support of regular classroom staff. Ideally, this type of commitment to teacher support would be coupled with staff who are knowledgeable and skillful in the areas of instructional and behavioral support. In schools where such circumstances exist, it would not seem unreasonable for parents and teachers to expect higher rates of academic, behavioral, and social success for students with ADHD.

SUMMARY

Children with ADHD frequently experience difficulty in the areas of classroom behavior, academic performance, and scholastic achievement. Maximizing each child's likelihood for school success will require a variety of behavioral, instructional, and learning strategies aimed at the prevention and management of problems in these areas. This chapter has provided a review of effective behavior management interventions and instructional strategies, as well as promising instructional and self-management strategies. The need for systematic teacher support was also noted. In addition to further research on promising intervention approaches, the challenge before us is one of integrating the various strategies into treatment programs that are based on individual student needs, such that all students with ADHD experience success in school.

5

Medication Therapy

The prescription of psychostimulant medication is the most frequent treatment for ADHD, with approximately 750,000 children (or greater than 2% of the school-age population) being treated with these drugs annually (Safer & Krager, 1988). Psychostimulant medication use has grown steadily throughout the last decade, particularly among middle and high school populations (Safer & Krager, 1988). The average duration of medication use is between 2–7 years depending upon the age of the child (Safer & Krager, 1988). Further, more research has been conducted on the effects of stimulant medications on the functioning of children with ADHD than any other treatment modality for any childhood disorder (Barkley, 1990).

Numerous investigators have consistently demonstrated short-term enhancement of the behavioral, academic, and social functioning of the majority of children being treated with stimulant compounds (see DuPaul & Barkley, 1990, for a review). However, the limitations of pharmacotherapy (e.g., possible side effects, lack of evidence of long-term efficacy) have led to the adoption of multimodal treatment approaches for ADHD (Barkley, 1989; Satterfield, Satterfield, & Schell, 1987). Stimulants appear to exert greater behavior-changing effects when combined with other effective treatment approaches, such as behavior modification (Gittelman-Klein et al., 1980; Pelham & Murphy, 1986). Given the demonstrated efficacy and widespread use of psychotropic medications in treating ADHD, it is important for school-based personnel to become familiar with (1) the types of medications used to treat ADHD, (2) possible behavioral effects and side effects associated with stimulant medications, (3) factors to consider in recommending medication trials for individual children, (4) methods to assess treatment response within school settings, (5) how to communicate assessment data to physicians and other medical professionals, and (6) the limitations of pharmacotherapy.

TYPES OF PSYCHOTROPIC MEDICATIONS EMPLOYED

Central Nervous System Stimulants

Psychostimulant medications are so named because of their demonstrated ability to increase the arousal or "alertness" of the central nervous system (CNS). Their effects on children with ADHD are not paradoxical as they exert similar physiological and behavioral effects with the normal population (Rapoport et al., 1980). Given the structural similarity of psychostimulants to certain brain neurotransmitters (e.g., dopamine), they are considered sympathomimetic compounds (Donnelly & Rapoport, 1985). The three most commonly employed CNS stimulants are methylphenidate (Ritalin), dextroamphetamine (Dexedrine), and pemoline (Cylert). Of the three medications, methylphenidate is the most widely employed, being used with over 90% of children treated with stimulants (Safer & Krager, 1988). Other types of stimulants (e.g., caffeine) are not discussed here because they have not been found to be as effective as the above medications nor are they typically used clinically.

Pharmacology

The primary mode of action of dextroamphetamine is an enhancement of catecholamine activity in the CNS, probably by increasing the availability of norepinepherine and/or dopamine at the synaptic cleft (Donnelly & Rapoport, 1985). The precise mechanism is still poorly understood. Methylphenidate is structurally similar to dextroamphetamine and is a piperidine derivative (Donnelly & Rapoport, 1985). Its specific mode of action is even less clearly understood than that of dextroamphetamine. It may be that methylphenidate has a greater effect on dopamine activity than other neurotransmitters, but this remains speculative at the present time (Barkley, DuPaul, & Costello, 1993). Pemoline is similar in function to the other stimulants, but is structurally dissimilar and has minimal sympathomimetic effects (Donnelly & Rapoport, 1985). The specific mechanism of action of pemoline is not well understood.

The specific locus of action of the psychostimulants within the CNS is speculative. Early investigators hypothesized that brainstem activation was the primary locus, while, more recently, the midbrain or frontal cortex has been implicated (Barkley et al., 1993). Recent studies of cerebral blood flow have shown that activity in the area of the striatum and the connections between the orbital–frontal and limbic regions is enhanced during stimulant medication treatment (Lou, Henriksen, & Bruhn, 1984; Lou, Henriksen, Bruhn, Borner, & Nielsen, 1989). Further, increased brain metabolic activity in the bilateral orbital–frontal area and in the left Rolandic and parietal areas has been found in seven adults with ADHD following a single dose of methylphenidate (Redman & Zametkin, 1991).

It has been hypothesized that stimulant medications serve to "canalize" or decrease fluctuation and variability in arousal, attention, and CNS reactivity (Gualtieri, Hicks, & Mayo, 1983). This may enhance the persistence of responding and increase cortical inhibition. Other investigators (Haenlein & Caul, 1987) propose that the stimulants decrease the threshold for reinforcement through enhancing arousal of the CNS behavioral activation (i.e., reward) system. Persistence of responding is thereby increased as activities in which the organism engages become more reinforcing.

Pharmacokinetics

Stimulant medications are typically administered orally, are quickly absorbed from the gastrointestinal tract, readily cross the blood-brain barrier, and are eliminated from the body within 24 hours (Diener, 1991). Methylphenidate reaches peak plasma levels within 1.5–2.5 hours after ingestion. The plasma half-life is 2–3 hours and the drug is entirely metabolized within 12–24 hours, with almost none of the compound appearing in the urine (Diener, 1991). The behavioral effects of methylphenidate occur within 30–60 minutes postingestion, peak within 1–3 hours, and are dissipated within 3–5 hours (Barkley et al., 1993). The plasma half-life of sustained-release methylphenidate (Ritalin SR, 20 mg) has been found to range between 2 to 6 hours, with a peak plasma level reached within 1–4 hours. Behavioral effects of this preparation appear to occur within 1–2 hours, peak within 3–5 hours, and gradually diminish until approximately 8 hours postingestion (Barkley et al., 1993). Considerable interindividual variability exists with respect to these time-response parameters (Pelham et al., 1987).

Dextroamphetamine reaches peak plasma levels in children within 2–3 hours, with a plasma half-life of 4–6 hours (Barkley et al., 1993). As with methylphenidate, the behavioral effects of this drug are noticeable within 30–60 minutes, peak within 1–2 hours postingestion, and diminish within 4–6 hours (Dulcan, 1990). There is considerable interindividual variability in the time response to dextroamphetamine.

Pemoline has a shorter half-life (7–8 hours) with children than with adults (11–13 hours) and reaches peak plasma levels within 2–4 hours after ingestion (Sallee, Stiller, & Perel, 1992). The time-course and response characteristics of the behavioral effects of pemoline have not been documented as well as they have been with the other stimulants, however recent research indicates that pemoline effects on cognitive functioning (e.g., paired-associates learning) occur within 2 hours after oral ingestion and are sustained for at least 6 hours (Pelham et al., 1990; Sallee et al., 1992). The half-life of this drug possibly increases with chronic use, which may lead to a buildup in plasma levels, thereby explaining its considerably delayed behavioral effects (up to 3–4 weeks) relative to other stimulant medications (Dulcan, 1990).

Unfortunately, knowledge of peak or absolute blood levels of these medications does not aid in predicting behavioral effects, beyond knowledge of the dose administered (Kupietz, 1991; Swanson, 1988). Therefore, where behavioral change is the primary goal of treatment, obtaining medication blood levels plays no role in establishing the therapeutic response for an individual child, beyond knowledge of the oral dose itself (Barkley et al., 1993). Where changes in learning performance are more important, blood levels eventually may provide more promising information about establishing a therapeutic dose range, however inter- and intraindividual variability in blood level parameters is quite common (Kupietz, 1991). Thus, drawing blood to guide therapeutic adjustments to stimulant medication for individual children typically is not recommended (Shaywitz & Shaywitz, 1991; Swanson, 1988).

Behavioral tolerance to stimulant medications has not been well researched, however anecdotal evidence indicates diminished efficacy over prolonged administration, particularly for pemoline (Barkley et al., 1993). In addition to physical factors, tolerance effects may result from noncompliance with the prescribed regimen, situational factors such as a stress event (e.g., a geographic move, parental divorce, change in classroom placement), weight gain, or altered caregiver expectations (Dulcan, 1990).

Dose Ranges

The CNS stimulants, their available tablet sizes, and typical dose ranges are displayed in Table 5.1. Fixed dose ranges, as opposed to those based on body weight (i.e., mg/kg), are given to reflect typical prescribing practice. Also, recent research indicates that gross body weight is not a significant predictor of dose response to methylphenidate in the pediatric age range (Rapport, DuPaul, & Kelly, 1989). Once a child's optimal dose is established, as discussed below, medication is usually dispensed twice per day (at breakfast and lunch) except for pemoline, which is given once per day in the morning. Given the relatively short behavioral half-lives of these compounds, school personnel have a greater opportunity to observe the child with ADHD when medicated than do parents and therefore must be included in the assessment of treatment response.

TABLE 5.1. Stimulant Medications, Tablet Sizes, and Dose Ranges

Brand name[a]	Tablet sizes	Dosage regimen	Dose range[b]
Ritalin (methylphenidate)	5 mg 10 mg 20 mg SR, 20 mg	Twice daily Once daily	2.5–25 mg 20–40 mg
Dexedrine (dextroamphetamine)	5-mg spansule 10-mg spansule 15-mg spansule 5-mg tablet 5 mg/5 ml (elixir)	Once daily Twice daily	2.5–25 mg 2.5–25 mg
Cylert (pemoline)	18.75 mg 37.50 mg 75 mg	Once daily	18.75– 112.5 mg

[a]Generic name in parentheses.
[b]Dose range for each administration is provided.

Both methylphenidate and dextroamphetamine are available in short-acting and sustained-release forms. Because the behavioral effects of the latter compounds purportedly last longer (i.e., 8 hours post-ingestion) than the short-acting derivatives, they have several advantages including the preclusion of noontime medication administered at school and greater confidentiality of treatment (DuPaul & Barkley, 1990). However, recent investigations have indicated that the time to peak effects and total duration of action of sustained-release methylphenidate vary considerably across indvidual children (Pelham et al., 1987). Some studies (e.g., Pelham et al., 1987) have found that sustained-release methylphenidate is less efficacious than the standard preparation of the drug for some children, whereas others (e.g., Fitzpatrick, Klorman, Brumaghim, & Borgstedt, 1992) have found the two preparations to be relatively equivalent in behavioral effects. Given the equivocal results of research on sustained-release compounds, the short-acting forms of these medications are preferred except in situations where in-school administration of the drugs is significantly problematic (e.g., no school nurse is available to dispense the medication or for teenagers who may be more prone to teasing and censure by peers).

Tricyclic Antidepressant Medications

Antidepressants, such as desipramine (Norpramin) and imipramine (Tofranil), are slower-acting medications that have been shown to produce behavioral effects similar to those of the stimulants with children with ADHD (see Pliszka, 1987, 1991, for reviews). For instance, both antidepressant medications have been found to result in improved teacher ratings of inattention, hyperactivity, and aggression in up to 70% of treated children. Further, these medications may be particularly helpful for children who are nonresponders to stimulants (Biederman, Baldessarini, Wright, Knee, & Harmatz, 1989). Desipramine has been found to enhance performance on laboratory-based measures of short-term memory and visual problem-solving, but does not affect learning of higher-order relationships unless combined with methylphenidate (Rapport, Carlson, Kelly, & Pataki, 1993).

Potential side effects of antidepressant medications include increases in blood pressure and heart rate as well as possible slowing of intracardiac conduction (Ryan, 1990). Thus, a child's response to these medications requires more intense monitoring (e.g., frequent electrocardiograms) than is necessary with the stimulants. Desipramine has also been associated with growth deficits, although these are not as pronounced as those found with the stimulant medications (Spencer, Biederman, Wright, & Danon, 1992). Tricyclic antidepressants remain a viable treatment alternative if a child does not respond to stimulant medication or exhibits characteristics (e.g., motor tics, anxiety disorder symptoms) predictive of an adverse stimulant response (Pliszka, 1987).

Alternative Medications

Other Antidepressant Medications

Monoamine oxidase inhibitors (MAOIs) have been found to be clinically effective for problems related to ADHD (Rapoport, 1986; Zametkin, Rapoport, Murphy, Linnoila, & Ismond, 1985). Unfortunately, certain dietary and multidrug restrictions must be followed when MAOIs are administered, thus rendering the use of MAOIs problematic, given the impulse control problems of children with ADHD (Hunt, Lau, & Ryu, 1991). Nortriptyline has been found to be helpful in reducing tics associated with Tourette's Syndrome and symptoms of ADHD in a majority of children with both ADHD and Tourette's (Spencer, Biederman, Wilens, Steingard, & Geist, 1993). Bupropion, a relatively new antidepressant, has been found to be mildly effective, at best, in reducing ADHD symptomatology (Casat, Pleasants, Schroeder, & Parker, 1989; Simeon, Ferguson, & Van Wyck Fleet, 1986). There is a possibility that bupropion may exert both antiaggressive and antihyperactive effects in some children with ADHD (Hunt et al., 1991).

Clonidine

Initial investigations indicate that clonidine may be useful in treating children with ADHD who are extremely hyperactive and aggressive or who have exhibited motor tics and/or a poor response to psychostimulant medications (see Hunt et al., 1991, for a review). For example, Hunt, Mindera, and Cohen (1985) obtained clonidine-induced enhancement of teacher and parent ratings of hyperactivity and conduct problems in 70% of children treated. It should be noted that when the effects of clonidine are directly compared to those of methylphenidate, the latter is found to be superior (Hunt et al., 1991). However, clonidine may be preferred in certain situations due to the continued effects in the evening and an absence of sleep or appetite disturbance sometimes found with methylphenidate. In fact, the combination of clonidine and methylphenidate may be helpful in those cases where methylphenidate alone has led to side effects such as insomnia (Hunt et al., 1991). The most frequent side effect of clonidine is sedation and sleepiness. In addition, because it is an antihypertensive agent, it may lead to low blood pressure, but the latter is rarely clinically significant (Hunt et al., 1991).

Although these and other initial results are promising, most of the available research with medications other than stimulants has been conducted with small samples employing only teacher and parent ratings as outcome measures. Further, some initial studies did not employ double-blind methodology, a crucial control in pharmacological research. Effects on academic performance and cognitive functioning must be studied prior to these compounds being considered viable alternatives to stimulant medications. In addition, the magnitude of treatment effects associated with alternative drugs and stimulants need to be compared directly within large samples of children with ADHD. Pending the results of such investigations, stimulants remain the medication of choice for the treatment of ADHD. For this reason, the remainder of this chapter will focus on CNS stimulants, primarily methylphenidate.

BEHAVIORAL EFFECTS OF STIMULANTS

Based on the empirical literature, it is estimated that between 70–80% of children with ADHD treated with stimulant medications respond positively to one or more doses (Barkley, 1977). The remainder either exhibit no change or their ADHD symptoms worsen with treatment, thus implicating the need for alternative medications or treatment approaches. Thus, it is not guaranteed that a given child with ADHD will respond to a particular stimulant nor should medication response be used as a confirmation of diagnosis (i.e., a positive response does not confirm an ADHD diagnosis, nor does a negative medication response indicate that a child does not have ADHD). Further, a lack of response or adverse effects associated with one of the stimulants does not rule out the possibility of a positive response to one of the remaining medications in this class (Elia & Rapoport, 1991). At the present time, methylphenidate is by far the most commonly employed stimulant; it is prescribed in greater than 90% of children receiving such medications (Safer & Krager, 1988).

The effects of stimulant medications upon nearly every area of behavioral, emotional, and physical functioning of children with ADHD have been investigated (for reviews, see Gadow, 1986; Gittelman-Klein & Klein, 1987; Rapport & Kelly, 1991; Ross & Ross, 1982). The areas of greatest potential concern to school professionals will be reviewed briefly below.

Behavioral Control and Attention

Stimulant medications have been found to have positive effects on the ability of children with ADHD to sustain attention to effortful tasks (Barkley, DuPaul, & McMurray, 1991; Douglas, Barr, O'Neill, & Britton, 1986; Rapport et al., 1987) and to inhibit impulsive responding (Brown & Sleator, 1979; Rapport et al., 1988). In many cases, attention to assigned classwork is improved to the extent that the child's behavior appears similar to his or her "normal" classmates (Abikoff & Gittelman, 1985b; DuPaul & Rapport, 1993). Further, these medications significantly reduce disruptive motor activity, especially task-irrelevant movements during work situations (e.g., Cunningham & Barkley, 1979). Problems with aggression (Hinshaw, 1991; Klorman et al., 1988), classroom disruptive behavior (Barkley, 1979), persistence with frustrating tasks (Milich, Carlson, Pelham, & Licht, 1991), and noncompliance with authority figure commands (Barkley, Karlsson, Strzelecki, & Murphy, 1984) also have been shown to improve with these medications. These effects on behavioral control and sustained attention are strongest at the higher doses and are ubiquitous across home, clinic, analog classroom, and school settings. Similar behavioral effects have been obtained for adolescents with ADHD, however the percentage of positive responders is lower (i.e., 50–70%) than among elementary school children (Evans & Pelham, 1991; Pelham, Vodde-Hamilton, Murphy, Greenstein, & Vallano, 1991).

Effects on Cognitive and Academic Performance

Stimulant medication effects on the cognitive performance of children with ADHD traditionally have been studied using laboratory-based paradigms such as the Paired Associates Learning test (Swanson & Kinsbourne, 1975) and tests of short-term recall (Sprague & Sleator, 1977). Salutary effects of methylphenidate on children's cognitive functioning have been found on tests of verbal retrieval (Barkley, DuPaul, & McMurray, 1991; Evans, Gualtieri, & Amara, 1986), paired associates learning (Rapport et al., 1985), stimulus equivalence learning (Vyse & Rapport, 1989), and short-term recall of visual stimuli (Sprague & Sleator, 1977). In general, the dose–response effects of methylphenidate on cognitive performance have been found to be linear, with the greatest enhancement occurring at the highest doses (see Rapport & Kelly, 1991; Solanto, 1991, for reviews). It is important to note, however, that these dose–response effects have been delineated at the group level and there are substantial differences in dose responsivity across individual children, as will be explicated below.

Reviews of stimulant medication effects on the academic performance of children with ADHD have generally concluded that this area of functioning is not impacted significantly by pharmacotherapy over the long term (Barkley & Cunningham, 1978). Of course, the studies conducted through the late 1970s had primarily utilized traditional academic achievement tests (e.g., Wide Range Achievement Test) or intelligence batteries. Such measures may not be sensitive enough to detect short-term or more subtle changes in cognitive functioning associated with treatment. Several additional factors limit the utility of norm-referenced achievement tests for treatment evaluation purposes, including (1) a failure to adquately sample the curriculum in use, (2) the use of a limited number of items to sample various skills, (3) the use of response formats that do not require the student to perform the behavior (e.g., writing) of interest, and (4) an insensitivity to small changes in student performance (Marston, 1989; Shapiro, 1989).

More recent studies conducted by several independent research teams have found acute methylphenidate-induced improvements in academic productivity and accuracy among large samples of children (Douglas, Barr, O'Neill, & Britton, 1988; Pelham, Bender, Caddell, Booth, & Moorer, 1985; Rapport et al., 1987, 1988) and young adolescents with ADHD (Evans & Pelham, 1991; Pelham et al., 1991). Attention to teacher lectures, completion of study hall assignments, and quiz and test scores among junior high school students with ADHD also are enhanced by methylphenidate (Pelham et al., 1991). As with other domains, these effects have been strongest in the higher dose range when analyzed at the group level. Rather than standardized achievement tests, these investigators employed written tasks assigned by each child's classroom teacher to assess academic performance. Although such measures may be more sensitive to treatment-related change and presumably possess greater ecological validity than do published, norm-referenced instruments, their reliability (i.e., stability over time) must be established prior to evaluating intervention effects. It remains to be seen whether short-term improvements in academic performance lead to greater scholastic success in the long run, however these results would indicate a high probability of obtaining such findings if medication dosage is initially determined based on the enhancement of academic functioning rather than simply behavioral control, as has been done in the past (Rapport & Kelly, 1991).

Effects on Social Relationships

Methylphenidate has been found to significantly improve the quality of social interactions between children with ADHD and their parents, teachers, and peers. For example, several studies have shown that stimulants increase children's compliance with parent or teacher commands and enhance their responsiveness to the interactions of others (see DuPaul & Barkley, 1992b, for a review). These same investigations found that negative and off-task behaviors are reduced in compliance situations, resulting in a decrease in the frequency of authority figure commands and an increase in positive adult attention to child behavior.

Similar results have been obtained for the peer relations of children with ADHD. When treated with methylphenidate, children with ADHD are found to be less aggressive with others, to behave more appropriately with other children, and to be accepted to a greater degree by their peers (Cunningham, Siegel, & Offord, 1985; Gadow, Nolan, Sverd, Sprafkin, & Paolicelli, 1990; Hinshaw, 1991; Pelham & Hoza, 1987; Whalen et al., 1989). The effects of methylphenidate on the prosocial behavior of children with ADHD remains unclear as some studies have found no change in the frequency of initiating interactions with others (Hinshaw, Henker, Whalen, Erhardt, & Dunnington, 1989; Wallander, Schroeder, Michelli, & Gualtieri, 1987), whereas a reduction in positive interactions with peers has been found by others (Buhrmester, Whalen, Henker, MacDonald, & Hinshaw, 1992). Beyond direct effects on social behavior, methylphenidate has been found to enhance other areas of functioning that may indirectly impact social status. For example, a group of children with ADHD was found to pay attention better during softball games (e.g., greater recall of the game score) when receiving methylphenidate versus a placebo (Pelham, McBurnett, et al., 1990).

Dose Response and Individual Responsivity

Beyond a delineation of specific behavioral effects, the results of empirical investigations of stimulants with children with ADHD have led to a number of important conclusions regarding the general properties of these drugs. First, methylphenidate-induced changes in a specific behavioral realm vary across dose in a systematic fashion, at least at the group level of analysis (e.g., Barkley, DuPaul & McMurray, 1991; Pelham et al., 1985; Rapport et al., 1985; Sprague & Sleator, 1977). For most areas of functioning (i.e., cognitive, social, behavior control) these dose–response effects have been linear, with higher doses leading to the greatest change. Second, at an individual level of analysis, separate classes of behavior may be affected differently by methylphenidate even at the same dose (Rapport et al., 1987, 1988; Sprague & Sleator, 1977). For instance, a given child may show the greatest improvement in academic performance at a different dose than at the level of medication that was optimal for impulse control or sustained attention. Finally, although linear dose–response effects are consistently found at the group level of analysis, individual children vary considerably with respect to behavior change across doses (Douglas et al., 1986; Pelham et al., 1985; Rapport et al., 1987, 1988). Even when children share similar characteristics (e.g., diagnosis, age, and body weight), there may be considerable variability in dose responsivity, presumably due to individual differences in CNS functioning (Rapport, DuPaul, & Kelly, 1989).

To illustrate the idiosyncratic nature of methylphenidate effects, Figure 5.1 presents school-based, dose–response data for three individual children with ADHD who were participants in a study conducted by Rapport and colleagues (1989). Behavioral changes for three measures are presented including percentage of on-task behavior during independent work, percentage of academic work completed correctly based on the Academic Efficiency Score (AES), and teacher ratings on the Abbreviated Conners Teacher Rating Scale (ACTRS) (Werry, Sprague, & Cohen, 1975). A double-blind, placebo-controlled experimental design was employed wherein each child received four active methylphenidate doses (i.e., 5 mg, 10 mg, 15 mg, 20 mg) and an inert placebo in a randomly determined sequence. The children were of similar age and body weight, but exhibited rather dramatic differences in methylphenidate response. For example, *S-1* (Figure 5.1, top) evidenced attentional and behavioral improvement as a direct function of increasing dose, peaking at the highest dose or 20 mg (i.e., linear dose–response effects). Alternatively, improvements in *S-2*'s classroom behavior and performance were obtained up to the 15-mg dose, where peak effects were evidenced, followed by a decrement at the 20-mg dose. The latter is referred to as a quadratic response because there was one change in the slope of the dose–response curve. Finally, *S-3* did not exhibit academic or behavioral change until a "therapeutic threshold" was attained at 10 mg, with little in the way of further enhancement at the higher doses (i.e., a threshold

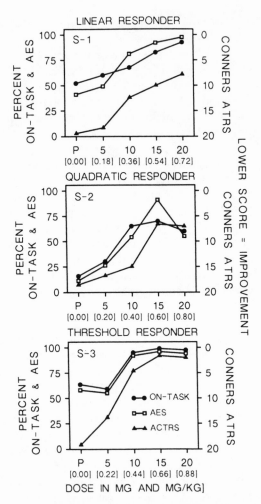

FIGURE 5.1. Dose–response curves of three dependent measures for three individual children of similar body weight (M = 25 kg). Percentage of on-task frequency and AES are plotted along the left-hand ordinate. Total score on the ACTRS is plotted on the right-hand ordinate. Improvement for all three measures is indicated by an upward movement on the axis. From "Attention Deficit Hyperactivity Disorder and methylphenidate: The relationship between gross body weight and drug response in children" by M. D. Rapport, G. J. DuPaul, and K. L. Kelly, 1989, *Psychopharmacology Bulletin, 25,* 285–290. Reprinted by permission of authors.

response). Thus, the dose–response profile and optimal or therapeutic dose differed for the three children.

Normalization of Classroom Functioning

Although the *statistical* significance of the behavioral effects of methylphenidate have been demonstrated reliably, the *clinical* significance of behavioral changes for individual children with ADHD has been demonstrated less frequently. Some investigations have indicated that the task-related attention (Loney, Weissenburger, Woolson, & Lichty, 1979; Whalen et al., 1978; Whalen, Henker, Collins, Finck, & Dotemoto, 1979) and aggressive behaviors (Hinshaw et al., 1989) of children receiving methylphenidate is statistically indistinguishable from those of their normal peers. Abikoff and Gittelman (1985b) found that 60% of children treated with methylphenidate evidenced "normalized" behavior in attention span and impulse control in the classroom. Similarly, Pelham and colleagues (1993) found that approximately 60% of children receiving 0.6 mg/kg methylphenidate were rated by teachers to behave "very much like . . . normal child[ren]" when interacting with peers and adults.

A recent investigation examined the degree to which methylphenidate normalized the classroom behavior and academic functioning of 31 children with ADHD based on comparisons with a normal control group of 25 children (DuPaul & Rapport, 1993). Subjects with ADHD participated in a double-blind, placebo-controlled trial in which they received each of four doses (5, 10, 15, and 20 mg) of methylphenidate and a placebo. Dependent measures included teacher ratings of social conduct, direct observations of classroom on-task behavior, and accuracy on independent academic tasks. Between 61 and 78% of the sample obtained scores within the normal range of functioning at one or more doses of methylphenidate depending upon the specific measure employed (see Figure 5.2). Although these results provide further evidence of the strong therapeutic effects of stimulant medication, concomitant interventions will be necessary for many children with ADHD, even for those whose classroom performance is normalized by methylphenidate.

Combination of Medication and Behavior Therapy

The two most common interventions for ADHD are stimulant medication and behavior modification strategies (Barkley, 1990; Pelham & Murphy, 1986). In fact, the combination of these interventions has been found to be more effective than the use of either treatment in isolation (see Pelham & Murphy, 1986, for a review) and is now considered the optimal approach to treating ADHD for many children (Barkley, 1990).

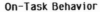

On-Task Behavior

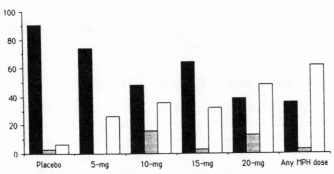

Academic Efficiency Score

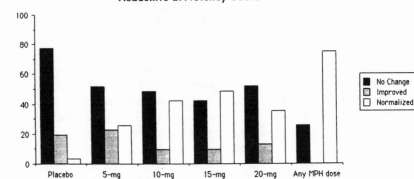

■ No Change
▨ Improved
□ Normalized

Abbreviated Conners Teacher Ratings

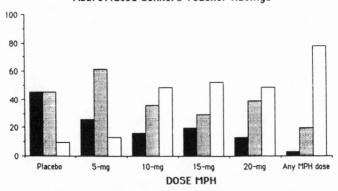

DOSE MPH

FIGURE 5.2. Percentage of children with ADHD exhibiting no change, clinically significant improvement, and normalized school behavior across three classroom variables as a function of placebo and methylphenidate dose. From "Does methylphenidate normalize the classroom performance of children with attention deficit disorder?" by G. J. DuPaul and M. D. Rapport, 1993, *Journal of the American Academy of Child and Adolescent Psychiatry, 32,* 190–198. Copyright 1993 by the American Academy of Child and Adolescent Psychiatry. Reprinted by permission.

148

There are important shortcomings of each treatment when used alone including that the effects are limited to the times when the interventions are active, each is ineffective for a significant minority of children with ADHD, and the long-term effectiveness of both treatments has not been documented (Hoza, Pelham, Sams, & Carlson, 1992; Pelham & Murphy, 1986). Fortunately, the combination of behavioral and pharmacological treatments may minimize the limitations of each treatment while maximizing the chances of obtaining clinically significant changes (Pelham & Murphy, 1986).

Surprisingly few controlled studies have examined the effects of combining behavior modification and stimulant medication in treating ADHD, however most of these have found the treatment combination to be superior to the use of either intervention alone, with medication generally more effective than behavior modification (Pelham & Murphy, 1986). Unfortunately, most of these studies have employed between-groups designs, thus ignoring individual differences in response to treatment. Recent single-subject investigations have shown that dosage is an important variable in determining the reponse of individual children with ADHD to this treatment combination (Abramowitz, Eckstrand, O'Leary, & Dulcan, 1992; Hoza et al., 1992). For example, Abramowitz and colleagues (1992) evaluated changes in the classroom off-task behavior of three boys with ADHD as a function of varying dosages of methylphenidate (placebo, 0.3 mg/kg, and 0.6 mg/kg) combined with either immediate or delayed reprimands from the teacher. The results are displayed in Figure 5.3 and indicate that response to the combination of interventions varied across children. Steven responded best to the combination of a low dose of methylphenidate and a low "dose" of behavioral intervention (i.e., delayed reprimands), as displayed in the top graph of Figure 5.3. Alternatively, Tony evidenced an optimal response to the high dose of methylphenidate in combination with either immediate or delayed reprimands (see middle graph in Figure 5.3). Finally, Kevin exhibited the least off-task behavior when treated with delayed reprimands combined with either a low or high dose of methylphenidate (see bottom graph in Figure 5.3).

The results of the above and similar investigations indicate that some children will require low intensity behavior modification (e.g., home-based daily report card) in combination with a low dose of methylphenidate, while the ADHD symptoms of another child may be severe enough to warrant a high dose of methylphenidate along with more intensive behavior modification (e.g., classroom-based response cost system). Further, the use of one treatment may result in an adjustment in dosage of another intervention. For example, implementing a behavior modification system may allow for a reduction in the amount of medication that a child may

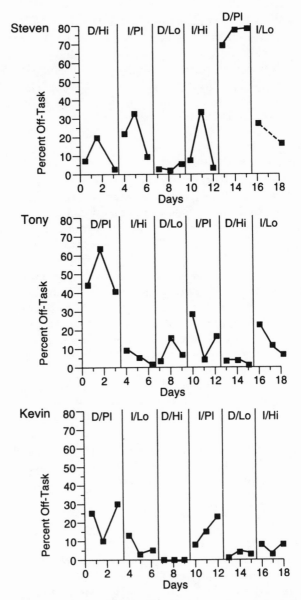

FIGURE 5.3. Off-task rates of three children treated with verbal reprimands and methylphenidate. D = delayed reprimands; I = immediate reprimands; Pl = Placebo; Lo = 0.3 mg/kg methylphenidate; Hi = 0.6 mg/kg methylphenidate. From "ADHD children's responses to stimulant medication and two intensities of a behavioral intervention" by A J. Abramowitz, D. Eckstrand, S. G. O'Leary, and M. K. Dulcan, 1992, *Behavior Modification, 16,* 193–203. Copyright 1992 by Sage Publications. Reprinted by permission.

require. The titration of various strengths of each intervention must be conducted on an individual basis as the response to the combination of treatments will vary according to organismic (e.g., severity of ADHD-related behaviors) and environmental (e.g., classroom placement) factors (Pelham, 1989).

POSSIBLE SIDE EFFECTS OF CENTRAL NERVOUS SYSTEM STIMULANTS

The most frequently reported acute side effects to methylphenidate and other stimulants are appetite reduction (particularly at lunch) and insomnia (Gittelman & Kanner, 1986). Other treatment emergent effects reported in the literature include increased irritability, headaches, stomachaches, and, in rare cases, motor and/or vocal tics (Barkley, 1977). Remarkably few studies have explicated the percentage of cases experiencing possible side effects across a dose range of methylphenidate. A recent investigation examined the prevalence of parent- and teacher-reported side effects to two doses (i.e., 0.3 mg/kg and 0.5 mg/kg) of methylphenidate in a large sample of children with ADHD (Barkley, McMurray, Edelbrock, & Robbins, 1990). These investigators found that over half of the sample exhibited decreased appetite, insomnia, anxiousness, irritability, or proneness to crying with both doses of methylphenidate. It should be noted that many of these apparent side effects (especially those associated with mood) were present during the placebo condition and may represent characteristics associated with the disorder rather than its treatment. Stomachaches and headaches were reported in about one-third of the subjects. The severity of these side effects was mild in most cases, increased as a function of dose, and did not necessarily result in the discontinuation of treatment. Further, it is apparent that the frequency and severity of possible side effects should be assessed during nonmedication or pretreatment conditions to establish whether they are truly associated with drug ingestion (Barkley, McMurray, et al., 1990).

Other possible treatment emergent effects that should be monitored include a behavioral rebound in the late afternoon and the onset or exacerbation of motor and vocal tics (Barkley et al., 1993). The behavioral rebound phenomenon is typically described as a deterioration in conduct (exceeding that which is observed during baseline or placebo conditions) that occurs in the late afternoon and evening following daytime administrations of medication (Johnston, Pelham, Hoza, & Sturges, 1987). Studies that have examined this phenomenon have indicated that it occurs in about one-third of children treated with methylphenidate and that the magnitude of the rebound varies considerably across days for individual children (Johnston et al., 1987). Further, a late afternoon administration of a small dose of methylphenidate may reduce the severity of rebound effects (DuPaul & Barkley, 1990).

It has been estimated that 1% of children with ADHD treated with stimulants will develop a tic disorder and that in 13% of the cases these drugs may exacerbate preexisting tics (Barkley, 1989). Although the vast majority of such reactions subside once pharmacotherapy is discontinued, there are a few reports in the literature where the tics apparently did not diminish in frequency and severity following the termination of treatment (e.g., Bremness & Sverd, 1979). Thus, it is important to screen children with ADHD for a personal or family history of tics or Tourette's syndrome prior to initiating stimulant therapy and to proceed cautiously, if at all, with such treatment in those with positive histories (Comings & Comings, 1984).

Clinical observations have documented an increase in "overfocused" behavior among some children with ADHD treated with methylphenidate (Solanto, 1984). This constriction of cognitive functioning may be demonstrated in a variety of ways including persistence at a task for an abnormally long period of time, a disregard for relevant peripheral stimuli, or an inability to shift cognitive set to adapt to situational demands (Solanto & Wender, 1989). Empirical investigations have failed to document the occurrence of this phenomenon at a group level of analysis; however, at least one study has indicated that a subgroup of children with ADHD may demonstrate overfocused performance as a function of methylphenidate (Solanto & Wender, 1989). This subgroup may include children who are less hyperactive and who demonstrate better baseline performance on cognitive testing relative to other children with ADHD. These findings provide a strong rationale for individualized assessment of academic and cognitive performance across doses when evaluating response to psychotropic medications.

The only long-term side effect of stimulant medication that has been well documented is suppression of height and weight gain. Studies examining this phenomenon have indicated that the probability of growth suppression increases with higher doses, is greater with dextroamphetamine than methylphenidate, and is higher during the first year of treatment (Greenhill, 1984; Mattes & Gittelman, 1983). A rebound in growth following discontinuation of treatment or habituation to this effect seems to occur thereafter, with little appreciable alteration in eventual adult height or weight (Greenhill, 1984; Reeve & Garfinkel, 1991). Other possible long-term side effects that have been proposed, primarily in the popular media, include drug addiction, depression, or other emotional difficulties (e.g., Bacon, 1988; Toufexis, 1989). These claims have no basis in the empirical literature and should not be considered actual treatment risks.

FACTORS TO CONSIDER WHEN RECOMMENDING A MEDICATION TRIAL

School psychologists and other educational professionals are in an ideal position to advocate for the appropriate treatment of a child with ADHD, given their opportunity to observe the student's functioning in the setting where the greatest problems with inattention, impulsivity, and overactivity typically occur (i.e., the school). The decision to initiate a trial of medication should not be an automatic response following the diagnosis of ADHD and obviously must be made in concert with a number of individuals, including the child's physician and parents. Prior to reaching this decision point, comprehensive physical and psychological examinations should be conducted to establish the presence and severity of ADHD symptomatology (see Chapter 2) as well as to identify any factors (e.g., motor tics, heart condition) that may rule out the use of stimulant medication. In concert with the child's physician, the psychologist should consider the following factors (from Barkley, 1990) prior to recommending a trial of medication:

1. *Severity of the child's ADHD symptoms and disruptive behavior.* As would be expected, the greater the severity of attention and behavior control difficulties, the more likely a medication trial will be necessary as a supplement to other treatment modalities (e.g., behavior modification program). Further, the more severe the ADHD symptomatology, the greater the probability of a positive response to methylphenidate (Taylor et al., 1987).

2. *Prior use of other treatments.* If other interventions (e.g., classroom behavior management program, parent training) have not been implemented, a trial of medication may be postponed, particularly if the child's ADHD is relatively mild. Alternatively, if limited success has been obtained with other interventions, then medication may need to be considered as an adjunctive treatment.

3. *Presence of anxiety disorder symptoms.* Children who present with both ADHD and internalizing symptoms (e.g., Overanxious Disorder, frequent psychosomatic complaints) are less likely to respond positively to stimulant medications and may exhibit a better response to an antidepressant (Pliszka, 1987). The latter assumptions have not been supported consistently by empirical research, however, so the presence of internalizing symptoms does not completely rule out the use of a stimulant medication.

4. *Parental attitude toward use of medication.* Parents who are strongly antimedication should be offered the opportunity to research the advantages and disadvantages of pharmacotherapy. Specifically, they should be provided with literature that clearly describes the behavioral

effects, side effects, and treatment monitoring practices associated with medication (see Barkley, 1991b). They *should not be coerced* into a medication trial given the higher likelihood of low treatment compliance in such cases.

5. *Adequacy of adult supervision.* The parents must be functioning at such a level that they will adequately supervise the administration of the medication and guard against its abuse. Further, all adults associated with the child's treatment program (i.e., physician, teacher, psychologist, parents) must make an ongoing investment of time necessary to determine the short- and long-term efficacy of the medication regimen.

6. *Child's attitude toward medication.* It is important that the use of medication be discussed with the child and the rationale for treatment be fully explained, particularly with older children and adolescents (see Whalen & Henker, 1980, for a thorough discussion of possible attributional effects associated with medication). In cases where children are antimedication or oppositional, they may sabotage efforts to use it (e.g., refuse to swallow the pill).

Regardless of whether stimulant medication treatment is employed and successful, the school psychologist is in a singular position to implement additional therapies for the child with ADHD. It is imperative that other interventions (e.g., behavior modification programming) are utilized prior to or in addition to medication in an effort to optimize the child's classroom functioning (Barkley, 1990; Pelham & Murphy, 1986). In fact, as mentioned earlier, the concomitant use of behavioral strategies and stimulant medication may lead to additive behavioral effects, thus minimizing the medication dose and/or the intensity of employed contingencies (Abramowitz et al., 1992; Hoza et al., 1992).

ASSESSMENT OF MEDICATION EFFECTS IN CLASSROOM SETTINGS

The methods used to monitor medication response in children with ADHD vary widely in content and quality. Unfortunately, all too frequently titration of dosage and long-term assessment of efficacy are based solely on the subjective reports of parents, thereby increasing the chances of erroneous decisions (Gadow, 1981). A recent survey of a large national sample of pediatricians indicated that slightly over half of the respondents employed objective teacher and parent rating scales to determine medication efficacy (Copeland, Wolraich, Lindgren, Milich, & Woolson, 1987). Although this certainly represents an improvement over previous practice, a large percentage of physicians prescribing stimulant medications do not collect objective data to establish treatment efficacy, optimal dose, or the need for a change in dosage. School professionals can have an impact on this practice to a large degree by communicating with physicians regarding changes in children's school performance associated with pharmacotherapy.

Because the response to stimulant medication is frequently idiosyncratic and dose specific, it is imperative to collect objective behavioral data across several doses, including a period of time when the child is not receiving active medication. Under ideal circumstances, a child's optimal dose should be established in the context of a double-blind, placebo-controlled assessment paradigm that includes multiple measures collected across several settings (e.g., home, school). This type of evaluation not only involves the aggregation of objective, quantitative data regarding a child's treatment response, but also controls for the biases inherent in some assessment measures (e.g., parent and teacher rating scales). Further details with respect to designing such an evaluation are discussed below and can be obtained by consulting several recent papers on this topic (Barkley, Fischer, et al., 1988; Gadow, 1993; Gadow, Nolan, Paolicelli, & Sprafkin, 1991; Rapport, 1987a).

In many instances, professionals do not have the resources and time to conduct elegant, placebo-controlled medication evaluations. Nevertheless, as a team the school psychologist and physician can collect objective data in a cost-effective fashion that would aid greatly in making medication-related decisions. Several steps are involved in this process including (1) designing a dosage sequence wherein the child receives one of several doses (including a baseline or nonmedication condition) every day for a week at each dose, (2) collecting objective measures of treatment response across dosage conditions, (3) assessing parent, teacher, and child perceptions of possible side effects across doses (including when the child is not medicated), and (4) communication between the physician and psychologist both during and after the medication trial to determine whether a child responds positively, which dose optimizes his or her performance, and whether the severity of a possible side effect warrants discontinuing the trial. If possible, those adults who are directly evaluating changes in the child's performance (e.g., teachers) should be kept "blind" to the medication condition. For instance, even during a nonmedication phase the child may continue to go to the nurse's office for his or her noontime administration (and take a vitamin instead of methylphenidate), thereby keeping the medication condition unknown from the teacher's perspective.

Although the teacher is not informed of the child's medication status, it is important to provide some information to the teacher about the positive changes and side effects usually associated with stimulants. A handout for teachers regarding stimulant treatment of ADHD is provided in Appendix 5.1. This information will help the teacher to focus on those behavioral changes that are most relevant to this treatment.

Measures of Medication Response

Several objective measures should be collected across medication conditions to assess treatment-related change including teacher and parent ratings of behavioral control and side effects, as well as direct observations of classroom behavior and academic performance. For youngsters with ADHD—Predominantly Inattentive Type or ADDnoH, ratings and observations of changes in attention span and work productivity will suffice as these children do not typically exhibit significant problems with behavior control (Barkley, DuPaul, & McMurray, 1990). In some cases, these techniques may be supplemented by the administration of clinic-based tasks such as the Continuous Performance Test (Rosvold et al., 1956), MFFT (Kagan, 1966), or additional tests of attention span, impulse control, and cognitive performance. Alternatively, the time and expense involved to include the latter instruments, as well as their questionable ecological validity (Barkley, 1991a; DuPaul, Anastopoulos, et al., 1992), limit their utility in making medication-related decisions. The core components of a school-based medication trial are listed in Table 5.2 and discussed below.

Teacher Rating Scales

A plethora of teacher rating scales have been found to be useful in evaluating the effects of stimulant medication, including the CTRS-R (Goyette et al., 1978), ACTRS (Goyette et al., 1978), ADD+H Comprehensive Teacher Rating Scale (Ullmann, Sleator, & Sprague, 1985), Teachers Self-Control Rating Scale (Humphrey, 1982), and the ADHD Rating Scale (DuPaul, 1991a). The inclusion of one of these questionnaires can provide a measure of treatment-induced reductions in the frequency and/or severity of behavioral control difficulties from the teacher's perspective. These brief rating scales are preferred to more comprehensive, broadband measures (e.g, CBCL) because the former provide more circumscribed information about medication response and are more practical for teachers to complete on a repeated basis. Measures such as the SSQ (Barkley, 1990) and the SSQ-R (DuPaul & Barkley, 1992a) can be included to assess changes in the pervasiveness of behavior problems and attentional difficulties across situations. Treatment-induced changes in academic productivity and accuracy can be assessed, in part, by using the

TABLE 5.2. Measures to Assess Medication Response

1. Teacher rating scales

    a. Conners Teacher Rating Scale–Revised (Goyette et al., 1978).
    b. ADD+H Comprehensive Teacher Rating Scale (Ullmann et al., 1985).
    c. ADHD Rating Scale (DuPaul, 1991a).
    d. School Situations Questionnaire (Barkley, 1990) or Questionnaire–Revised (DuPaul & Barkley, 1992a).
    e. Academic Performance Rating Scale (DuPaul et al., 1991).
    f. Side Effects Rating Scale (Barkley, 1990).

2. Parent rating scales

    a. Conners Parent Rating Scale–Revised (Goyette et al., 1978).
    b. Home Situations Questionnaire (Barkley, 1990) and/or Questionnaire–Revised (DuPaul & Barkley, 1992a).
    c. ADHD Rating Scale (DuPaul, 1991a).
    d. Side Effects Rating Scale (Barkley, 1990).

3. Direct observations of school performance

    a. Classroom Observation Code (Abikoff et al., 1977).
    b. ADHD Behavior Coding System (Barkley et al., 1988).
    c. Classroom Observations of Conflict and Attention Deficit Disorders (Atkins et al., 1985).
    d. On-Task Behavior Code (Rapport et al., 1987).
    e. Code for Observing Social Activity (Sprafkin et al., 1986).

4. Academic performance measures

    a. Percentage of assigned work completed correctly.
    b. Curriculum-based measurement.

5. Self-Report rating scales

    a. ADHD Self-Report Rating Scale (Appendix 5.2).
    b. Piers–Harris Children's Self-Concept Scale (Piers, 1984).

APRS (DuPaul, Rapport, & Perriello, 1991). All of these questionnaires have been found to possess adequate levels of reliability and validity (Barkley, 1990), however it is recommended that teacher questionnaires be administered twice during baseline conditions to assess possible "practice" effects that are frequently obtained with these measures (Barkley, 1988a).

Parent Rating Scales

There are a number of parent questionnaires that have been documented to be sensitive to stimulant medication effects with this population such as the CPRS-R (Goyette et al., 1978), the Werry–Weiss–Peters Activity

Rating Scale (Routh et al., 1974), and the ADHD Rating Scale (Barkley, DuPaul, & McMurray, 1991). The HSQ (Barkley, 1990) and/or HSQ-R (DuPaul & Barkley, 1992a) may be used to assess the situational pervasiveness of behavior control and attentional difficulties, respectively. As with the teacher questionnaires, all of these instruments have demonstrated reliability and validity for the purpose of assessing intervention effects (Barkley, 1990).

Direct Observations of School Performance

School professionals are in a unique position relative to other mental health professionals because they have the opportunity to observe children in one of their most important natural environments. Thus, questionnaires completed by parents and teachers can be supplemented with behavioral observations that are presumably not subject to the possible biases associated with rating scales. A variety of coding systems have been developed for observing the behavior of students with ADHD (see Chapter 2) including the Hyperactive Behavior Code (Jacob et al., 1978), the Classroom Observation Code (Abikoff, Gittelman-Klein, & Klein, 1977; Abikoff & Gittelman, 1985b), the ADHD Behavior Coding system (Barkley, 1990), and Classroom Observations of Conflict and Attention Deficit Disorders (COCADD) (Atkins et al., 1985). The use of such systems can provide valuable information regarding the frequency (usually in the form of percentages) of occurrence of various behaviors (e.g., on-task, fidgets) over the course of the observation period. One alternative to the above coding systems is the simple recording of off- versus on-task behavior (i.e., visual attention to task materials), which has been found to be quite sensitive to the dose effects of methylphenidate (Rapport et al., 1987, 1988). The latter requires very little training and is likely to engender more than adequate levels of interobserver reliability.

Medication effects on children's social interactions also should be investigated. A variety of observational coding systems have been developed for this behavioral domain (see Hops & Greenwood, 1988, for a review) and have been adapted for evaluating stimulant medication effects (e.g., Pelham & Milich, 1991). For example, direct observations of social behavior using the COSA (Sprafkin et al., 1986) or the coding system described in Appendix 2.3 could be conducted in relatively unstructured settings such as the school lunchroom and/or playground. The COSA has been found to be sensitive to the effects of stimulant medication (Gadow et al., 1990), and it allows one to document changes in both aggressive (e.g., physical aggression) and prosocial (e.g., appropriate social interaction) behaviors as a function of treatment.

Academic Performance Measures

Information regarding the child's academic performance should be gathered in conjunction with behavioral observations. For example, the percentage of work that the child completes relative to the amount assigned and the percent accuracy of work could be calculated following the observation session. Such data are highly sensitive to MPH dose effects and can indicate when a medication-induced "cognitive decrement" or "overfocusing" phenomenon has occurred (Rapport et al., 1987, 1988). Under the latter conditions the child may show behavioral improvements but a diminishment of academic productivity and/or accuracy. Baseline stability and interobserver reliability should also be asssessed for these measures. Curriculum-based measurement strategies (Shinn, 1989) are potentially appropriate techniques to assess medication-related changes in this functioning area as well (DuPaul, Stoner, Tilly, & Putnam, 1991).

Self-Report Ratings

For older children and adolescents (e.g., over the age of 9 years old), it may be helpful to obtain self-report ratings of treatment-related changes in behavioral control, academic performance, and self-esteem. Although the reliability of self-report data in this population may be suspect (Barkley, 1990), self-report ratings may serve two purposes. First, these data provide information about areas of functioning (e.g., depressive symptoms, self-esteem) that is not available through other modalities. Second, the student is directly involved in the medication evaluation process, thus the chances of cooperation and compliance with the treatment regimen are increased. Questionnaires that could be used for this purpose include the Piers–Harris Children's Self-Concept Scale (Piers, 1984) and the ADHD Self-Report Rating Scale (see Appendix 5.2; DuPaul, Kwasnik, Anastopoulos, & McMurray, 1993).

Assessment of Possible Side Effects

The child's teacher and parents should be asked to complete a brief Side Effects Rating Scale (Barkley, 1990) on a weekly basis. Older children (i.e., those over the age of 9 years old) should also be asked to complete this questionnaire. These ratings provide information regarding the number and relative severity of possible treatment emergent effects (e.g., irritability, insomnia, appetite reduction). Parents can provide the most useful information in this domain as they have the greatest opportunity to observe the activities most likely to be affected (e.g., eating, sleeping).

As mentioned previously, it is crucial to obtain such ratings during a nonmedication condition as many behaviors that are possible side effects (e.g., irritability) could be occurring in the absence of treatment as well.

Medication Evaluation Procedure

Prior to the initiation of the medication evaluation, comprehensive physical and psychological evaluations are conducted to establish the need for a trial of stimulant medication, as outlined above. The steps to a school-based medication evaluation are presented in Table 5.3. Once a medication trial has been agreed upon, the school psychologist should contact the child's physician to discuss and establish the sequence of dosages, which vary as a function of the age of the child. Using methylphenidate (Ritalin) as an example, the doses used would vary for preschoolers (2.5, 5, 7.5 mg), elementary school students (5, 10, 15 mg), and middle and high school students (10, 15, 20 mg). The dosage sequence should be randomized with the stipulation that the highest dose is never administered as the first dose. A nonmedication condition, preferably a placebo, is also included in this sequence. Both the physician and school psychologist record the dosage sequence and store this information in a safe place until after the medication assessment is completed.

The physician prescribes 1-week's worth of medication at each of the doses, including a placebo, if possible. The parent then has the pre-

---

TABLE 5.3. Steps to School-Based Medication Evaluation

1. Parent obtains prescription (e.g., Ritalin, 5 mg) from pediatrician.
2. Staff member not involved directly with evaluation (e.g., school nurse) and physician determine order of administration of several doses (e.g., 5, 10, 15, 20 mg) including a nonmedication trial.
3. Parent (or school nurse) administers dose according to predetermined schedule on a daily basis.
4. Assessment measures collected on a weekly (daily) basis:
    a. teacher ratings
    b. parent ratings
    c. side effects ratings
    d. observations of classroom behavior by independent observer during individual written seatwork
5. Assessment measures must be taken to reflect the child's behavior during the active phase of the medication (i.e., 2–4 hours postingestion).
6. Determine if there are significant changes in behavior (especially academic) at any dose.
7. Determine the lowest dose that brings about the greatest change with the fewest side effects.
8. Report results to child's pediatrician.

scription filled at the pharmacy, and, if possible, the medication is packaged in opaque, gelatin capsules. If the latter packaging is possible, the capsules are dispensed in vials that are labeled by week of the medication trial rather than by dosage to maintain the "blind." The parent and school nurse dispense the medication according to the schedule determined. The typical dosing schedule for methylphenidate and dextroamphetamine is once in the morning and once at lunchtime with approximately 4 hours between medication admininistrations. Although daily changes in dosage are recommended by some researchers in this area (e.g., Pelham & Milich, 1991), it is often more practical to make these changes on a weekly basis because, for instance, this would preclude asking teachers to provide behavior ratings on a daily basis.

Parent, teacher, and self-report ratings are completed on a weekly basis throughout the medication evaluation. Dosage changes should occur on Saturdays so that all ratings are completed on the last day of each dosage week (i.e., Fridays). If dosage changes occur on Saturdays, the parent is able to observe for possible side effects and contact the physician in a timely fashion. If observed side effects are severe enough, further administration of this dose would be omitted. It is optimal for the ratings to be completed with the parents, teacher, and child remaining unaware of the medication dose to minimize measurement error due to rater bias. The best way to accomplish this is for the pharmacist to package the medication in opaque capsules and to use an inert placebo (e.g., lactose powder) during one of the "medication" weeks. If this is not possible then the teacher and child may be kept blind by having the nurse dispense a vitamin tablet during the placebo or nonmedication week. Pill counts should be used, whenever possible, to document compliance with medication administration. If the medication is not being dispensed in a consistent fashion at home, then both doses should be administered at school, if possible.

Regardless of the coding system employed, behavioral observations should be conducted at a time of the school day when the child is engaged in independent seatwork, because this is typically one of the more problematic situations for students with ADHD. Observations of social behavior in the school lunchroom and playground may also be helpful. Further, observations should take place on as many days as possible during each dosage condition approximately 1.5–3 hours after medication ingestion to coincide with the time of peak behavioral effects. Observation periods should be between 15–20 minutes apiece. Also, observations should be conducted several times during baseline conditions to establish a stable trend (i.e., consistency in the data) prior to introducing treatment conditions. Interobserver reliability checks (e.g., conducted by a teacher aide or guidance counselor) should be obtained as frequently as possible, ideally at least once per dosage condition, throughout the medication trial to ensure the integrity of the data.

Academic performance data should be collected following each observation period. For example, the amount and accuracy of work completed during the observation session may be calculated before leaving the classroom. In addition, brief curriculum-based measurement probes could be conducted following an observation session. Care should be taken to collect such data from several students in the classroom so that the child with ADHD is not aware that he or she is being singled out for observation.

COMMUNICATION OF RESULTS
WITH PRESCRIBING PHYSICIAN

Throughout the course of the medication trial, the school professional should be in communication with the prescribing physician, especially when questions arise concerning possible side effects. At the conclusion of the treatment evaluation, it is best if a written summary of the results is forwarded to the physician to facilitate discussion during a follow-up telephone conversation (see Chapter 7 for additional discussion of communication with physicians). Two major questions should be addressed in the report: (1) Are there clinically significant changes in the child's behavior control and academic performance at any active dose of the medication? and (2) If so, what is the lowest dose, that is, the minimal effective dose (Fielding, Murphy, Reagan, & Peterson, 1980), that brings about the greatest change with the fewest side effects? These questions are addressed by systematically comparing assessment data collected during active medication conditions with those data obtained during nonmedication conditions. Significant changes are indicated when there is a change of 1 standard deviation from placebo to active dose conditions. Alternatively, reliable change indices (Jacobsen & Truax, 1991) could be calculated for each variable to determine clinical significance. Finally, comparison to a normative sample or to normal peers from the same classroom is helpful in determining the clinical significance of obtained treatment effects.

A sample summary of results for Judy, a 9-year-old girl with ADHD who participated in a 4-week trial of methylphenidate, is presented in Table 5.4. Data are summarized across four dosage conditions (i.e., placebo, 5, 10, and 15 mg methylphenidate), which were administered under double-blind conditions in a randomly determined sequence. Significant changes in objective ratings and direct observations of classroom behavior are identified by scores that are underlined (i.e., representing

TABLE 5.4. Sample Summary of Results for a Trial of Methylphenidate

Measure	Placebo	5 mg	10 mg	15 mg
		Dose		
Parent ratings				
CPRS-R[a]	7.0[b]	6.0	<u>3.0</u>[c]	<u>2.0</u>
Side effects—total	11.0	9.0	8.0	<u>2.0</u>
Side effects—severity	3.4	3.3	<u>1.1</u>	<u>1.0</u>
Teacher ratings				
CTRS-R[d]	14.0	15.0	<u>9.0</u>	<u>4.0</u>
SSQ—problem settings	8.0	8.0	<u>3.0</u>	<u>0.0</u>
SSQ—mean severity	5.1	4.9	<u>1.3</u>	<u>0.0</u>
APRS[e]	49.0	51.0	58.0	<u>67.0</u>
Behavioral observations				
Percent on-task	60.3	68.9	<u>80.0</u>	<u>89.7</u>
Academic completion[f]	49.7	<u>59.8</u>	<u>95.0</u>	<u>98.0</u>
Academic accuracy[g]	62.0	61.0	<u>78.0</u>	<u>88.5</u>

[a]CPRS-R Impulsivity–Hyperactivity Factor.
[b]Values are raw scores for all variables.
[c]Underlined values represent change of greater than one standard deviation relative to placebo.
[d]CTRS-R Hyperactivity Index.
[e]Academic Performance Rating Scale Academic Productivity Score.
[f]Percentage of work completed relative to classmates.
[g]Percent correct on academic work.

a change of one standard deviation from placebo or, in the case of direct observations, 10% change from placebo values). Judy evidenced appreciable improvement in behavioral control across settings during both the 10- and 15-mg conditions, with no apparent increase in possible side effects. Her academic performance was optimally affected at the latter dose, which resulted in a recommendation for her to receive methylphenidate 15 mg twice per day for the remainder of the school year.

The report to the physician should include a brief table of assessment results with a one to two page report highlighting the changes in each area of functioning at each dose level. A summary paragraph should be used to indicate the dose, if any, that school personnel felt was most helpful in enhancing the child's school performance (see Chapter 7). Obviously, the ultimate course of treatment is determined by the physician and parents of the child. A week or two after sending the report to the physician, a follow-up phone call is helpful in case the physician has any questions about the report or additional school-based information is necessary before a final medication decision can be reached. Finally, a postassessment feedback session should be conducted with the child's parents and teachers to discuss the results of the medication evaluation and answer questions about further treatment with medication (Gadow et al., 1991).

ONGOING MONITORING OF MEDICATION RESPONSE

Once a student's optimal dosage is established, then the measures described above should be collected periodically throughout the school year to evaluate the need for dosage adjustments or the onset of side effects. The vast majority of the measures need be readministered only every several months or so. It is usually a good idea for parents to complete the Side Effects Rating Scale on a monthly basis and submit this information to the physician.

Approximately every 6 months that a child is taking medication, the physician usually conducts a brief physical examination. During this time, the child's height, weight, blood pressure, and heart rate are recorded to determine potential side effects. For children receiving pemoline, liver functioning should be checked given the findings that this drug may adversely affect liver functions (*Physicians' Desk Reference*, 1993). Children receiving a tricyclic antidepressant (e.g., desipramine) should undergo a baseline electrocardiogram (ECG) with followup ECGs obtained with dosage changes or every few months, if normal, on a steady dose (Biederman, 1991). The school psychologist should attempt to collect relevant parent and teacher ratings prior to the 6-month checkup as well as provide any anecdotal information related to medication response to the physician.

When parents or teachers report that a previously effective dose "doesn't work anymore," the psychologist and physician should work in tandem to determine possible factors for this apparent deterioration in response before making dosage adjustments. Behavioral changes could be related to medication factors (e.g., a switch from trade name to generic forms of the medication, poor compliance with treatment) or environmental events (e.g., family stress events, increase in difficulty of academic material). It is important to carefully assess possible nonmedication factors that could account for a deterioration in functioning. Ofttimes, parents and teachers of children with ADHD may be unrealistic in their expectations regarding the amount and consistency of behavioral improvements associated with pharmacotherapy. Thus, they should realize that, even when medicated, children will experience occasional "bad days" regardless of the dosage being employed.

LIMITATIONS OF STIMULANT
MEDICATION TREATMENT

As with most treatment regimens, there are factors associated with psychotropic medications that limit their overall effectiveness. Some of these factors have been discussed above, including possible short- and long-term side effects as well as, in the case of the stimulants, a relatively short duration of action on behavior. Further, these medications do not "teach" the child to compensate for symptoms of their disorder and thus must be supplemented by skill-building strategies such as behavior modification programming (O'Leary, 1980). Of greatest concern is the lack of data supporting the long-term efficacy of stimulant medication treatment. In fact, most longitudinal studies conducted to date have not found significant differences between groups of children with ADHD who have or have not been treated with stimulants (e.g., Weiss, Kruger, Danielson, & Elman, 1975). Although these studies have been criticized for myriad methodological shortcomings (e.g., insensitive outcome measures), their results reinforce the fact that no single treatment modality, even one with demonstrated short-term efficacy, is sufficient in bringing about durable reductions in ADHD symptomatology.

Given the short intervals of behavior control resulting from a once- or twice-daily dose of stimulant medication, much of the drug's influence has dissipated by the time the child is home from school. Further, the family will witness the brunt of any side effects (e.g., insomnia) resulting from pharmacotherapy. As a result, families of children with ADHD will need more professional help to deal with the child's behavior problems at home (see Chapter 6). School professionals should be knowledgeable of the professional resources in the mental health community so that appropriate referrals on behalf of the family can be made (Barkley, 1979).

Although objective data are used to determine medication response, treatment decisions often rely heavily on clinical judgment (Gadow et al., 1991). For example, there are many times where treatment-related changes vary across areas of functioning or sources of data (e.g., parents, teachers). In such situations, the psychologist and physician must decide which measures are most important to the decision and this can vary as a function of treatment priorities and the child's strengths and weaknesses. Specifically, those domains that address the child's greatest pre-treatment difficulties are given the most weight in reaching decisions regarding dosage (Pelham et al., 1993). In addition, the child's response to other interventions and the degree to which additional improvement is necessary to move the child into the normal range of functioning is also taken into account (Pelham, Vodde-Hamilton, et al., 1991).

SUMMARY

Various psychotropic medications have been used to enhance the attentional, behavioral, and academic functioning of children with ADHD. CNS stimulant medications are the most effective medication for the symptomatic management of children with ADHD. Among positive treatment responders, stimulant medications significantly enhance the attention span, impulse control, academic performance, and peer relationships of children with ADHD, although effects on the latter two functioning areas must be replicated further. Side effects (e.g., insomnia, appetite reduction) are relatively benign and are more likely to occur at higher dose levels. Given that the behavioral effects of stimulants are moderated by dose and individual responsivity, each child's treatment response must be assessed in an objective manner across a range of therapeutic doses. School professionals can play a major role in evaluating stimulant-induced changes in the classroom performance of children with ADHD and providing objective outcome data to the prescribing physician. Because the overall efficacy of stimulant medication treatment is limited by a number of factors, other interventions (e.g., behavior modification) are likely to be necessary to optimize the probability of long-term improvements in the behavioral and academic status of children with ADHD.

APPENDIX 5.1
Stimulant Medication Treatment of ADHD:
A Teacher Handout

Children with ADHD exhibit significant problems with inattention, impulsivity, and overactivity. One of the most effective interventions for this disorder is the use of central nervous system (CNS) stimulant medications. The latter include Ritalin (methylphenidate), Dexedrine (dextroamphetamine), and Cylert (pemoline). Of the three medications, Ritalin is by far the most commonly prescribed. CNS stimulants purportedly increase the availability of certain neurotransmitters (i.e., dopamine and norepinepherine) in specific parts of the brain. This results in a greater level of CNS arousal and, hence, increased attention and behavior control. It was once believed that these medications exerted a paradoxical (i.e., sedating) effect in children with ADHD and that this response was diagnostic. On the contrary, these medications act to stimulate brain activity not only in youngsters with ADHD but most other children and adults as well. Thus, one cannot diagnose a child as having ADHD based on his or her response to stimulant medication.

BEHAVIORAL EFFECTS

The primary behavioral effects of stimulants include enhanced attention, decreased impulsivity, and reduced task-irrelevant motor activity. Students are more likely to complete assigned tasks accurately, are more compliant with classroom rules, and evidence fewer aggressive behaviors. They may also show improved handwriting and fine motor skills as well as greater acceptability by their classmates. In fact, some studies have shown that for a majority of treated children, stimulant medication can lead to changes in attention span and academic productivity such that levels of functioning in these areas are no different from their peers. It is important to note, however, that these medications do not cure ADHD and a child should be expected to evidence the usual "ups and downs" of behavior control even when a positive response has been obtained. Further, these medications are never to be used as the sole treatment for ADHD. Ofttimes, when combined with other interventions (e.g., classroom behavior modification program), medication effects on behavior control are enhanced.

The behavioral effects of Ritalin and Dexedrine usually last between 3–4 hours after ingestion. Thus, most children take these medications twice per day (i.e., in the morning before school and at lunchtime). This effectively covers the school day, but teachers should be aware of a possible drop-off in effectiveness toward the latter stages of the morning. There are also sustained release versions of Ritalin and Dexedrine that are taken once per day with behavioral effects lasting up to 8 hours. However, some children do not respond as well to these sustained release medications.

Approximately 70–80% of children with ADHD between the ages of 5–12 years old who receive stimulant medication evidence a positive response. For adolescents, the percentage of positive responders is somewhat lower (i.e., 60%). Thus, it can be assumed that the majority of students with ADHD who are treated with a stimulant will respond positively. Response to these medications varies as a function of the dose. Some children will respond to lower doses, while others will require higher doses to achieve the same effects. Dose response to stimulants varies widely across individual children and cannot be predicted on the basis of a child's age or body weight. Specifically, the strength of obtained behavioral effects can range across children and doses from mild (i.e., minimal positive change in behavior) to strong (i.e., normalization of behavior control). Thus, most physicians will try a range of doses of a specific stimulant in an effort to determine a child's optimal dose.

In those instances when a child with ADHD does not respond to a particular stimulant, this is indicated by no change or, in some cases, a worsening of the core characteristics of ADHD (i.e., inattention, impulsivity, and overactivity). Usually, the physician will try an alternative stimulant when this occurs. For instance, some children who do not respond to Ritalin can be successfully treated with Dexedrine. If none of the stimulants work, some physicians may prescribe other medications such as tricyclic antidepressants (e.g., Norpramine). Thus, when a child's behavior is not affected by the first medication prescribed, there are other alternatives.

SIDE EFFECTS

The primary acute side effects of stimulant medications are insomnia and appetite reduction. One of these side effects is likely to occur in about 50% of children treated with Ritalin, particularly at higher doses and during the initial stages of treatment. In most cases, however, effects on sleep and appetite are quite mild and do not require discontinuing treatment. Other, less common side effects include stomachaches, headaches, and increased anxiety or sad mood. Some children treated with Ritalin will experience a "behavioral rebound" effect in the late afternoon when the medication is wearing off. The rebound effect is indicated by a worsening of the child's behavior and mood to an extent beyond what was evident prior to taking medication. The latter can be dealt with by reducing the dosage or by adding a late-afternoon administration of the medication. A very small number (i.e., less than 5%) of children treated with stimulants will exhibit motor and/or vocal tics (i.e., repetitive motor movements or vocal noises). Usually, these will disappear after reducing the dosage or discontinuing the medication. In some cases, albeit very few, these tics will continue even when treatment is terminated.

One potential side effect that may be most prominent in school settings is an "overfocusing" effect. The latter refers to instances when a child may be exhibiting exemplary behavior control, but appears to be concentrating too hard on tasks with minimal output. In some children, this overfocused effect may be indicated by appearance (e.g., "glassy" eyes, restricted emotional expressions), while in others this may be signalled by a drop-off in academic performance (e.g., amount of work completed correctly). This reaction is usually a result of the child receiving a dose of medication that is too high.

Teachers and other school professionals should be aware of the possible side effects of stimulant medications. When these are observed, the child's parents, physician, and/or the school nurse should be informed. This is especially the case when the child begins to exhibit tics or overfocused behavior. Care should be taken to evaluate possible side effects in comparison to the child's behavior without medication. In other words, sometimes what appears to be a side effect of medication is actually a behavior associated with ADHD that was evident prior to the initiation of treatment. For instance, some children with this disorder are prone to irritable moods regardless of whether they are receiving stimulant medication or not.

ROLE OF SCHOOL PROFESSIONAL IN TREATMENT

It is quite important that teachers and other school professionals are in communication with a child's parents and/or physician whenever stimulant medication is prescribed. This is true for at least two reasons. First, these medications are most active in affecting a child's behavior during the school day. In fact, many parents do not have the opportunity to see medication effects on their children's behaviors. Second, children with ADHD evidence their greatest problems in school settings, and thus the success of treatment is determined, in part, by changes in a child's school performance.

School professionals can play a role in three stages of treatment. First, teacher input should be sought prior to initiating medication treatment. This is necessary to address whether the child has ADHD and, if so, whether medication treatment is needed. If this information is not actively sought by the child's physician, then someone from the school should contact the physician to provide school data. Second, changes in the student's behavior control and academic performance should be among the primary measures used to determine the best dose of medication. Objective information (e.g., rating scales completed by the teacher) about the child's classroom performance is invaluable in making medication-related decisions. Finally, once a child's dosage is determined, teachers should communicate any significant changes in student performance that may occur during the school year. Although such changes are not always related to medication, sometimes a drop-off in behavior control may indicate that an adjustment in dosage is necessary. Thus, the school and physician should be communicating throughout the various stages of medication treatment.

APPENDIX 5.2
ADHD Self-Report Rating Scale

Your name: _____ Age: _____ Grade: _____
Date: _____   Week #: _____

Circle the Number in the One Column That Best Describes You This Past Week.

	Not at all	Just a little	Pretty much	Very much
1. Often fidget or squirm in my seat.	0	1	2	3
2. Difficulty staying in my seat.	0	1	2	3
3. Problems concentrating on one thing because other things get my attention easily.	0	1	2	3
4. Difficulty waiting for my turn in groups.	0	1	2	3
5. Often speak out of turn.	0	1	2	3
6. Difficulty following directions.	0	1	2	3
7. Difficulty paying attention to my work.	0	1	2	3
8. Often begin a new activity before I finish another one.	0	1	2	3
9. Difficulty playing quietly.	0	1	2	3
10. Often talk a lot.	0	1	2	3
11. Often interrupt or butt into other people's activities.	0	1	2	3
12. Often have problems listening when other people are speaking.	0	1	2	3
13. Often lose things necessary for tasks.	0	1	2	3
14. Often do things that might be dangerous without thinking ahead.	0	1	2	3

6

Adjunctive Interventions for ADHD

Children with ADHD often display problems with inattention, impulse control, and activity level across home, school, and community environments. Beyond the core behaviors that define ADHD, these children may exhibit difficulties in peer relationships, frequent noncompliance with authority figure commands, conduct problems such as lying and stealing, and poor homework completion and study skills. Unfortunately, no single treatment modality, including psychostimulant medication, is sufficient for ameliorating the myriad problems related to ADHD. The chronic and potentially debilitating nature of difficulties associated with ADHD requires the use of multiple interventions implemented across settings over a long period of time. In addition, treatment strategies should focus on multiple target behaviors so as to maximally impact the child's overall functioning. For many children with this disorder, a "prosthetic" environment must be engineered over the long term both at school and at home (Barkley, 1989).

Previous chapters have detailed the use of classroom-based behavioral procedures and psychotropic medications in the treatment of ADHD. Certainly, the combination of these therapeutic modalities represents the optimal intervention approach for ADHD at the current time (Barkley, 1990; DuPaul & Barkley, 1993; Pelham & Murphy, 1986; Rapport, 1987a). Nevertheless, adjunctive interventions will be necessary, in many cases, as a function of the severity of ADHD symptoms and the presence of additional behavioral difficulties. In this chapter, several therapeutic strategies that can supplement classroom behavioral programming and pharmacotherapy will be delineated. First, school-based training of social skills will be discussed. The potential uses of peer tutoring and computer-assisted instruction to address the academic performance deficits associated with ADHD will be outlined as well. Next, home-based interventions such as parent training and behavioral family therapy are detailed, especially in relation to their impact on school performance. In the final section of the chapter, we will review treatments for ADHD that have minimal or no demonstrated efficacy, yet often are touted as effective in the popular media. The implementation of these latter interventions often diminishes the time and resources available for proven treatments, thus it is important to make parents, teachers, and other school personnel aware of the relative support in the research literature for each of the therapies discussed in this book.

SCHOOL-BASED INTERVENTIONS

A variety of classroom-based interventions were described in detail in Chapter 4, including token reinforcement programming, home–school communication systems, and self-management training. Several other treatment strategies can be useful in addressing problems related to ADHD. Social skills training techniques such as modeling, behavioral rehearsal, and reinforced practice have been proposed to ameliorate the social relationship difficulties often exhibited by children with ADHD. In addition, technologies designed to improve academic competencies, such as peer tutoring and computer-assisted instruction, may yield positive results for children with ADHD. Each of these treatment modalities is reviewed briefly in this section.

Social Skills Training

As discussed in Chapter 1, children with ADHD frequently have difficulties getting along with their peers and sustaining close friendships with others. Their problems with inattention and impulse control disrupt their "social performance" in a number of areas (Guevremont, 1990). First, they may enter ongoing peer activities (e.g., board or playground games) in an abrupt, disruptive manner that ultimately may lead to their peers becoming dissatisfied with the activity. For example, a child with ADHD is not likely to ask permission before trying to join a game and then may participate in a manner contrary to established rules. Second, they frequently do not follow the implicit rules of good conversation. A child with this disorder is likely to interrupt others, pay minimal attention to what others are saying, and to respond in an irrelevant fashion (i.e., non sequitur) to the queries or statements of peers. Third, these children are more likely than their normal counterparts to solve interpersonal problems in an aggressive manner. This is not surprising given the strong association between ADHD and physical aggression. Thus, arguments and fights with peers are common. In addition, children with ADHD are prone to losing control of their temper and becoming angry quite easily. Teasing and other forms of provocation that might be ignored or dealt with in an appropriate fashion by most children may be reacted to in a swift and violent manner by many youngsters with this disorder.

Given the variety of social performance problems that children with ADHD may display, they are more likely than their normal counterparts or even aggressive children to be rejected by their peers (Barkley, 1990). Of greater concern is the well-established finding that a child's rejected status often is stable over the course of development (Parker & Asher, 1987). Thus, interventions designed to address these myriad difficulties must be implemented for a sufficient duration to counteract the high risk for problematic outcome. What makes attempts to intervene in this area so difficult, however, is that children with ADHD do not appear to have deficits in social *skills* per se. They are able to state the rules for appropriate social behavior as well as their peers are. What sets them apart from their typical peers is that they often do not act in accord with these rules. These deficits in social *performance* are more difficult to ameliorate than skills problems for two primary reasons. First, most currently available social relationship interventions target deficits in skills rather than performance. Further, because social performance problems occur across settings (e.g., classroom, playground, neighborhood), interventions addressing these difficulties must be implemented by a variety of individuals in a cross-situational fashion.

In addition, interventions that target social knowledge and the acquisition of prosocial behaviors in group therapy formats (i.e., traditional social skills training) have not been found to lead to durable changes in interpersonal functioning in real-world environments. Although impressive gains in conversation skills, problem solving, and anger control have been obtained during training sessions themselves, rarely do these improvements continue once the child leaves the therapy room (DuPaul & Eckert, in press; Guevremont, 1990).

The lack of maintenance and generalization of social skills training curricula has led to proposals for a more comprehensive approach to social relationship intervention with this population. One of the more ambitious programs, developed by Guevremont (1990), consists of three interrelated treatment components: (1) social skills and cognitive-behavioral training, (2) generalization programming, and (3) strategic peer involvement. Although this program was originally designed to be implemented in an outpatient clinic setting, it could readily be adapted to the school environment. In fact, school-based skills training ultimately may be more effective than clinic-based training in bringing about generalization of treatment effects and eliciting the involvement of children's natural peer groups (Guevremont, 1990). Each of the components of this social relationship training program is described in greater detail below.

Skills Training Program

Four major skill areas are covered in this portion of the training program including social entry, conversational skills, conflict resolution, and anger control (Guevremont, 1990). These components are designed to address each of the major social performance difficulties that are associated with ADHD, as delineated above. Instruction in each of these skill areas is conducted in the context of group training sessions. Sessions are relatively brief (e.g., 30–45 minutes) to conform with the shorter attention spans of the participants. Training occurs once per week, at a minimum, and more frequently when conducted in school settings. Typically, groups meet in a room separate from the classroom to permit discussion of confidential topics as necessary, while allowing participants to engage in a variety of activities (e.g., role-playing). Professionals conducting the social skills sessions should have some training in behavioral and cognitive-behavioral interventions and have a working knowledge of the research literature on social skills training with children and adolescents. Generally, these groups are led by school psychologists, social workers, or guidance counselors.

The initial session of the social skills training involves cooperative activities to foster group cohesion as well as the delineation of the purpose and goals of future sessions. Regardless of the specific topic area, subsequent training sessions follow a similar format as presented in Table 6.1 (Guevremont, 1990). Group rules and contingencies (e.g., points that can be traded for back-up rewards are awarded for following rules) are reviewed at the start of each session to promote compliance with training activities. The specific social skill (e.g., controlling anger during interpersonal conflict) that is to serve as the focus of the session is discussed in detail. Next, the therapist provides step-by-step instructions in how to enact a particular skill set and models the component behaviors for the group. Participants then are asked to role-play the skill behaviors with the therapist and then with each other. The therapist provides coaching and feedback to group members as the role-plays are enacted. Points are awarded for exemplary performance of skills during role-plays. If possible, the child-to-child role-plays are videotaped to facilitate later review and provision of feedback from other group members. At the conclusion of the training session, the therapist summarizes the skills that were practiced and assigns homework. Typically, the latter involves children attempting to practice the specific social skills in the natural environment

TABLE 6.1. Sequence of Activities for Social Skills Training Sessions

1. Review of group rules and behavior management system.
2. Introduction, rationale, and group discussion of social skill.
3. Verbal instruction on the performance of the skill; step-by-step components are discussed and posted on a blackboard or sign.
4. Modeling by the therapists; participants observe the therapists acting out each of the steps involved in performing a social skill.
5. Role-playing between a therapist and one participant; the therapist and a single group member participate in a brief role-play.
6. Coaching and feedback; the therapists provide verbal feedback to each child and offer suggestions through verbal instruction and further modeling.
7. Child-to-child role-playing; child dyads are formed to practice the social skills while therapists and other group members provide feedback.
8. Videotaping; child-to-child role-plays are recorded and reviewed while further feedback is provided.
9. Summary of the skills focused on during the session.
10. Assignment of homework.
11. Delivery of consequences.

Note. From *Attention-Deficit Hyperactivity Disorder: A handbook for diagnosis and treatment* (p. 552) by R. A. Barkley, 1990, New York: Guilford Press. Copyright 1990 by The Guilford Press. Reprinted by permission.

(e.g., neighborhood, school playground) and keeping a diary or journal describing the relative success experienced as a result. To ensure compliance with homework, the diaries are reviewed in detail at the beginning of the following training session.

The first component of social skills training focuses on entry into peer group activities (Guevremont, 1990). Participants are instructed in and have the opportunity to practice the steps to successful group entry, including (1) passive observation of group activities, (2) initiate conversations with a group of peers, (3) ask permission to join the activity, and (4) follow the rules of the activity. The participants are provided with coaching and feedback regarding these skills as they role-play various scenarios of their own design. Peer group entry skills serve as a focus of between two to four sessions depending upon the group's speed of acquisition of component behaviors.

Training in conversational skills is the next major component of the social skills program (Guevremont, 1990). Participants are encouraged to share conversation as opposed to monopolizing it, as many children with ADHD are wont to do. Children receive instruction, modeling, coaching, and feedback in the practice of several verbal and nonverbal skills crucial to engaging in socially appropriate conversations. The verbal skills are (1) question others about themselves, (2) provide information about oneself, and (3) make suggestions, invite initiation of activities, give assistance, or provide feedback (i.e., make leadership bids). The primary nonverbal behaviors to be learned include (1) make eye contact when speaking or listening and (2) proper body orientation (e.g., facing the peer with whom one is talking). As with peer entry skills, conversation behaviors are the focus of training for two or three sessions depending upon the pace of the group.

Among the more difficult skills for children with ADHD to enact is the proper resolution of interpersonal conflict. Thus, the third component of social skills training is instruction and practice in the use of social problem-solving strategies (Lochman & Curry, 1986; Spivack & Shure, 1974). Participants are encouraged to utilize the following steps in attempting to resolve disagreements with peers: (1) identify the problem and set goals, (2) generate alternative solutions to conflict (i.e., brainstorming), (3) delineate potential consequences of each proposed solution, and (4) choose a plan and evaluate the results. The overall goal is to promote greater reflective thinking in conflict situations, thus increasing the probability that the child will choose a solution that will produce a favorable outcome (Guevremont, 1990). Given the difficulties that children with ADHD have in inhibiting impulsive behavior, particularly aggressive responses, training in conflict resolution skills may need to take place over three to five sessions.

The final component of social skills training is the promotion of greater anger control abilities (Guevremont, 1990). There are two phases to anger control training. First, children are taught to identify common environmental events (e.g., peer teasing) that lead to anger, to recognize internal events (i.e., cognitive, affective, physiological) that are associated with anger, and to think about the sequelae (e.g., getting into a fight with peer) of getting angry. These steps are intended to increase each participant's awareness of his or her own triggers for anger as well as to serve as a stimulus for discussion of more appropriate ways to deal with anger. These activities lead to the second component of anger control training, which is to practice coping skills and socially appropriate alternatives to aggressive behavior. Coping skills training typically includes the following steps: (1) recognize internal cues associated with anger, (2) use coping self-statements to inhibit open expression of anger, (3) generate a plan for responding to provocations (e.g., asking a peer to stop teasing), and (4) have a contingency plan (e.g., leaving the situation) if the child becomes too angry during enactment of the original plan.

After instruction, modeling, and guided rehearsal of coping skills, participants are sometimes asked to practice anger control strategies under simulated provocation conditions. For instance, each group member may be exposed to brief (1–2 minute) peer teasing sessions wherein other children verbally taunt him or her in an effort to induce anger (Hinshaw, Henker, & Whalen, 1984). The child being taunted is expected to practice coping skills in an effective manner. This exercise provides an opportunity for greater generalization to occur as it involves stimuli and behaviors that closely resemble the "natural" environment. Of course, peer teasing exercises should be undertaken with extreme caution and only under the careful supervision and structure provided by the therapist (Guevremont, 1990). The focus on anger control takes place over at least three or four sessions of the social skills training program.

Generalization Programming

Although the skills training package described above may lead to appreciable gains in socially appropriate behaviors exhibited in the training setting, such changes rarely transfer spontaneously to the real world (e.g., playground, neighborhood, classroom). Thus, a comprehensive peer relationship intervention program *must* include direct steps to promote maintenance and generalization of acquired social behaviors. Guevremont (1990) proposes that generalization programming can entail within-training strategies as well as structuring the environment to support enactment of prosocial behaviors.

Various procedures should be incorporated into the social skills training sessions themselves to increase the probability of generalization to real-world settings. These strategies could include (1) using real-life vignettes generated by the group participants for role-plays, (2) employing multiple exemplars and diverse training opportunities during modeling and role-plays, (3) assigning homework that incorporates self-monitoring and self-reinforcement procedures, and (4) having periodic booster sessions to reinforce and extend previous training. An example of a homework assignment to promote the use of problem solving is a daily problem-solving log incorporating self-monitoring procedures, as displayed in Figure 6.1.

One of the major reasons that appropriate social behaviors do not generalize to real-world environments is that adults (e.g., parents, teachers) and peers do not necessarily prompt and/or reinforce the desired behaviors on a consistent basis. Thus, continued use of newly acquired skills is unlikely to occur (Guevremont, 1990). Therefore, changes must be made to the child's natural environment such that the latter supports the ongoing use of appropriate interpersonal behaviors. Components of environmental programming might include (1) instructing parents and teachers to prompt children to enact the behaviors trained in the social skills sessions, (2) developing contingency management programs at home and at school to reinforce trained skills and decrease the

YOUR DAILY PROBLEM-SOLVING LOG

Date: _____

Describe the problem: _____

_____

_____

Did you try to use problem solving?   Yes   No

What solutions did you think about using? _____

_____

_____

_____

What solution did you try? _____

_____

How did it work?

1	2	3	4
Not at all	Just a little bit	Pretty well	Great

Initials _____

FIGURE 6.1. A sample problem-solving log used to promote generalization of problem-solving skills. From *Attention-Deficit Hyperactivity Disorder: A handbook for diagnosis and treatment* (p. 567) by R. A. Barkley, 1990, New York: Guilford Press. Copyright 1990 by The Guilford Press. Reprinted by permission.

probability of verbal and physical aggression (e.g., token reinforcement plus response cost for specific social behaviors), and (3) teaching children to elicit reinforcement from others in the environment, based on their engaging in prosocial behaviors (Guevremont, 1990). Thus, parents and teachers are integral members of the "social skills treatment team" by serving as agents for generalization.

Strategic Peer Involvement

In addition to the child's parents and teachers, his or her peers should be enlisted to support the generalization of prosocial behaviors across settings. The inclusion of peers is quite important as they often are present in settings where adult monitoring and attention is remote (e.g., neighborhood games) and peers are the crucial determinants of whether changes in social behaviors are clinically significant (i.e., enhanced social acceptance and increased friendships). Peers could be involved in all phases of social skills intervention (Guevremont, 1990). First, nonhandicapped peers can participate as role models in the skills training sessions. Through their participation in role-plays and providing feedback, they could serve in a "cotherapist" role. Substantial data exist indicating that models perceived as more closely resembling the observer are more likely to be imitated (e.g., Klingman, Melamed, Cuthbert, & Hermecz, 1984). Second, peers could serve as social skills tutors in the natural environment by prompting and reinforcing the enactment of social behaviors that have been targetted in the training sessions. Once again, this would require training the non-ADHD peers in the parameters of acting as cotherapists. Finally, parents can structure home-based friendship training experiences by supervising their child with ADHD in the context of highly structured, noncompetitive activities with a small group of peers (Guevremont, 1990). In many cases, this would be preferable to encouraging children with ADHD to participate in community-based activities such as athletic teams or scouting, which may be less closely supervised and inherently more competitive.

Interventions Designed to Improve Academic Performance

There are several properties of instruction that have been found to enhance the attention span and academic performance of students with ADHD (also see Chapter 4). First, tasks that require active responses to academic material help to channel potentially disruptive behaviors into constructive responses (Zentall & Meyer, 1987). Second, children with ADHD exhibit higher rates of appropriate responding when performance feedback is immediate and administered individually rather than delayed and delivered in a group setting (Pfiffner & Barkley, 1990). Finally, students with attention problems are more likely to succeed on academic tasks that are well matched to their abilities and when instructed at their pace of learning (Pfiffner & Barkley, 1990). Thus, successful instruction of students with ADHD should provide opportunities for active responding under conditions of frequent, immediate performance feedback using individualized academic content that is presented at a pace that the student can control. Unfortunately, it frequently is difficult to incorporate such instruction in regular classroom settings given inherent limitations on the teacher's time and resources. There are alternatives to traditional, teacher-mediated instruction that may enhance the academic performance of children with ADHD, including peer tutoring and computer-assisted instruction.

Peer Tutoring

Peer tutoring has been applied successfully across many academic areas (e.g., reading, math, spelling) with students of varying cognitive and academic abilities (Greenwood, Maheady, & Carta, 1991; Kohler & Strain, 1990). In fact, several studies have indicated that achievement gains associated with peer tutoring are superior to those engendered by traditional teacher lecturing or mastery learning approaches (Greenwood et al., 1991). This instructional approach also appears to possess a higher degree of efficiency in terms of teacher time and effort (Kohler & Strain, 1990) and monetary costs (Levin, Glass, & Meister, 1984) relative to teacher-mediated interventions (e.g., contingency management programming). Peer tutoring seems to have great potential for the classroom instruction of children with ADHD because it incorporates active responding to academic material under conditions of frequent, immediate feedback using individualized academic content presented at the student's pace. Students with behavior disorders have, in fact, exhibited improvements in academic performance and behavior control as a function of receiving and providing peer tutoring (e.g., Kohler, Schwartz, Cross, & Fowler, 1989). The results of a recent case study (DuPaul & Henningson, 1993) imply that peer tutoring procedures are helpful for students with ADHD.

Training Students in Classwide Peer Tutoring   The first step in using this intervention is to train the student(s) with ADHD and his or her classmates in peer tutoring procedures. The content, format, and process of peer tutoring training sessions are based on the ClassWide Peer Tutoring (CWPT) procedures described by Greenwood, Delquadri, and Carta (1988). Typically, three or four 20-minute training sessions are conducted covering the following topics: rationale for and overview of peer tutoring, practice of tutoring procedures, and methods to determine progress (i.e., awarding points to the tutee). Training sessions involve brief didactic descriptions of behaviors to be trained (e.g., how to present academic material to the tutee), modeling of the behaviors by the teacher and selected students, followed by structured rehearsal of the tutoring techniques by the entire class. In conjunction with training, teachers are provided with copies of the peer tutoring manual developed by Greenwood, Delaquadri, and Carta (1988), which contains detailed, step-by-step guidelines to the implementation of this intervention across academic content areas. During the training phase, the consultant meets with the teacher on a regular basis (e.g., at least weekly) to review the progress of training and discuss potential or actual problems with implementation of peer tutoring (e.g., interpersonal disagreements between tutors and tutees).

Process of Peer Tutoring Once peer tutoring procedures are formally implemented, all students in the classroom are randomly paired with another classmate. Peer tutoring procedures are implemented for one academic subject (e.g., mathematics) at a time. The tutor and tutee are seated at separate, adjacent desks during tutorial sessions. The tutor is provided with a "script" of academic material (e.g., ten math problems) related to the current content of instruction in the classroom. Items are dictated to the tutee one at a time from the script. The tutee then responds orally to the presented item, using a blank piece of paper when necessary (e.g., to work out math problem). Two points are awarded by the tutor for each correct, initial response. Alternatively, the tutor provides the correct answer when errors are made and offers the tutee the opportunity to practice the correct response. The tutee is eligible to earn one point after practicing the correct response three times. No points are awarded if the student is unable to answer correctly three times. The item list is presented as many times as possible for 10 minutes. The two students then switch roles with the tutor now receiving instruction from the tutee for 10 minutes.

Teacher's Role during Peer Tutoring During the tutoring sessions, the teacher monitors the behavior of tutoring pairs throughout the classroom and provides assistance, as necessary. Bonus points are awarded to tutorial pairs on a random interval basis if proper instructional procedures and behavior control are exhibited. At the conclusion of each 20-minute peer tutoring session, the teacher reviews and records the number of points earned by each tutorial pair and praises their efforts. Points are recorded on a cumulative basis throughout the week. To increase motivation for following tutorial procedures, the class is usually divided into two teams and separate point totals are tallied for each team. At the conclusion of each week, members of the team with the most points are declared the "winners," but all students are praised for their efforts.

Monitoring Progress A variety of measures are used to document progress associated with peer tutoring. These include tallying of peer tutoring points on an individual student basis, conducting curriculum-based measurement probes (Shinn, 1989) several times per week, and the administration of teacher-made tests on academic material practiced during peer tutoring sessions both prior to and following each week's tutorial sessions. These data are readily obtained and can be graphed for individual students, especially those with ADHD, to document progress, determine whether changes in instructional practice and content are necessary, and enhance motivation to participate in peer tutoring sessions. The specific monitoring procedures will vary across classrooms as a function of available teacher and consultant time, as it is important to keep ongoing assessment as simple and efficient as possible.

Case Example of Implementation   Don was a 7-year-old boy who was referred by his classroom teacher to an outpatient psychiatry clinic due to problems with attention span, impulse control, and activity level. In particular, he was reported to pay minimal attention to teacher instruction and, as a result, was seen to be underachieving academically, particularly in mathematics skills. Don was diagnosed as having ADHD based on a diagnostic interview with his mother using DSM-III-R criteria (American Psychiatric Association, 1987), developmentally deviant parent and teacher ratings of ADHD symptoms, and direct observations of a high frequency of off-task and fidgety behavior in a clinic analog setting using the ADHD Behavior Coding System (Barkley, 1990). Don had never been referred for an assessment regarding learning difficulties by school personnel. Don had never received stimulant medication for his ADHD nor was pharmacotherapy implemented during the case study.

The case study was conducted in Don's regular education, second-grade classroom. During the period of time that the study was conducted (i.e., mathematics instruction), there were 28 other students, a regular education teacher, and a special education teacher present in the classroom.

Several measures were used to document changes in Don's classroom performance as a function of CWPT. These included observations of Don's behavior during mathematics instruction using a modified version of the ADHD Behavior Coding System (see Appendix 2.1). Two ADHD-related behaviors (i.e., on-task, fidgets) were recorded using a 30-second partial interval coding system. The percentage of observation intervals that on-task and fidgets occurred was determined for each intervention component. Curriculum-based measurement (CBM) probes were conducted to document changes in mathematics skills as a function of peer tutoring. The dependent measure was digits written correctly.

An ABAB reversal experimental design was used to evaluate the effects of peer tutoring on Don's classroom performance. During baseline (i.e., "A" phases), typical classroom instructional procedures (e.g., didactic lecture with question and answer periods) were used. CWPT was used during the active intervention conditions (i.e., "B" phases).

The percentage of observation intervals during which on-task and fidgety behavior was coded is displayed across observation sessions in Figure 6.2. Don's attention during instruction and levels of motor restlessness were highly variable across days during the first baseline condition. On the average, he exhibited on-task behavior during only 39% of the observation intervals while displaying relatively high rates ($M = 31\%$) of fidgety behavior. A dramatic increase in on-task behavior and reduction in motor restlessness were observed during the first peer tutoring condition. Don's attention to instruction was more consistent than dur-

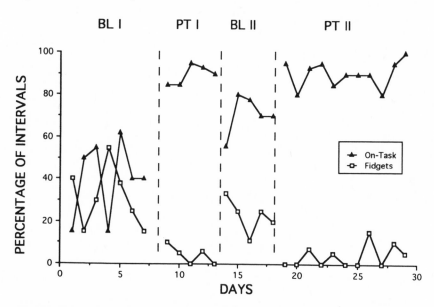

FIGURE 6.2. The frequency of two ADHD-related behaviors are displayed for Don across school days. The percentage of intervals that on-task and fidgety behaviors were observed is graphed relative to the ordinate. BLI = Baseline I; PTI = Peer Tutoring I; BLII = Baseline II; PTII = Peer Tutoring II. From "Peer tutoring effects on the classroom performance of children with attention-deficit hyperactivity disorder" by G. J. DuPaul and P. N. Henningson, 1993, *School Psychology Review, 22*, 134–143. Copyright 1993 by the National Association of School Psychologists. Reprinted by permission.

ing the first baseline, with 89% of the intervals being coded as on-task. Fidgety behavior was observed during an average of 4% of the intervals and was less variable across days than during baseline. The reinstitution of baseline conditions (i.e., teacher-directed instruction) resulted in a decrease in on-task behavior (M = 70%) and an increase in task-irrelevant activity (M = 23%). It is interesting to note that the frequency of these behaviors did not return to preintervention levels and was more consistent than during the first baseline condition. Finally, when CWPT sessions were reimplemented, attention to instruction (M = 90%) and motor activity (M = 3.8%) were improved and highly similar to those behaviors displayed during the initial peer tutoring phase.

The number of digits correct on CBM math probes are displayed across days in Figure 6.3. Don's performance on these probes was largely inaccurate and quite variable during the first baseline condition, ranging from 0 to 10 correct (M = 5). Only three math probes were conducted during the first peer tutoring phase, however Don's performance was

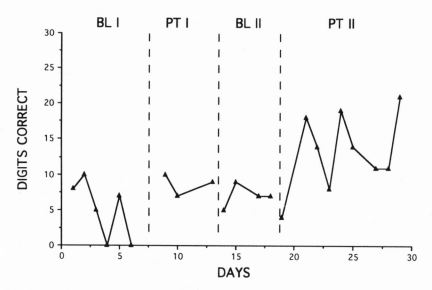

FIGURE 6.3. The number of digits correct on curriculum-based math probes are displayed for Don across school days. BLI = Baseline I; PTI = Peer Tutoring I; BLII = Baseline II; PTII = Peer Tutoring II. From "Peer tutoring effects on the classroom performance of children with attention-deficit hyperactivity disorder" by G. J. DuPaul and P. N. Henningson, 1993, *School Psychology Review, 22,* 134–143. Copyright 1993 by the National Association of School Psychologists. Reprinted by permission.

more consistent across days, ranging from 7 to 10 digits correct ($M = 8.6$). A return to baseline resulted in only a slight dropoff to an average of 7 digits correct. CBM data were available on a more regular basis during the second peer tutoring phase. During this condition, Don's accuracy on CBM probes increased over time as he obtained an average score of 13.3 digits correct.

Beyond the inclusion of successful instructional procedures, there are a number of practical advantages to CWPT as an intervention for ADHD. First, the teacher's time is used in a more efficient manner than teacher-mediated academic tutoring and/or contingency management programs. A readily available classroom resource (i.e., other classmates) is used to provide individualized instruction and ongoing performance feedback, thus freeing the teacher to structure and supervise the learning of the entire classroom. Second, students and teachers typically report a high level of satisfaction with peer tutoring (Greenwood et al., 1991), thus presumably enhancing their compliance with prescribed procedures. Third, CWPT can be used for instruction in a variety of academic subject areas in both elementary and secondary school settings (Greenwood,

Carta, & Hall, 1988). Fourth, the use of a classwide intervention prevents the potential social stigma that a child with ADHD might experience if a teacher-mediated behavioral program was instituted on an individual basis. In a related manner, the opportunity to provide tutoring to other students could positively impact the child's social functioning (e.g., encouraging cooperative behavior) and self-esteem. Finally, typical students (i.e., those not identified with ADHD or other difficulties) can profit from classwide peer tutoring as the latter has been associated with improvements in the academic performance of both high- and low-functioning students (Greenwood et al., 1991).

Computer-Assisted Instruction

In comparison to traditional educational strategies, computer-assisted instruction (CAI) would seem to have several advantages in teaching students with ADHD. Positive features of CAI include the use of individualized instruction that is self-paced, provision of immediate feedback for academic behavior, frequent opportunities for academic responding, and the use of consistent correction procedures (Budoff, Thormann, & Gras, 1984). In addition, CAI is presumably more stimulating and motivating than typical seatwork activities to children with attention problems. Thus, CAI includes all of the instructional features that have been found to promote success in children with ADHD. Surprisingly, we were unable to locate any research studies that have examined the use of CAI with students who have received a diagnosis of ADHD. Despite the lack of empirical data with this specific population, CAI has been studied with various groups of "difficult-to-teach" students (e.g., those identified with learning disabilities), and the results of this work are summarized below.

CAI has been found to increase attention to academic tasks among students with learning difficulties. For instance, a group of difficult-to-teach high school students receiving CAI were found to be actively engaged during instruction at a higher frequency than a similar group of students who were instructed in a traditional fashion (Reith, Bahr, Polsgrove, Okolo, & Eckert, 1987). Further, students receiving CAI were off-task during only 3.7% of the class period, whereas their counterparts who did not receive CAI were inattentive for more than 16% of the time. Extrapolating from these results, CAI has the potential to enhance the active engagement with academic materials of children with ADHD.

CAI has been used to accomplish a variety of educational tasks, including drill-and-practice, tutoring, teaching problem-solving strategies, and practicing writing skills (Reith & Semmel, 1991). Drill-and-practice has been the most common use for CAI. Computer-based activities are designed to help students practice skills that they have been taught previously through teacher-mediated instruction. The extant data indicate that drill-and-practice sessions are helpful in increasing fluency in math skills and word decoding, with equivocal results for spelling skills (Reith & Semmel, 1991). The greatest weakness of CAI in this area has been a lack of generalization of skill fluency to non-computer-based activities.

For tutoring activities, the computer interacts with the child by posing questions and providing feedback contingent upon student responses (Reith & Semmel, 1991). Given the opportunity to precisely structure instructional materials and to provide relatively immediate feedback, CAI appears to incorporate appropriate teaching strategies for children with learning difficulties. In fact, some studies have found that the combination of tutorial activities and drill-and-practice on the computer has led to significant gains in the fluency of math skills among difficult-to-teach students, resulting in levels similar to those of their classmates (Hasselbring, Goin, & Bransford, 1988).

Computers can be used to provide direct instruction in problem-solving skills to difficult-to-teach students. This instruction is then followed by opportunities for the student to practice problem solving in novel, computer-based simulation activities (Reith & Semmel, 1991). In fact, one study has found that the combination of direct instruction and simulation activities was effective in teaching problem-solving skills in health-related areas (Woodward, Carnine, & Collins, 1986).

Word processing skills can be taught to children to enhance the quantity and quality of their writing. The assumption is that computer-based writing will result in a more readable text and will make revising written products less aversive (Reith & Semmel, 1991). Despite the inherent potential of word processing training, there is little research available to support these claims.

In a recent review of CAI research with difficult-to-teach students, Reith and Semmel (1991) concluded that the efficacy of computer-based instruction is dependent upon a number of variables including teacher behaviors during CAI, provision of CAI in groups, the quality of available software, and the degree to which CAI is integrated with teacher-mediated instruction. These conclusions imply that the potential use of CAI for students with ADHD must be considered in relation to the following question: Under *what* grouping condition, using *which* software, for *what* instructional activity in *which* subject area, employing *what* kind of teacher supervision and feedback, can CAI be used to meet *which* specific instructional objective(s)?

Until research studies specifically addressing these issues are conducted with students who have ADHD, practitioners interested in the use of CAI are advised to attend to the following guidelines based on Reith and Semmel's (1991) review:

1. Although individual sessions with the computer are ideal, most classrooms are not equipped with enough machines to provide all students access to one-to-one instruction. Fortunately, several studies have indicated that significant achievement gains can be attained even when students work with computers in dyads or triads. Homogeneous groups are preferred because they have been found to promote greater enhancement of academic responding. Finally, when students with ADHD are receiving CAI in groups, it is wise for them to have frequent access to the keyboard to facilitate sustained attention and motivation to continue the task.

2. Given that there are more than 10,000 educational software products currently on the market (Office of Technology Assessment, 1988), there is wide variety in the quality of available software. Prior to use, software should be evaluated as to technical adequacy (e.g., clear screen displays, consistency of successful "runs") and educational quality (e.g., use of sound educational principles, effectiveness in teaching skills). For students with ADHD, it is particularly important that educational tasks be stimulating and interesting and that frequent, immediate feedback for academic responding is provided. As suggested by Budoff and colleagues (1984), further educational features that should be included are (1) opportunity for flexible programming, (2) student or teacher control of task presentation rate, (3) length of lesson commensurate with student's attention span, and (4) rate and type of reinforcement under teacher control. Finally, on-screen directions should be in simple English and the software should allow the printing of records of CAI sessions (Reith & Semmel, 1991). The Office of Technology Assessment (1988) recently published a description of some of the best educational software programs.

3. CAI seems best suited for a combination of tutoring and drill-and-practice in previously taught concept areas. Math and language arts skills are the subject areas most likely to be enhanced using CAI. Further, computer-based instruction in problem-solving strategies could be helpful, although it is important to keep in mind that programming for generalization of such skills to real-world settings must be incorporated.

4. Teachers must be encouraged to provide supervision and feedback to students during CAI activities. Some studies have indicated that teachers spend little time monitoring or interacting with students during computer-based lessons (Reith & Semmel, 1991). This lack of interaction may compromise the integrity (i.e., the student does not complete the lesson as prescribed) and, ultimately, the efficacy of this intervention. Further, teachers should endeavor to use CAI in such a fashion that it is consistent with present student functioning and is consonant with teacher-mediated instruction. CAI should be an integral, related component of instruction rather than an "add-on" or "busy work" activity.

5. Educational objectives should be specified prior to computer-based instruction, with ongoing assessment (e.g., curriculum-based measurement) conducted to document effectiveness.

HOME-BASED INTERVENTIONS

Parent Training

It is often important for parents of children with ADHD to receive supportive instruction in behavior management strategies designed to enhance their children's attention to household tasks and rules. In some instances, school psychologists or social workers provide parent training services in the school setting, especially when these services are not available in the community (e.g., with a clinical child psychologist). When school-based parent training is provided, there usually is an emphasis on helping parents to supervise the completion of academically relevant tasks such as homework and studying for tests. A number of programs for providing parent training in behavior modification strategies have been developed (e.g., Forehand & McMahon, 1981).

Barkley (1987, 1990) has adapted the Forehand and McMahon (1981) parent training program to more specifically address the core problems related to ADHD. This training program, as described below, can be conducted with individual parents or in a group format. Usually the child does not participate in the training, except in cases where the therapist wants the parent to practice management skills *in vivo*. Training sessions last 1–1.5 hours for an individual family and 1.5–2 hours for groups of parents.

Each training session follows a similar sequence of activities, including a review of the information covered the previous week, a brief assessment of whether any critical events occurred since the previous meeting, and a discussion of homework activities that were assigned at the end of the last session. The therapist then provides instruction with respect to particular management methods that the parents are to practice during the subsequent week. Following didactic instruction, the therapist models the appropriate behavior(s). The parents rehearse the management strategies and receive feedback and further guidance from the therapist. At the end of the session, additional practice of management skills is assigned as homework for the coming week. Written handouts detailing the session's techniques and procedures are distributed for review.

Parent training is usually provided over the course of eight or nine weekly sessions. At the conclusion of the initial course of training, follow-up meetings are scheduled every several months to provide booster sessions in management techniques and to support maintenance of acquired skills. The content of each of the sessions is briefly described, below. For more detailed information regarding parent training, the reader should consult Barkley (1987, 1990).

Session 1: Overview of ADHD

The initial session is intended to provide parents with information regarding the characteristics, prevalence, possible etiologies, and effective treatment of ADHD. The emphasis is placed upon coping with rather than curing the disorder through the creation of a therapeutic home environment.

Session 2: Understanding Parent–Child Relations and Principles of Behavior Management

Based on Bell and Harper's (1977) model of the reciprocal nature of parent–child interactions, four major factors are discussed as contributing to child misbehavior. These factors include characteristics of the child and parents, familial stressors, and situational antecedents and consequences. The rationale for parent training is thereby established as the need for parents to modify the way that they respond to their children's behavior. General principles of behavior management (e.g., positive and differential reinforcement) are outlined to set the stage for parents to practice these principles in subsequent weeks.

Session 3: Developing and Enhancing Parental Attention to Child Behavior

Patterson (1976) has demonstrated that the value of parental attention is diminished greatly in the families of children with behavior problems and is unlikely to be useful in reinforcing appropriate behavior. Thus, parents are instructed to employ a "special time" activity designed to increase both the amount and quality of parental attention to their children. The child chooses a one-to-one activity with the parent and the latter issues no commands or questions while praising any appropriate behavior that occurs.

Session 4: Attending to Appropriate Behavior

The parents are instructed to use positive attending skills to reinforce child behaviors occurring outside the context of the special time activity described above. Specifically, positive attention to compliance with parental commands as well as spontaneous adherence to household rules is emphasized. Finally, the parents receive information and the opportunity to practice the forms (e.g., stated request vs. asking a favor) and timing (e.g., after distractions have been reduced) of commands that increase the probability of child compliance.

Session 5: Establishing a Home Token Reinforcement System

The initiation of a structured, home token economy system is designed to augment parental attention to appropriate and compliant behavior, while introducing highly predictable, frequent, and immediate consequences for specific behaviors. This can be a useful procedure for impacting on school-related tasks such as homework completion and studying for tests. The use of privileges and rewards as back-up reinforcers increases the potency of reinforcement strategies.

Session 6: Using Response Cost and Time-Out from Positive Reinforcement

Until this point in training, the use of positive reinforcement has been emphasized with no instruction in punishment strategies. This session introduces two mild punishment techniques, response cost and time-out, that may be used as *adjuncts* to positive disciplinary methods. Response cost involves the removal of tokens and time-out is the withdrawal of attention from the child for short intervals contingent upon inappropriate behavior. Parents are instructed in the use of these two aversive procedures to reduce noncompliance with commands and household tasks.

Session 7: Managing Misbehavior in Public Settings

Most children with ADHD exhibit behavior control difficulties in public places, such as stores, restaurants, churches, or the homes of others. If the parents have developed the skills necessary to implement behavior management procedures at home, then they are instructed in the use of similar strategies in public settings. First, parental anticipation of such problems is emphasized. Then, parents are encouraged to formulate a plan of action to address public displays of misbehavior. Specifically, parents are advised to increase their use of praise and positive reinforcement for appropriate behavior, and to use response cost and/or time-out from positive reinforcement for rule infractions. In addition, a home–school communication program (e.g., daily report card system; see Chapter 4) can be designed such that home-based contingencies are used to enhance the child's performance at school.

Session 8: Managing Future Misbehavior

The final session of the parent training program is used to review the important principles of behavior management that were incorporated into each of the methods parents were taught to employ. Examples of anticipated or hypothetical problems are generated by the therapist and the parents are asked to develop a plan to handle such problems. Finally, the steps in gradually fading the use of the home token reinforcement system are discussed to discourage abrupt withdrawal of contingency management procedures.

At least one follow-up session is held approximately 4–6 weeks after the formal training is completed. This is to provide support for continued use of management procedures as well as to troubleshoot additional behavior problems that may have arisen. Parents are encouraged to contact the therapist for additional booster sessions, as necessary.

Despite its substantial research record in the treatment of noncompliance in children (Forehand & McMahon, 1981), the child management program outlined above has begun only recently to receive empirical evaluation in the treatment of ADHD. Although there is preliminary evidence that this treatment approach is effective (e.g., Anastopoulos, Shelton, DuPaul, & Guevremont, 1993; Horn, Ialongo, Popovich, & Peradotto, 1987), many questions remain, given the relatively small number of empirical studies and the numerous differences in methodology that exist across investigations. In particular, future research will be necessary to examine the durability over time and the generalization across settings of obtained treatment effects with this population. Training programs to promote parent support in enhancing the academic and homework performance of their children also need to be developed (e.g., Olympia, Jenson, Clark, & Sheridan, 1992). Further, this training paradigm may be useful in training teachers to use behavior management principles. Despite the need for further research, parent training in behavior modification strategies is an integral and, ofttimes, necessary component of a multimodal treatment program for ADHD.

Behavioral Family Therapy for Adolescents

Teenagers with ADHD often exhibit higher rates of disruptive, noncompliant behavior; rebelliousness; conduct problems; and conflicts with family members than non-ADHD adolescents (Barkley, Anastopoulos, Guevremont, & Fletcher, 1991; Robin, 1990; Weiss & Hechtman, 1993). Interpersonal conflict is particularly prominent in families of adolescents with both ADHD and ODD as these families are more likely to exhibit aversive behaviors (e.g., insults, complaints) in discussions than are parent–teen dyads in groups of ADHD only or normal control adolescents (Barkley, Anastopoulos, Guevremont, & Fletcher, 1992). Possible treatment approaches to address parent–adolescent conflict include the most common interventions for ADHD (i.e., stimulant medication and contingency management) as well as various forms of family therapy (e.g., structural family therapy; Minuchin, 1974).

A behavioral family therapy approach known as problem-solving and communication training (PSCT) (Robin & Foster, 1989) combines elements of contingency management training and structural family therapy. Specifically, PSCT involves skill-building techniques such as instruction in problem solving and appropriate communication behaviors, as well as prescribed changes in family systems and coalitions. In many cases, cognitive therapy procedures are employed to restructure the irrational belief systems of family members (Robin & Foster, 1989).

Although the use of PSCT in treating the families of adolescents with ADHD has not been studied extensively, the results of an initial investigation of its efficacy are promising. Barkley, Guevremont, Anastopoulos, and Fletcher (1992) found PSCT to be as effective as contingency management training and structural family therapy in reducing the number of conflicts and the intensity of anger during conflict discussions at home. In addition, PSCT significantly improved the quality of parent–adolescent communication according to the independent reports of 21 teenagers with ADHD and their mothers. Improvements also were reported by parents with respect to their adolescent's school adjustment and in the broad-band dimensions of both internalizing (e.g., depression) and externalizing (e.g., conduct problems) symptomatology. This treatment was rated positively by all family members on consumer satisfaction questionnaires and obtained improvements were maintained at a 3-month follow-up. Unfortunately, treatment effects were not obtained on direct observations of parent–adolescent conflict, did not result in clinically significant change for most of the sample, and PSCT appeared to worsen the degree of irrational beliefs that some mothers held about their teenagers' conduct problems. The authors attributed the latter findings to the brevity of treatment (i.e., an average of nine sessions) and suggest that the course of PSCT should be lengthened with this population. It also is possible that greater treatment effects could be obtained if PSCT is combined with other treatment modalities (e.g., contingency contracting).

Parent Support Groups

It usually is quite helpful for parents of children with ADHD to interact with other parents of similar children to share frustrations, successes, and advocacy strategies. In the past decade, a number of national parent organizations have been founded to play a supportive role, to serve as a clearinghouse for information about ADHD, and to lobby political groups for greater services for this population. One of the fastest growing national parent organizations is the Children with Attention Deficit Disorders (Ch.A.D.D.) organization based in Plantation, Florida.[1] Ch.A.D.D. was founded in 1987 and currently has over 14,000 members with chapters in 46 states, as well as in the District of Columbia, the Bahamas, and the Virgin Islands. In addition to publishing a quarterly newsletter, this organization sponsors an annual conference on ADHD that draws a national audience. Ch.A.D.D. members include not only parents but teachers and health care professionals working with children with ADHD. Organizations such as Ch.A.D.D. serve an important role in the overall treatment of ADHD as they provide valuable information about the disorder as well as guidance for its members in advocating for proper educational and therapeutic intervention for their children.

INTERVENTIONS WITH LIMITED OR NO EFFICACY

A number of treatments for ADHD have been proposed and promoted over the years that either have been found, via controlled research, to have minimal efficacy in ameliorating attention deficits or have not been subjected to controlled empirical investigation. Despite a lack of demonstrated efficacy, many of these interventions (e.g., dietary management) are quite popular and are commonly employed. In general, continued support for these treatments is derived from theory, "expert opinion," and/or face validity (i.e., the approaches appear to make great intuitive sense and consequently have tremendous consumer appeal). Although ineffective treatments are rarely physically harmful, their use diverts valuable time, energy, and resources from the implementation of more effective therapies. Thus, it is important for school practitioners to be aware of ineffective treatment modalities and to discourage their use whenever necessary. Of course, this should be done in a sensitive manner, while offering alternative, better-supported interventions.

Treatments that have minimal or no established efficacy for children with ADHD include relaxation training, play therapy, prescription of megavitamins, amino acid supplementation, ocular motor exercises, and sensory integration training. Currently, the most popular interventions

1. Information about joining CH.A.D.D. or a local chapter of this organization can be obtained by contacting the CH.A.D.D. national office at (305) 587-3700 or by writing their office at 499 Northwest 70th Avenue, Suite 308, Plantation, FL 33317.

in this category are various dietary regimens, individual psychotherapy, and electroencephalogram (EEG) biofeedback. The use of each of these therapies in treating children with ADHD is discussed below.

Dietary Management

The most well-known dietary approach to the treatment of ADHD is the Kaiser Permanente diet prescribed by Feingold (1975). Feingold's hypothesis was that ADHD and other childhood disorders are often caused by ingestion of foods containing additives and salicylates by children who are physiologically intolerant of such chemicals. He believed that these children have a natural toxic reaction to salicylates and additives that results in or exacerbates the occurrence of hyperactivity. Thus, the Feingold diet consists primarily of eliminating foods that contain certain chemicals and additives from the diet in order to reduce hyperactive behavior.

Initial results supporting the veracity of Feingold's theory came from his own clinical case studies, in which he claimed that treated children exhibited dramatic changes in behavior within 1–4 weeks of initiating the diet (Feingold, 1975). It was argued that the ability to turn the symptoms of ADHD on and off at will using this diet demonstrated a causal relationship between the variable being manipulated (i.e., the diet) and the children's observed behavior pattern (Conners, 1980). However, these claims, coupled with a lack of methodological control, led other researchers to initiate investigations aimed at validating his assertions. Although a few studies provided tentative support for Feingold's hypothesis (e.g., Swanson & Kinsbourne, 1980), the majority of controlled investigations found few, if any, positive effects of the Feingold diet on hyperactive behavior (e.g., Gross, Tofanelli, Butzirus, & Snodgrass, 1987; Weiss et al., 1980). Although a small percentage (< 10%) of preschoolers may evidence minor increases in activity or inattentiveness associated with food additives, there remains little evidence that such substances play a causal role in ADHD or that the Feingold diet is a viable treatment for this disorder (Barkley, 1990).

It is commonly believed that sugar ingestion causes hyperactivity and that reducing sucrose in the diet will ameliorate ADHD symptoms (Smith, 1975). In our experience, parents and teachers alike often adhere to this theory. Nevertheless, there is minimal empirical evidence to support the causal role of sugar in leading to ADHD and even fewer data indicating that a reduction in sugar significantly impacts attention and behavior control problems in this population (Barkley, 1990). Milich, Wolraich, and Lindgren (1986) reviewed the research literature in this area and found that the results of controlled investigations of dietary regimens were inconclusive. Further, studies were as likely to find *improvements* in behavior control associated with increased sugar ingestion as they were to find exacerbation of hyperactivity and attention deficits. It appears, then, that although reduction of sugar may promote a healthier lifestyle, it has minimal impact on the problematic behaviors associated with ADHD.

Individual Psychotherapy

By the time they reach late adolescence, approximately 63% of students with ADHD will have received an average of 16 months of individual psychotherapy (Barkley, Fischer, et al., 1990). This finding is ironic given that studies examining the effectiveness of various forms of individual psychotherapy for ADHD, including cognitive therapy (Abikoff, 1985), have provided uniformly disappointing results (O'Malley & Eisenberg, 1973; Weiss, Minde, Werry, Douglas, & Nemeth, 1971). These results are not surprising when examined from current etiological perspectives. ADHD is not considered to be an emotional disturbance, per se, and one should not expect counseling to alleviate core symptoms. Existing data should not be interpreted, however, as disparaging the use of counseling as an *adjunctive* treatment for children with ADHD. In fact, individual counseling may be useful to help children deal with *associated* emotional difficulties accompanying ADHD (e.g., low self-esteem) and could serve an important role in a comprehensive treatment program (Barkley, 1990).

EEG Biofeedback

A treatment for ADHD that has become popular in recent years has been the use of EEG biofeeedback. Claims have been made, primarily in the popular press, that this treatment leads to signficant improvements in academic performance and behavior control that are equivalent to those associated with stimulant medication, that are generalized across settings, and that are maintained over time (Adduci, 1991). The assumption underlying this intervention is that the brains of children with ADHD may show decreased brain electrical activity in certain regions of the brain (i.e., frontal lobes) associated with inhibition control and sustained attention (Lubar, 1992). Thus, this treatment involves attaching electrodes from an EEG machine to the child's head such that brain wave activity from various regions of the brain is detected. A biofeedback machine provides information to the child about the type of brain activity that is being detected. The child is trained to use various relaxation training techniques to alter brain wave activity in desired directions (i.e., beta wave activity purportedly associated with sustained attention). The treatment typically takes place over 40–80, 40-minute training sessions that are held 2–3 times per week (Lubar, 1992).

Although the assumptions upon which EEG biofeedback is based may be viable, there are important limitations associated with it that detract from its endorsement as an effective therapy for ADHD (Barkley, 1992). First, claims for the efficacy of EEG biofeedback are based on the results of several uncontrolled case studies. To date, no studies employing placebo control groups or attention control conditions have been conducted. The positive results of case studies may have been due to the nonspecific effects of receiving therapist attention. Second, EEG biofeedback training as described by Lubar (1992) typically involves other interventions, such as academic tutoring and positive reinforcement for complying with training. It is unclear, therefore, whether treatment outcome is specifically related to EEG biofeedback alone. Third, according to the proponents of EEG biofeedback, hundreds of children have been treated successfully. Yet, published data are available for only about 10 children. There are no reports as to the relative percentage of children who are positive responders to this therapy nor as to possible side effects of EEG biofeedback. Finally, the diagnostic status is unclear for many of the children reported upon in case studies of EEG biofeedback. Specifically, measures that are typically used to classify children as ADHD (e.g., structured diagnostic interview, behavior ratings by parents and teachers) were not used in these studies. Thus, until well-controlled studies of EEG biofeedback training are completed, there is no reason to view this as an effective treatment for ADHD (Barkley, 1992).

Factors to Consider before Recommending a Treatment

Due to the plethora of proposed treatments for ADHD, it is not possible to discuss the relative merits of every one of these techniques. Nevertheless, it is important to enumerate several guidelines that can be employed when considering the use of a new or alternative therapy for ADHD, because using them may detract from treatment efforts in more effective directions (Goldstein & Ingersoll, 1992).

1. If the developer or a proponent of a particular therapy states that the treatment cures ADHD or that it can be used alone to treat this disorder, then an automatic red flag should be raised. Even well-researched, effective treatments for ADHD (e.g., stimulant medication) do not lead to irreversible improvements in children's functioning and must be supplemented by a variety of treatments implemented across settings. Thus, claims of cures must be approached with a high degree of caution.

2. Treatments that are touted as effective and potentially curative for a variety of disorders (e.g., ADHD, learning disabilities, autism, *and*

depression) should also be approved warily (Goldstein & Ingersoll, 1992). It is highly unlikely that one specific therapy would lead to clinically significant results in treating children with a variety of disorders. Such claims should prompt an automatic red flag and further information regarding the empirical underpinnings of the therapy should be obtained.

3. It is incumbent upon the developer or proponent of a novel treatment to demonstrate its therapeutic efficacy in the context of a controlled, experimental design using reliable and valid dependent measures. It is not enough to offer case study data or testimonials from satisfied clients. Further, data should be available that allow direct comparison of the effects of novel therapies relative to those associated with established, effective interventions. Thus, "Where are the data?" is one of the first questions to ask proponents of a new treatment for ADHD.

4. The quality of experimental research investigating a novel treatment may be assessed by asking several questions. Were the subjects classified as ADHD using reliable and valid indices of the disorder? Were the dependent measures collected so as to reduce possible biases (e.g., behavioral observations conducted by individuals who were unaware of the clinical population being studied and the treatment being investigated)? Are threats to the internal validity (e.g., maturation) of the treatment controlled for? How generalizable are the obtained results to other children with ADHD? Was the clinical significance (e.g., normalization) of the obtained findings assessed? Did the investigators examine the generalization of treatment effects across settings (e.g., home and school) and over time (e.g., follow-up assessment)?

5. Whenever school professionals encounter novel treatments that are not substantiated by empirical evidence, it is important to communicate their skepticism to parents and educators of children with ADHD. Parents of these children may be particularly prone to accepting new therapeutic approaches because of their frustrations in dealing with ADHD-related difficulties and their knowledge of the limitations of currently available treatments. Further, in our experience, these parents often lack a clear understanding of the necessity for and requirements of the scientific study of treatments.

SUMMARY

The chronic exhibition of ADHD-related behaviors across settings and caregivers necessitates the implementation of a multimodal treatment program over several years or longer. A number of adjunctive intervention approaches can supplement the use of classroom behavior modification strategies and psychotropic medications. Additional school-based treatments may include social skills training and interventions specifically designed to enhance academic performance (e.g., peer tutoring, CAI). Home-based treatments include parent training in behavior modification techniques, behavioral family therapy for adolescents with ADHD, and parental participation in support organizations (e.g., Ch.A.D.D.). Over the years, a number of therapies for ADHD (e.g., Feingold diet) have been proposed that either have not been subjected to empirical investigation or have been found ineffective in the treatment of this disorder. Given the popularity of some of the latter therapies, it is important that the school-based professional is cognizant of both empirically sound and less efficacious interventions in order to more effectively advocate for the appropriate treatment of students with ADHD.

7

Communication with Parents, Professionals, and Students

The assessment of ADHD and related problems is a multimethod, multi-informant process. This process involves the communication of information, observations, and opinions among parents, teachers, psychologists, and physicians (also see Chapter 2). The design, implementation, and evaluation of interventions for ADHD involves similar processes and communications. Professionals should engage in clear and ongoing communication with parents, teachers, and other professionals involved with identified children because of several issues critical to assessment, diagnosis, instructional planning, intervention management, and professional service delivery in general.

Concerns regarding a child's problem behavior(s) are typically raised first by school professionals and/or parents. In addition, medical professionals (e.g., pediatricians, psychiatrists) are often involved with students who are diagnosed with ADHD. Together, these persons will make screening, referral, classification, and intervention decisions. Constructive interactions among these involved parties rely on clear and specific communications despite differing vocabularies, perspectives, and backgrounds.

Furthermore, the diagnosis of ADHD is based on a psychiatric classification system (DSM-III-R and soon DSM-IV). However, the identified children and their parents interact most frequently with school-based education professionals, while also being served in many cases by community-based physicians and mental health professionals. One cannot assume equivalent understanding of the psychiatric classification system across involved individuals. Therefore communication (and, in some cases, professional training) is necessary regarding the DSM system, its research base, DSM terminology, implications for treatment planning, and related issues.

Clearly, the design and evaluation of medical, behavioral, and educational interventions for children with ADHD requires a great deal of communication. The development of interventions often is a clinic-based or office-based activity, whereas an intervention's behavioral effects and any undesirable side effects are experienced in home, classroom, and community settings. Thus, the evaluation of intervention effects requires communication among physicians, parents, teachers, and other professionals.

Last, but not least, the ethical principles and standards for practice of school psychologists (National Association of School Psychologists, 1992b) indicate that communication with parents, children, and other professionals, is an expected component of appropriate school practitioner practice.[1] These guidelines for professional conduct specify that the purpose(s) and possible consequences of the professional's involvement, as well as intervention options and alternatives, be discussed with parents and students. Guidelines are also provided regarding the development of relationships between professionals (e.g., school psychologists and pediatricians) when such relationships are in the best interest of the students being served. In the latter sections of this chapter, pertinent examples of these guidelines are provided as introductory statements.

This chapter identifies and discusses several important issues related to communication about ADHD between school professionals and others involved with identified students including parents, other professionals, and the children themselves. Primary attention is given to the following: (1) the relationship between a diagnosis of ADHD and educational services, (2) the responsibilities of education professionals, (3) issues surrounding stimulant medication treatment, and (4) issues specific to communication with parents, physicians, other professionals, and children. Perhaps we are stating the obvious, however we believe that by discussing and clarifying these issues, professional and parental actions as well as decision making can be facilitated, resulting in improved outcomes for children.

DSM DIAGNOSES AND EDUCATIONAL SERVICES

How does a DSM diagnosis or other classification relate to educational service delivery? The usefulness of diagnostic classification systems of childhood problems has been debated for years (Garmezy, 1978; Gresham & Gansle, 1992a, 1992b; Hynd, 1992; Martens, 1992; Reynolds, 1992; Schact & Nathan, 1977; Shapiro, 1992), yielding a wide range of

---

1. The American Psychological Association, the Council for Exceptional Children, and other professional organizations have similar ethical guidelines.

professional opinions. In fact, the DSM-III-R (American Psychiatric Association, 1987) states that a diagnosis is merely a starting place for planning services:

> Making a DSM-III-R diagnosis represents only an initial step in a comprehensive evaluation leading to the formulation of a treatment plan. Additional information about the person being evaluated beyond that required to make a DSM-III-R diagnosis will invariably be necessary.
> . . . the clinical and scientific considerations that were the basis of the DSM-III-R classification and diagnostic criteria may not be relevant to considerations in which DSM-III-R is used *outside clinical or research settings, e.g., in legal determinations.* (p. xxvi; italics added)

From an educational decision-making standpoint, it must be recognized that the DSM system of classification is tied to assessment tools and procedures that are *nomothetic* in their foundations and assumptions. In psychology and education, reliable and valid nomothetic assessment yields information useful for comparing children with one another along the measured dimension or construct (e.g., intelligence). For example, a child who earns a score at the 37th percentile on an intelligence test has performed less well than a comparable child who earns a score at the 78th percentile. Developing an instructional intervention or planning an educational program for either child based solely on this information is not defensible. However, information based on nomothetic assessment procedures can be used in a reliable and valid manner for making screening, referral, and classification decisions.

By comparison, intervention or educational planning and evaluation decisions are more readily linked to assessment tools and procedures that are *idiographic* in their foundations and assumptions. Idiographic assessment does not focus on classification of behavior, but is concerned with the behavior of individuals over time. When the idiographic assessment measure has accuracy and utility, it can yield information useful for the development of effective instructional and intervention programs. For example, accurate assessment information regarding a child's ongoing and differential performance in two different reading curricula could be directly relevant to instructional planning decisions. (For a thorough comparison of nomothetic and idiographic approaches to assessment, see Barrios & Hartmann (1986), Cone (1986), and Johnston & Pennypacker (1980).) Based on the child's reading performance, a decision to provide instruction within the curriculum that will yield higher rates of success would seem reasonable. Intervention outcome evaluations, comparing a child's behavior or performance over time, also need to be grounded in idiographic assessment information, although information yielding peer comparisons might also be useful for some types of educational decisions.

A primary limiting factor preventing direct links between diagnosis and intervention is the great variability in the behavior of children diagnosed with ADHD (Barkley, 1990; Frick & Lahey, 1991). That is, all children diagnosed with ADHD do not display the same problem behaviors, nor do they experience the same difficulties, if any, in school. In assessment terms, Haynes (1986) has referred to the variability among persons classified in the same manner as an issue of "diagnostic homogeneity." Specifically, Haynes noted, "If individuals placed in a particular classification category . . . are homogeneous on dimensions of topography, etiology, and response to treatment, categorization is sufficient for description and intervention design, and the benefits of additional preintervention assessment are reduced" (p. 391). Given that children with ADHD lack homogeneity in behavioral topography and response to treatment (Barkley, 1988a), intervention design, implementation, and evaluation requires a good deal more professional effort than does diagnosis or classification. In part, the focus of this effort must depend on professional training and responsibilities.

These issues should be discussed openly at various stages of the assessment process. When a child is exhibiting significant attention and/ or behavior control problems, the first step is to collect screening information (see Chapter 2). Sometimes, at this stage, the child's parent or teacher specifically questions the presence of ADHD, as though this is all that needs to be determined. This provides an opportunity to put the diagnostic process into perspective. Specifically, it should be communicated clearly that evaluation data are being collected not simply to arrive at a diagnosis but, more importantly, to gather information that will lead to effective intervention. Similarly, when the multimethod assessment and interpretation of results (i.e., Stages 2 and 3, see Chapter 2) are concluded, it is helpful to reiterate that a diagnosis is simply a "way station" between the referral and the design of an intervention program. Further, it should be stated that the value of the diagnosis is its utility in directing further assessment activities, suggesting risks for associated behavior or learning difficulties, and increasing the probability of choosing effective treatment strategies. Finally, it must be stressed with school team members that ongoing assessment of the child's functioning will be necessary to evaluate the relative efficacy of intervention procedures. If these points are communicated effectively, the focus of the evaluation team can be shifted away from a search for a diagnosis towards the development of a potentially successful treatment protocol.

Communication around these issues can help to identify and clarify the expectations held by parents, teachers, and others regarding the use and benefits of various assessment procedures. Identifying and clarifying these expectations should result in improved understanding of the need for links between assessment, intervention, and education in serving students with ADHD.

EDUCATIONAL TRAINING AND RESPONSIBILITIES

The primary professional responsibilities of education professionals involve the development and delivery of curricula and instruction. As such, educators deal with issues of what to teach (curricula and instructional objectives), how to teach (materials, procedures, and methods), when to teach (instructional organization), who will teach, and where to teach (instructional environment). Decisions surrounding these issues are important for all students, including those identified with ADHD, and these parameters arguably define the domain of education. When education professionals are involved with children diagnosed with ADHD, their primary professional responsibility must be to promote the child's learning and achievement. In addition, because the diagnosis and treatment of ADHD nearly always involves pediatricians, psychiatrists, and clinical psychologists, collaborative efforts at assessment and treatment will need to be developed and maintained.

The wide range of issues and concerns requiring professional involvement with children diagnosed with ADHD clearly warrants interdisciplinary collaboration. Also warranted are frank discussions about appropriate roles and responsibilities for the professionals involved. School psychologists and special educators, in particular, may be faced with challenging demands for service delivery in light of recent decisions regarding the eligibility for special education services of children identified with ADHD under the "Other Health Impaired" category of the IDEA (Hakola, 1992; see also Chapter 3, this volume). For example, legal and ethical mandates likely will necessitate professional development efforts to obtain additional training in the DSM psychiatric classification system, developmental psychopathology, psychopharmacology, and the methods and models of clinical psychology and psychiatry.

Additionally, a reexamination of educational service delivery models may be prompted. That is, the fields of school psychology and special education, and to some degree education in general, have recently addressed and in some cases adopted noncategorical, outcomes-oriented models of service delivery (Bardon, 1988; Reschly, 1988; Reynolds, 1988; Stoner & Green, 1992b). To date, however, limited professional consideration has been given to how such models might accommodate children with ADHD (e.g., compare Hakola, 1992, with Stoner & Carey, 1992).

Noncategorical service delivery is intended, in part, to prevent an overemphasis on the diagnosis and classification of children, which may preclude school psychologists taking a more active role in developing and implementing effective interventions. To further illustrate this point, suppose that school professionals are involved with a child who is accurately diagnosed with ADHD. Does this disability necessarily represent a handicapping condition and therefore warrant special services? It has been argued that a recognizable disability, such as ADHD, only becomes a handicap in a nonaccommodating environment (Kameenui & Simmons, 1990; Shinn, 1989). That is, if a school is providing instructional and social support such that a student with a recognized disability is not considered to be handicapped (i.e., his or her performance meets or exceeds expectations; is commensurate with same age, typical peers), then that school should be recognized as providing exemplary services. Of course, given evidence that a student is not meeting the expectations of his or her current environment, reasonable attempts should be made to support the student (and teacher) toward meeting those expectations (e.g., matching instructional materials with current academic skills, providing more frequent positive and corrective feedback, enhancing motivation to engage in academic work, increasing opportunities to practice newly acquired skills and knowledge) and achieving academic success. The emphasis here is on encouraging schools to allocate limited resources primarily to procedures that monitor and foster the individual social and academic progress of all students (Reschly, 1988).

These service delivery issues will need to be discussed among all interested parties so that expectations and responsibilities of each team member may be clarified. Clarification of team member expectations and responsibilities must be established at a minimum of three points in the evaluation and treatment process. Prior to conducting a multimethod evaluation of ADHD (Stage 2 of assessment process; see Chapter 2), the specific responsiblities of each school-based professional should be delineated clearly. Further, the theoretical and professional biases of each team member should be elicited openly and discussed. The latter will not necessarily lead to a complete resolution of potential conflicts (e.g., professional "turf" issues), but discussion will increase the awareness of similarities and differences among the positions of all team members. This is, at least, the first step in promoting greater teamwork in service delivery.

The second point where service delivery issues will need to be discussed is when the intervention plan is designed (Stage 4 of the assessment process; see Chapter 2). At this point, decisions must be made not only about which treatments to recommend, but also about who will implement each intervention. There may be initial confusion among some team members as to what ADHD is and the most effective treatments for this disorder. In particular, questions surrounding the use of stimulant medication may arise. It may be helpful to provide all interested parties with written information (e.g., see Appendix 5.1) and/or suggested readings (see Appendix 7.1) about ADHD and its treatment. The appointment of a case manager (see Chapter 8 for further discussion of the role of a case manager) will facilitate treatment planning as well as enhance the maintainence of consistent service delivery. Given that some treatments for ADHD (e.g., stimulant medication) are provided by community-based professionals, the need for the school to "speak with one voice" is particularly crucial. Potential disagreements among team members should be elicited actively and resolved prior to implementing treatment procedures. It has been our experience that although the latter may delay service delivery, it often prevents more serious and time-consuming conflicts from occurring once treatment is begun.

Service delivery expectations and responsibilities should be discussed periodically in the context of ongoing evaluation of the treatment strategies. Several meetings per year should be held so that the school-based team, including the parent(s), may discuss the efficacy of each specific intervention and the need for adjustments in programming. This provides the opportunity to make changes in specific responsibilities among team members, if necessary. It is particularly important for those team members (i.e., teachers and parents) who are performing the bulk of the direct intervention to receive reinforcement and support for their efforts. Further, if possible, responsibilities should be rotated among team members to enhance collegiality and prevent the potential "burnout" of a specific individual.

ISSUES SURROUNDING STIMULANT MEDICATION TREATMENT

As discussed in Chapter 5, the most frequent intervention for ADHD is stimulant medication, typically methylphenidate. By all accounts, the use of stimulant medication in the treatment of ADHD-related problems is common and affects the lives of a significant number of school-aged children. Further, stimulant medication treatment needs to be undertaken with caution as beneficial effects do not occur for all treated children, and for those who do benefit, medication response will be dose- and behavior-specific. Finally, some children will experience adverse effects related to stimulant treatment.

The use of stimulant medication treatment (SMT) for problems of children's inattention, overactivity, and impulsivity has been controversial (Bacon, 1988; Toufexis, 1989). Concerns that have arisen around SMT primarily involve discrepancies between defensible professional practices and the personal beliefs of involved parents, educators, and other professionals regarding several key issues, including (1) the potential benefits of treatment, (2) the potential harmful effects of treatment, and, (3) the values of parents, educators, and other professionals involved in intervention decision-making. Communication and discussions of each of these issues will be critical where stimulants are being considered in the case of a child with ADHD.

Potential Benefits of SMT

Numerous research investigations conducted since the 1960s have documented positive, short-term benefits of stimulants for *most* children diagnosed with hyperactivity and/or attention problems. These outcomes have been demonstrated in the following areas: (1) academic performance (Rapport, DuPaul, et al., 1986), (2) social interactions (Whalen et al., 1987), and (3) responses to individually administered, performance assessment tasks such as the MFFT (Brown & Sleator, 1979; Rapport et al., 1988) and Paired Associates Learning tests (Swanson & Kinsbourne, 1975). However, it also has been demonstrated that response to stimulants varies from child to child (even those of the same body weight) and across target behaviors for any given child (Rapport et al., 1988). As such, the determination of stimulant treatment outcomes for individual children must be made cautiously and requires the generation and analysis of individual outcome data (see Chapter 5 for details of school-based medication evaluation).

Potential for Adverse Effects

Of concern to parents and professionals considering stimulant treatment for children are potential adverse effects of medication. Children treated with stimulants may experience adverse physical side effects such as appetite suppression, nausea, headaches, irritability, insomnia, growth suppression, and, in rare instances, motor or vocal tics (see Chapter 5). Further, in a minority of cases, stimulant treatment may result in an "overfocused" child who appears to be overly attentive to specific stimuli and is slow to orient to alternative activities or tasks. Although problems such as these typically have been reported at relatively high doses of medication, they may occur at low doses as well. These possibilities and the monitoring systems aimed at detecting potential adverse outcomes need to be discussed among professionals and parents.

Values Conflicts: Assumptions on Which Treatment Is Based

From a personal values standpoint, some parents and professionals are resolute in their opposition to using stimulant treatment with children. These values take various forms and are difficult to attribute to any single source or concern. Rather, support for a values position against the use of medication can be found in a variety of professional and popular publications. For example, one researcher (O'Leary, 1980) has argued that identified children need to learn social and self-management skills, rather than to be chemically quieted. Correspondingly, a popular book published in the 1970s (Schrag & Divoky, 1975) asserted that stimulant medication, widespread testing, labeling, and "behavior modification" with children were all methods of inappropriate institutional control of human rights. More recently, legal suits against prescribing physicians and the picketing of professional conferences have been supported by an organization within the Church of Scientology, the Citizens Commission on Human Rights. This group alleges that the use of stimulants and other psychotropic medications for childhood problems is turning school children into drug addicts. As discussed in Chapter 5, these criticisms of stimulant medication are not supported by the empirical literature. Unfortunately, these value-laden critiques are unlikely to be influenced by objective outcome data. However, from an empirical perspective, reliable and valid data regarding meaningful treatment outcomes can and should be critical determinants of parent and professional decision making about the therapeutic usefulness of stimulant medications.

For any given child, reasoned judgments may be made regarding the benefits and costs of stimulant medication treatment using outcome data. Further, by focusing on a range of carefully measured outcomes (e.g., academic performance, social behavior, adverse physical effects), both the misgivings and the goals of involved parents and professionals may be addressed. Thus, if a child's physician and the school-based evaluation team agree that stimulant medication may be warranted, the student's parents should be provided with accurate and unbiased information regarding the costs and benefits of this treatment as well as how its efficacy will be evaluated. For example, the parents could be provided with a handout, similar to the one designed for teachers in Appendix 5.1, delineating the potential benefits and side effects of stimulants (see Barkley, 1991b, for a parent handout on stimulant medication).

The parents' decision about medication treatment should be viewed realistically. The initial decision is whether or not to conduct a *controlled trial* of stimulants, not to permanently and irrevocably place a child on medication. Also, the parents should be aware of the need for ongoing assessment of medication response that should occur on at least an annual basis. Thus, even if the initial trial of medication is successful, professionals should not communicate to the parents that pharmacological treatment is a permanent part of the treatment plan. Nevertheless, given the chronicity of ADHD symptoms it is realistic to assume that medication may be necessary for a minimum of 1 year.

School Involvement

Management and evaluation of stimulant treatment often involves activities within the school and classroom. Suggestions for school involvement and collaboration with prescribing physicians have been discussed fully in other places (Chapter 5, this volume; see also Gadow, 1993; Johnson, Kenney, & Davis, 1976) and include the following: (1) establishing district- or school-wide policy and communication systems for collaboration with community physicians, (2) establishing a system-wide outcome evaluation system for use with children being treated with stimulant medications, (3) delineating the specific roles of school system personnel in implementating and monitoring of medication trials, and (4) ensuring that all staff are appropriately trained to fulfill their responsibilities. School psychologists and school nurses should be qualified to facilitate the coordination and implementation of each of these suggestions within their districts.

In addition to discussions of assessment and diagnosis, educational responsibilities, and stimulant medication, involvement with children with ADHD requires education professionals to communicate specific information, requests (e.g., referrals for evaluation), and expectations to parents, other professionals, and children. These person-specific communications are the focus of the remainder of this chapter.

COMMUNICATION BETWEEN EDUCATION PROFESSIONALS AND PARENTS

The following excerpts from the National Association of School Psychologists (1992) outline the ideal approach for school practitioners:

> *Ethical Guideline C.1.* School psychologists explain all services to parents in a clear, understandable manner. They strive to propose a set of options which takes into account the values and capabilities of each parent.

Ethical Guideline C.4. School psychologists discuss recommendations and plans for assisting the student/client with the parent. The discussion includes alternatives associated with each set of plans, showing respect for the ethnic/cultural values of the family. The parents are advised as to sources of help available at school and in the community. (p. 11)

Communication with parents regarding the education of children with ADHD can be conceptualized broadly as intended to involve and support parents in a variety of activities that contribute to educational decision making. The time and effort necessary for these communications and activities will vary widely. For example, compare issues of due process notification and consent for assessment, with completion of a behavior rating scale or participating in a structured interview to derive goals for educational planning. Regardless of the time required, our goals should be to communicate as directly and clearly as possible with parents and to facilitate their involvement and understanding to the fullest extent possible. Particular attention is warranted to issues of due process notifications, parent involvement in educational decision making, and parent roles in educational program implementation.

Due Process Notifications

The IDEA of 1992, as well as its predecessors and related public laws (PL 94-142 and PL 99-457), ensures the rights of all children to a free and appropriate education, regardless of disability or handicapping condition. These laws require that parents be notified of and give consent to initial placement of children into special education programs, as well as to assessment activities that might lead to such changes (Bersoff & Hofer, 1990). Parental notification also is required as to when a conference will be held for purposes of discussing these decisions. Bersoff and Hofer (1990) discuss further that informed consent involves parental *knowledge* of the action(s) to be taken, *voluntariness* or freedom from coercion, and *capacity* or competence to provide consent. These procedural requirements can best be met through open and informative communication, which also facilitates involvement in educational decision making.

Involving Parents in Educational Planning and Decision Making

Five distinct and related types of educational decisions that can be facilitated by careful assessment have been delineated by Salvia and Ysseldyke (1991): screening, referral, classification or eligibility, instructional program planning (including placement decisions), and program evaluation (including student progress evaluation). It is incumbent upon professionals to clarify and discuss with parents the issues and procedures involved in assessment for each of these purposes, as well as how they relate to educational decision making. These discussions can help parents to be truly informed and knowledgeable consumers, who can better act in the best interest of the child(ren) being served.

As part of these discussions, professionals will probably want to clarify several aspects of their work. The following questions address issues to explain to parents:

> What is your model of (or general approach to) professional practice, and, based on the assumptions of that model, what are the implications for service delivery?
>
> With respect to assessment, what activities do you and your organization typically engage in when addressing issues of screening, referral, classification, and eligibility for programs?
>
> How will you convey to parents the concept that there is no "litmus test" for diagnosing ADHD, especially when you are faced with parents, teachers, and other professionals saying, "We really need to know whether or not this child has ADHD"?

When discussing a diagnosis of ADHD, parents will need to be informed as to the nature and implications of an ADHD diagnosis. For example, how was this diagnosis arrived at? How should parents view this problem? Should they view this as a medical disorder, developmental disorder, educational problem, or some combination of the three? What is the prognosis for children diagnosed with ADHD? In our experience, it is helpful to convey to parents of children with ADHD that they face two primary problems: first, their child is likely to present with *difficult-to-manage behavior,* and second, the child is likely to be *difficult to teach.* Intervention strategies and options for child management by parents and teachers, as well as by self-management and medication, may be appropriate to discuss at this point. Also, with respect to interventions, the importance of careful planning, implementation, and evaluation of intervention strategies should be conveyed to parents. Finally, professionals should do their best to expose myths regarding ADHD. For example, commonly held beliefs, such as that ADHD is caused by food allergies or that medication response is a diagnostic indicator of ADHD, can be discussed in the course of communications around the appropriate topic (e.g., etiology, assessment, intervention). Discussion of these issues can be facilitated by providing the parents with a brief factsheet about ADHD (see Barkley, 1991b) and/or a list of suggested readings (see Appendix 7.1).

Parent Involvement in Educational Programming

Professional–parent partnerships, attempting to foster a shared responsibility for student learning, are part of the spirit and the letter of the IDEA and its related public laws. Furthermore, it has been documented that parent involvement in educational and school-related activities enhances student achievement (Christenson, Rounds, & Gorney, 1992). However, as Epstein (1986) has pointed out, although parents want their children to succeed in school, in general parents are unclear as to how to assist their children achieve that success. Christenson, Rounds, and Gorney (1992) provide an excellent review of literature on those family/parent influences on achievement that have been documented to be both positively correlated with student achievement and manipulable. Of particular relevance here are parental influences involving school–home communications and the structuring of and participation in learning-related activities at home.

A variety of home–school communication strategies are available for consideration. For example, Turnbull and Turnbull (1986) describe and discuss the organization and utility of conferences, informal school visits, telephone calls, log books or notes (see Chapter 4 for discussion and examples of home–school notes), newsletters, and report cards as viable strategies. In addition, they suggest that school professionals solicit input regarding parent preferences for method and frequency of home–school communication. These strategies can be utilized to foster parental understanding of school programs, as well as to facilitate parental monitoring of student behavior and achievement. In addition, their use can facilitate parental ability to specifically discuss aspects of their children's schooling at home and to incorporate motivational and feedback strategies around schooling into their routines. Additionally, informed parents can recognize and celebrate student accomplishment(s) on a regular basis, as well as prevent problems and/or manage problems as they arise (see Reid & Patterson, 1991, for a discussion of the critical nature of parental monitoring in preventing patterns of antisocial behavior). An important aspect of these activities is that they help parents communicate to and teach children that education, learning, and socially appropriate behavior are valued at home.

Home-based learning activities also teach children that education and learning are valued. For example, parents can be involved in activities, such as monitoring homework completion and discussing school work, that are linked to children's classroom assignments and responsibilities. Additionally, parents can foster learning by ensuring that books are available at home; by reading, enjoying, and discussing books and other reading material themselves, and by providing a variety of opportunities for learning. However, it is quite likely that parents will need assistance in organizing and structuring such activities (Epstein, 1986; Christenson et al., 1992). Also, it should not be assumed that teachers are familiar with strategies to recommend to parents or comfortable with actually making such recommendations. Working together with parents, however, school psychologists, teachers, and administrators may help to promote parent involvement in activities likely to foster learning and achievement.

COMMUNICATIONS WITH PHYSICIANS AND OTHER PROFESSIONALS

National Association of School Psychologists (1992) professional practice standard 4.2.2. reads as follows:

> School psychologists establish and maintain relationships with other professionals (e.g., pediatricians) who provide services to children and families. They collaborate with these professionals in prevention, assessment and intervention efforts as necessary. They also cooperate with advocates representing children and their families. (p. 56)

In our experience with ADHD, educators' communication with and referrals to physicians center around two primary issues: the diagnosis of the disorder and medication treatment. In these instances, families should be involved in the decision-making process (e.g., to make a referral) and should be treated with dignity and respect. During this process, the person(s) making the referral should patiently help parents to understand the purpose of the referral. For example, it might be communicated to parents that "I/we are concerned about your son and believe that he may be diagnosable with ADHD. In many instances where professionals have such concerns, it is helpful to have the input and opinion of physicians. As such, I/we would like to refer you to your family pediatrician (or other medical professional) for a professional opinion regarding these concerns." If parents are in agreement with a referral, assistance should be offered to them in the form of a letter (or, in some cases, a phone contact) to the referee, conveying both the specific concerns being raised, and what questions the person making the referral would like to have answered (e.g., diagnostic classification). A sample referral letter is included as Appendix 7.2.

For children who already have been diagnosed with ADHD, a referral might be made to inquire about the appropriateness of a medication trial (see Appendix 7.3). Here, the referral might include information about other interventions that have been attempted or that are in place. In addition, school-based professionals might offer to systematically gather information that could be used to evaluate and monitor medication effects (e.g., using side-effects questionnaires, academic performance information, behavior rating scales). Appendices 7.4 and 7.5 comprise two sample letters discussing the evaluation of a medication trial and its results, respectively. In making professional referrals, it is important to keep in mind that appropriate referrals do not tell other professionals how to practice. Rather, referrals are requests for professional assistance in producing information to answer particular questions. The manner of producing the information or answering the question remains the professional's prerogative.

Finally, when school-based professionals are responsible for children who are being treated with psychoactive medications, a number of issues and questions should be discussed with parents and physicians. For example, who should be responsible for ensuring that a student takes his/her medication, and what happens if a student refuses to take prescribed medication? Who is responsible for assessing side effects and for monitoring the medication's effects on a student's social, academic, and physical functioning? Who will be making decisions about changes in the medication regimen? How will these tasks be accomplished? How will changes in the student's physical, social, and academic functioning be measured in valid and reliable ways? (See Chapter 5, this volume; Gadow, 1993; or Johnson et al., 1976, for some suggested answers to these questions.)

COMMUNICATIONS WITH STUDENTS

The following excerpts outline appropriate communication with students (National Association of School Psychologists, 1992):

> *Ethical Guideline B.2.* School psychologists explain important aspects of their professional relationships with students and clients in a clear, understandable manner. The explanation includes the reason why services were requested, who will receive information about the services provided, and the possible outcomes.
>
> *Ethical Guideline B.3.* School psychologists understand their obligation to respect the rights of a student or client to initiate, participate in, or discontinue services voluntarily.
>
> *Ethical Guideline B.4.* Recommendations for program changes or additional service will be discussed including any alternatives which may be available. (p. 10)

As with parents and physicians, students also should be treated with dignity and respect while they are involved in discussions and communications regarding assessment, diagnosis, and interventions, as well as the actual activities. First, in communicating the results and implications to a student diagnosed with ADHD, care should be taken to utilize language the student is likely to understand. Rather than telling a child that he or she has a disorder, the focus of the discussion should be on individual strengths and weaknesses. The student should be told what strengths and weaknesses were indicated by the evaluation. It should be pointed out that all of his or her classmates have individual strengths and weaknesses so that he or she is not unique in this regard. Weaknesses related to ADHD should be discussed in terms of problems sustaining attention, inhibiting impulses, and controlling activity level, especially in certain situations such as during independent seatwork. The student might be asked to enumerate specific examples of when, where, and how these problems are experienced on a daily basis. It should be emphasized that many students have weaknesses in these areas and that there are some ways to help with these difficulties. Discussion of various treatment modalities then ensues, explained in language that the child understands. For example, the use of stimulants would be framed in the context of trying to see whether medication would help the student to pay attention better and get more work done. If positive changes occur, the student is reminded that he or she was responsible for these improvements and the medication merely helped to make these changes possible.

With older adolescents (e.g., high school students), more specific information about ADHD should be communicated. Depending upon the cognitive abilities of the specific student, the handouts and readings recommended for parents and teachers might be provided. Several counseling sessions may be necessary to accurately communicate this information, answer student questions, and to provide emotional support. As with younger children, the emphasis of these discussions is not what the student does wrong, but rather that these weaknesses must be addressed in the long term with the help of teachers and parents.

In an ongoing fashion, time should be taken to involve students in service delivery decisions (e.g., intervention development and choices, when possible) as appropriate. As a general rule for educating students diagnosed with ADHD, in every possible way we want to convey encouragement, reinforce effort, plan for success, and provide constructive feedback and formative evaluation to promote success.

A primary consideration with children diagnosed with ADHD is the attributions that they develop for their behavior, achievement, and academic progress, especially when they are being treated with stimulant (or other) medication. A small, developing literature in this area (Pelham et al., 1992, Whalen, Henker, Hinshaw, Heller, & Huber-Dressler, 1991) suggests that children with ADHD rate both current and predicted behavior more favorably when they have taken medication. Although further work is needed in this area, the reported findings suggest it is important to consider and evaluate what "messages" children are receiving, or sending to others, with respect to attributing their behavior to medication or to their own competence. Thus, regardless of whether they have taken their medication or not, all students with ADHD must feel that they are responsible for their own behavior.

SUMMARY

The position that child advocacy and student outcomes should drive professional practice has several implications for the services provided by school psychologists to students who are, or may be, diagnosed with ADHD. It requires a focus on the identification and definition of problems and concerns, in addition to diagnoses. Thus, careful communication with parents, physicians, children, and others sets the agenda for assessment procedures and intervention activities.

Our comments regarding educational services for children diagnosed with ADHD have focused briefly on the linkages between diagnosis and educational programming, professional responsibilities, stimulant medication use, and communications with parents, physicians, and children. Other perspectives and issues are relevant and will arise to challenge professionals, parents, and children alike. The challenge for those involved will be to balance/divide their attention appropriately between the often competing needs to focus not only on legal or procedural requirements related to diagnosis and classification, but on student outcomes as well. The communication challenge will be to overcome the potential barriers raised by a lack of common vocabulary, training, and perspectives, while building effective interventions through collaboration. However, by initiating and promoting the discussions identified herein, parents, students, and professionals can contribute to improving meaningful student outcomes.

APPENDIX 7.1
Suggested Readings on ADHD
and Related Difficulties
for Parents and Teachers

Bain, L. J. (1991). *A parent's guide to attention deficit disorders.* New York: Dell.

Canter, L., & Hausner, L. (1988). *Homework without tears: A parent's guide for motivating children to do homework and to succeed in school.* New York: Harper & Row.

Forgatch, M., & Patterson, G. (1989). *Parents and adolescents living together: Part 2: Family problem-solving.* Eugene, OR: Castalia.

Fowler, M. (1992). *CH.A.D.D. educators manual: An in-depth look at attention deficit disorders from an educational perspective.* Plantation, FL: Ch.A.D.D.

Ingersoll, B. (1988). *Your hyperactive child: A parent's guide to coping with attention deficit disorder.* New York: Doubleday.

Parker, H. C. (1992). *The ADD hyperactivity handbook for schools: Effective strategies for identifying and teaching students with attention deficit disorders in elementary and secondary schools.* Plantation, FL: Impact.

Patterson, G., & Forgatch, M. (1989). *Parents and adolescents living together: Part 1: The basics.* Eugene, OR: Castelia.

Swanson, J. M. (1992). *School-based assessments and interventions for ADD students.* Irvine, CA: K.C.

APPENDIX 7.2
Referral Letter to a Physician

Dr. Janet Williams
755 E. 45th Street
Anywhere, USA 99999

Dear Dr. Williams:

We are writing with a referral question regarding one of your patients, Michael Winston. Michael is a first-grade student with us here at Edgars Elementary, and we have concerns as to whether he might have Attention-Deficit Hyperactivity Disorder (ADHD). Michael's teacher and our school psychologist have completed systematic observations of Michael's classroom behavior. As compared to his peers, Michael was observed to spend significantly less time engaged in assigned classroom tasks, and significantly more time out of his seat and fidgeting while in his seat. At this point, Michael is keeping up with his peers academically, but we are concerned that he frequently does not complete in-class assignments, or he completes them quite quickly with little attention to detail.

Although as yet we do not have a systematic intervention program for Michael, we are considering developing one. Before doing so, however, we would like your professional opinion as to whether Michael might be diagnosable with ADHD, and if so, we would appreciate your input as to potential directions for intervention. We would be pleased to provide other information at your request. Thank you for your assistance in this matter.

Sincerely,

School Psychologist   Teacher   School Principal

APPENDIX 7.3
Referral to Physician for Possible Medication Trial

Dr. James Smith
The Anytown Clinic
1162 Williams Street
Anytown, USA 99999

RE: Billy Buck

Dear Dr. Smith:

As you are aware, we have been working with the above-named student to address his problems with inattention, impulsivity, and overactivity in the classroom. Previously, you had identified Billy as having ADHD. We are writing to provide an update of his progress and to request your input regarding the need for additional intervention (e.g., stimulant medication).

Over the past several months, we have implemented a number of interventions designed to enhance Billy's academic performance and behavior control. These have included a token reinforcement program in the classroom, a home–school communication protocol, and the use of peer tutoring for certain subjects (e.g., math, spelling). Although these interventions have been helpful, Billy continues to display attention difficulties throughout the school day and also is very disruptive on the playground and in the lunchroom. We plan to modify and continue these interventions for the remainder of the school year. Nevertheless, we are requesting that you evaluate the need for a stimulant medication trial.

We have discussed the need for this referral with Mr. and Mrs. Buck. They are in agreement with us that further treatment appears to be necessary. Of course, as with previous cases, we are willing to provide objective data to you regarding Billy's response to stimulant medication.

If you need further information about Billy's school program, please do not hesitate to contact us at any time. We look forward to hearing from you in the near future.

Sincerely,

School Psychologist   Teacher   School Principal

APPENDIX 7.4
Description of Medication Trial to Physician

Dr. James Smith
The Anytown Clinic
1162 Williams Street
Anytown, USA 99999

Dear Dr. Smith:

We are pleased to be working with you and your patient, Thomas Jones, in evaluating the effects of stimulant medication on Thomas's academic and social functioning in school. Enclosed you will find a brief description of the project, its purpose, and goals. I am writing to ask your cooperation in prescribing the medication for the trial. Joan Williams, head pharmacist at the Health Center, has agreed to facilitate packaging of medication for the trial. Joan has agreed to label the separate bottles of medication with a code letter and dates (e.g., methylphenidate, dose A, week of April 14). Of the people involved in administering the medication trial, only you and the school principal will be aware of the actual dose on any medication day. Please write three separate prescriptions as follows, and specify that the prescription is to be filled by the Health Center:

Methylphenidate   5 mg; Dispense 6 doses.
Methylphenidate   10 mg; Dispense 6 doses.
Methylphenidate   15 mg; Dispense 6 doses.

Mrs. Jones will pick up the prescriptions from your office when they are ready. The dates and doses (randomly assigned) of Thomas's medication trial will be as follows:

Dates	Dose
Week of April 7	Baseline
Week of April 14, Monday thru Saturday	10 mg
Week of April 21, Monday thru Saturday	5 mg
Week of April 28, Monday thru Saturday	15 mg

We will provide you with a summary of the results of this evaluation upon completion of the trial. We look forward to working with you. Please contact us if you have any questions.

Sincerely,

School Psychologist   School Principal

APPENDIX 7.5
Report of Results of Medication Trial to Physician

Dr. James Smith
The Anytown Clinic
1162 Willams Street
Anytown, USA 99999

Dear Dr. Smith:

We have now completed the methylphenidate evaluation trial for your patient, Thomas Jones. The conditions and dates of the trial were as follows:

Dates	Dose
Week of April 7	Baseline
Week of April 14, Monday thru Saturday	10 mg
Week of April 21, Monday thru Saturday	5 mg
Week of April 28, Monday thru Saturday	15 mg

Ongoing measures consisted of Thomas's reading performance in passages sampled from his curriculum, math performance in basic math skill probes, teacher ratings of classroom behavior and performance, parent ratings of behavior, and side-effects ratings completed by Thomas and his mother. A graph of Thomas's reading data is attached. The overall results of the trial are summarized in the table that follows:

Measure	Optimal dose(s)
Daily curriculum-based reading performance	15 mg
Daily math performance	15 mg
Teacher ratings of classroom behavior	10 mg/15 mg
Parent ratings of behavior	15 mg/5 mg

With respect to side effects, some dizziness, irritability, stomachaches, and difficulty sleeping were reported by both Thomas and his mother at both the 10-mg and 15-mg doses. These problems were reported as minor to moderate in severity and tended to diminish over the course of each of these weeks.

The results of this evaluation indicate that the 15-mg dose of methylphenidate optimally enhanced Thomas's behavior across social and academic performance measures. Should methylphenidate be prescribed for Thomas at this dose, side effects should be carefully monitored. We hope that you find the results of this evaluation to be useful to you in your work with Thomas and his family. If we can be of further assistance with Thomas or other children, please do not hesitate to contact us.

Sincerely,

School Psychologist   Teacher   School Principal

THOMAS J.: READING PERFORMANCE

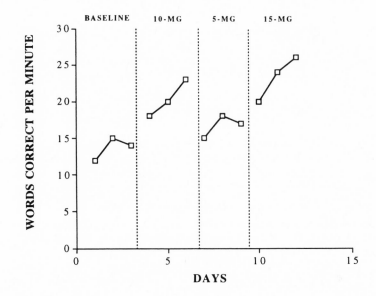

8

Conclusions and Future Directions

Meeting the needs of students with ADHD presents significant challenges to educational personnel. The hallmark characteristics of this disorder (i.e., inattention, impulsivity, and overactivity) often lead to disruptions of classroom decorum, academic underachievement, and difficulties making and keeping friends. Each of the characteristics comprising ADHD appears to exist on a continuum (i.e., normal curve) within the population such that the upper 2–5% of children in a given age and gender group could be diagnosed with the disorder. Further, an additional 5% of children in a given population, just out of the range of "clinically diagnosable" ADHD, present with significant, albeit less severe, attention and behavior control problems. Thus, in a regular classroom of 25 children, a teacher would be faced with at least 2 or 3 students who have notable difficulties attending to instructional activities and complying with classroom and school rules.

The academic performance of most children with ADHD is deficient because of their poor study habits; lack of work completion; and inconsistent accuracy on seatwork, homework, and tests. In addition, about one-third of these students are significantly below average in academic skills and, therefore, are identified as having a learning disability. Recent changes in the interpretation of federal guidelines have allowed for the provision of special education services to children with ADHD solely on the basis that this disorder limits their educational performance. Special education eligibility decisions should be made by conducting a reliable and valid assessment of ADHD and related problems, determining the degree to which the child's ADHD impacts his or her academic and social functioning, and evaluating the success of interventions in general education classrooms for ameliorating behaviors related to the disorder.

The first step in addressing the needs of children referred for problems consistent with ADHD is to conduct comprehensive psychological and, if necessary, educational evaluations. The school-based assessment of ADHD is comprised of multiple techniques used across a variety of settings (e.g., classroom, playground) and sources of information (e.g., parent, teacher, child). Following a teacher referral for possible ADHD, five stages of assessment are conducted including initial screening for ADHD symptoms, multimethod assessment, interpretation of results to reach a classification decision, development of a multimodal treatment plan, and ongoing monitoring of progress resulting from intervention(s).

A diagnosis of ADHD does not signal the end of the evaluation process nor is it the ultimate goal of an assessment. Rather, the value of the initial assessment lies in the determination of an intervention plan whose success is linked to the information gathered in the evaluation process. The use of behavioral methodologies including parent and teacher interviews, parent and teacher rating scales, direct observations of school behavior, and collection of academic performance data is the optimal way to address both diagnosis and intervention planning. These assessment data are collected throughout treatment to determine the efficacy and/ or limitations of the various components of an intervention program.

The most effective psychosocial interventions are those based on principles of operant conditioning and social learning theory. Typically, these include token reinforcement systems, response cost, and self-management strategies. Treatment targets include maladaptive behaviors (e.g., inattention to task) to be reduced, as well as competencies (e.g., academic performance, social acceptance) to be enhanced. In fact, when adaptive behaviors are increased, disruptive actions usually are diminished in frequency because of the inherent incompatibilities between these two classes of behavior. Therefore, positive reinforcement procedures are emphasized with the realization that mild punishment strategies will be necessary, in some cases, to curtail off-task and/or aggressive actions.

For many children with ADHD, the optimal treatment approach may be the combination of behavioral interventions with psychostimulant medication (e.g., methylphenidate). In school settings, stimulant medication may enhance attention span, task completion and accuracy, and compliance with classroom rules in the majority of treated children. Given that the behavioral effects of stimulants are moderated by dose and individual responsivity, each child's treatment response *must* be assessed in an objective manner across a range of therapeutic doses. School-based professionals should play a major role in helping physicians to evaluate stimulant-induced changes in children's behavior across a variety of crucial functioning areas (e.g., educational performance, social relationships, compliance with classroom rules). The same sources of data that were used in the initial evaluation of ADHD can be tapped on a continuous basis over several weeks to objectively determine whether an individual responds to pharmacotherapy and which dose optimizes the student's academic and social functioning.

Regardless of the well-established efficacy of stimulant medication and contingency management interventions, no single treatment approach will be sufficient in ameliorating ADHD-related difficulties. Chronic problem behaviors across settings and with different caregivers will probably necessitate implementating a multimodal treatment approach over several years or longer. A number of intervention strategies can be used to supplement the use of classroom behavior modification systems and psychotropic medications. These may include both school-based (e.g., social skills training) and home-based (e.g., parent training) treatments. The focus must be on designing an effective, comprehensive program to treat a variety of functional areas while acknowledging the necessity for long-term treatment. Concurrently, educators and parents, in particular, will need to set their sights on achieving short-term objectives throughout the school year to promote gradual improvements in the child's overall adjustment.

School-based professionals should carefully evaluate the documented efficacy of proposed treatments for ADHD as there are a number of therapies that have been touted as effective in the treatment of this disorder (e.g., Feingold diet) that actually have limited or no empirical support. Given the appeal of alternatives to medication or behavior modification among the general public, it is important that someone on the child's treatment team take a cautious, data-based stance towards newly proposed therapies that are purported to cure ADHD. Specifically, the quality and quantity of empirical support for the treatment should be evaluated closely. More often than not, it is necessary to point out the limitations of unsubstantiated treatment modalities so as to keep energy and resources focused on those interventions more likely to help the child.

Usually, a number of individuals are involved in the treatment of a child diagnosed with ADHD. Thus, the student and his or her parents often interact with both school-based (e.g., teachers, school psychologists, administrators, school nurse, guidance counselors) and community-based (e.g., physician, clinical psychologist) professionals. This necessitates adopting a team approach to treatment wherein the provision of services is coordinated across professionals through ongoing communication. Unfortunately, the latter is more of an ideal than a commonplace circumstance in the real world. Nevertheless, it is assumed that the more teamwork involved in treatment, the better the outcome for the child.

The team approach can be fostered by ensuring that all school professionals are aware of what ADHD is, how to identify students who may potentially require intervention, and how to treat problems related to the disorder. Educators aligned with both general and special education need to understand that ADHD-related behaviors are chronic and rarely fully eliminated, especially in the context of a single academic year. Thus, the focus of professional efforts is on modifying the classroom and school environment to meet the needs of students with this disorder so as to attain short-term goals. As short-term improvements in attention, impulse control, and activity level are achieved, gradual progress toward long-term amelioration of these problems occurs. However, in our experience, to maintain the motivation of the student and treatment team members, it is necessary to concentrate on making small gains rather than achieving a permanent cure within a short time period.

FUTURE DIRECTIONS FOR WORKING WITH STUDENTS WITH ADHD

Although there has been substantial progress over the past several decades in the school-based identification and treatment of students with ADHD, significant work remains to be done in a number of key areas. First, reliable methods to identify preschoolers with ADHD and to manage their behaviors in an effective fashion are sorely needed. A proactive approach to preventing school-related problems may be easier to adopt during this stage of development. Second, minimal attention has been paid to the difficulties and needs of middle, junior high, and senior high school students with ADHD. The latter typically exhibit myriad adjustment problems across academic, social, and behavioral areas of functioning. Given the greater emphasis on independence and individual responsibility for one's own behavior during the adolescent years, it is particularly crucial to determine the types of programming that will enhance scholastic success for these students. Third, the roles and responsibilities of school-based case managers must be delineated. Even during the elementary school years, students with ADHD work with a variety of professionals, thus implicating the need for someone to coordinate communication and services across home, school, and community environments. Next, instruction in how to meet the educational and behavioral needs of children with ADHD must occur at the preservice level of training (i.e., prior to receiving teacher certification) for both general educators and special education personnel. Currently, many teachers are not adequately prepared to work effectively with such children even after attending inservice workshops or reading relevant professional literature. Finally, empirical investigations are sorely needed to determine practical, time-efficient ways to manage the behavior control difficulties associated with ADHD, while simultaneously enhancing the academic and social competencies of children and adolescents with this disorder.

Preschoolers with ADHD

Children usually are not diagnosed with ADHD until the onset of formal schooling (i.e., kindergarten and first grade). In recent years, however, more children are entering day care and/or nursery school settings as early as infancy. Although preschool educational programs are typically play-oriented and offer more free choice activities than does later schooling, the preacademic tasks, social activities, and art projects comprising schooling during these years require sustained attention and compliance with rules for short periods of time. Thus, children with ADHD-related behaviors could significantly disrupt structured activities, transitions from one activity to another, and group interactions (e.g., circle times). Further, preschoolers who are motorically overactive and more impulsive than their peers may have difficulties sharing, waiting turns, and controlling frustration even during less structured activities such as free play. Therefore, it will be important to develop methods for early identification of such children in order to facilitate their adjustment to preschool settings.

The identification of ADHD among preschoolers is quite difficult because of the degree of variability in development and behavior control across children at this age. The following questions should be asked whenever a young child is exhibiting significant levels of inattention, impulsivity, and overactivity:

1. How much of the child's disruptive behavior is due to "immaturity"? Is the child immature in many areas of development in addition to attention span and distractibility? Have the child's behaviors improved over time and with careful attention to their amelioration? If not, a referral for an ADHD evaluation may be warranted.

2. Are the classroom expectations age-appropriate? For example, are children expected to sit still for too long? The curriculum may be too focused on academics and/or may be requiring skills beyond the child's instructional levels. Are the disruptive behaviors a function of frustration?

3. Are the classroom rules clear? Have these rules been taught to the children? Is the teacher's discipline style clear and consistent? Is the child oppositional and defiant toward the classroom rules?

Parents and professionals often are reluctant to have a child labeled at a young age. They and the child's teacher may be more comfortable waiting until kindergarten or first grade to see if the child "grows out of it" (i.e., behavior becomes less difficult to manage). However, if a child exhibiting ADHD-related behaviors receives no intervention during the preschool years, the "wait-and-see" approach may result in increased frustration in school activities, the development of poor peer relationships, and diminished self-esteem relative to school success. Thus, one must ask whether the benefits of identification and intervention at this age outweigh the costs.

Children with ADHD typically do not fully benefit from the preschool experience because they miss preacademic information due to inattention and may be excluded from playtime as punishment for disruptive behavior. Further, the classroom ecology is changed by the presence of a child with ADHD as the classwide level of disruption may increase. Thus, the preschool teacher must evaluate the physical space, the daily schedule of activities, and his or her teaching techniques to help the child with ADHD to succeed and to manage the class as a whole. To date, classroom interventions for ADHD in preschool settings have not been studied in any detail. Nevertheless, some possible modifications to the preschool classroom are identified below.

1. Redesign the physical space. Tables where more formal activities, such as those designed to teach early academic skills, are presented should be positioned away from indoor climbers, block areas, water tables, or other distractions (e.g., bright, three-dimensional bulletin boards). Use shelves or furniture as boundaries to play areas (e.g., book corner, dramatic play area) so that there are physical cues as to the type of play that is appropriate in a given area. These types of environmental arrangements may help the child to focus on one activity at a time while minimizing the probability of the child becoming distracted by other classroom activities.

2. Adopt a step-by-step approach to activity setup. For example, rather than setting up an art activity by placing paper, crayons, scissors, and glue on a table all at once, the teacher would provide materials necessary for only the first step in the process (e.g., paper and crayons for coloring). As children complete each step of the activity, materials successively are added and then removed from the table when no longer needed. This reduces distractions and minimizes potential disruptions. During the presentation of activity directions, the child with ADHD should be seated as close as possible to the teacher with an uninterrupted view of the teacher's demonstrations. Finally, chairs should be spaced so that children are not seated too close together.

3. Evaluate and modify the daily schedule and activity transitions. The teacher should be encouraged to examine critically the content and timing of scheduled activities. Although specific modifications will vary as a function of the classroom, several questions could be considered. Is it preferable to schedule two short circle times versus one longer one? The former may be more adaptable to children with a short attention span. What time of the day does the child sit better for activities? Perhaps the schedule could be adjusted based on observations of the child's

behavior. Must everyone actually form a line to go outside? Can transitions be shortened so that there is less waiting (e.g., to get everyone dressed to go outside, to serve snack to everyone)? Finally, it may be beneficial to "talk through" transition times. For example, impending transitions can be announced, as can the requirements for completing the present activity. Consistently using a transition cue, such as singing a pick-up song, flickering the lights, ringing a bell, or making announcements with a special puppet or prop, can be more successful than relying on verbal directions alone at transition times.

4. Vary the curriculum. To maximize interest level, the teacher should be encouraged to be creative in planning innovative and engaging activities (e.g., flannelboard stories, puppet shows) for the entire class and should include those of special appeal to the child with attention and behavior problems.

5. Give individual directions clearly. The teacher should not assume that the child will follow directions presented to the group on a consistent basis. While giving directions, the teacher should make eye contact and gently touch the child to encourage attention. Commands should be made in a straightforward, direct manner (e.g., "Johnny, please pick up these toys") rather than posed as a question or favor (e.g., "Johnny, could you do me a favor and pick up these toys?"). Multistep directions should be broken down into individual steps. Finally, the child should be asked to repeat directions to insure attention and understanding.

6. Increase the ratio of adults to children. Recruit and use volunteers (e.g., grandparents, college students) to provide the child with ADHD more individualized attention during structured activities, circle times, and transitions. Also, having extra help can ensure greater consistency and follow-through on any interventions that might be implemented.

Adolescents with ADHD

As students with ADHD move from elementary school to middle school and beyond, they face a plethora of developmental hurdles that are substantially higher for them than for their peers. Further, secondary settings are characteristically more demanding with respect to student organizational abilities, academic skills, and self-directedness. Specifically, secondary school students are expected to be able to study for tests and display adequate organizational skills (e.g., keep a neat notebook) as well as plan for their future beyond high school. It is presumed that if students with ADHD are able to meet the latter expectations that their chances for successful adjustment as adults are enhanced.

In most secondary schools, minimal instruction in study and organizational skills is provided. Students are assumed to develop these skills as they progress through the grade levels as a function of their burgeoning cognitive and emotional maturation. Although this assumption may be valid for many adolescents, it is clear that many students with ADHD do not acquire adequate study skills and that their academic performance is compromised accordingly (see Chapter 4 for additional discussion of study skills intervention). Thus, direct instruction in study and organizational strategies (for a review, see Gleason et al., 1991) must be provided to these students as early as possible in their schooling. Even though there is a dearth of empirical work in this area with the ADHD population, certain guidelines should be followed:

1. Initial instruction in how to study for tests and proper note taking should take place in the later elementary and early middle school years (i.e., fifth and sixth grades), when homework and long-term projects become more demanding. This instruction should be provided by either the regular classroom teacher or support personnel (e.g., guidance counselor, school psychologist) on an ongoing basis with ample opportunity for supervised practice.

2. Students with ADHD should be required to keep homework assignment books as soon as substantial amounts (i.e., more than 30 minutes per night) of such work are required. Both short- and long-term assignments should be recorded in this book. Initially, the teacher should check and initial the assignment book at the end of each school day to ensure that the correct assignments are recorded. Further, parents should review the assignment book prior to each homework session to make sure that the student understands what is required. Home-based contingencies (e.g., preferred free-time activities) should be directly linked to compliance with assignment book responsibilities. The latter component is crucial because many youngsters with ADHD will not consistently write down their assignments unless there is a direct pay-off for doing so. As the student demonstrates greater levels of individual responsibility in using the assignment book, the level of supervision by teachers and parents may be reduced. Nevertheless, students with ADHD should continue to be required to keep an assignment book throughout their schooling.

3. Compensations for the attentional and organizational deficits associated with ADHD should be made. First, these students should be allowed to tape-record lectures as a supplement to note taking. This is particularly helpful when the child is taught how to take notes by making transcriptions of the audiotaped lecture under the supervision of a teacher. Second, an extra set of textbooks should be kept at home during the school year to prevent missed opportunities to complete homework assignments due to "forgetting" appropriate texts.

4. Continued direct instruction and monitoring of study, note-taking, and organizational skills may be necessary across several grade levels and should be considered an integral component of school-based programming for many adolescents with ADHD.

Although the above suggestions for educational practice are presumed to lead to improved student outcomes, there are still important questions in this domain that remain to be answered. At the most basic level, what are the specific deficits that students with ADHD demonstrate in the areas of study and organizational skills? Do these deficits endure over time or are there some areas that improve or worsen as the child progresses through the grades? In terms of intervention, what are the best ways to teach study and organizational skills to this group of students? Should modes of instruction vary as a function of individual characteristics (e.g., presence of learning disabilities, grade level of the child)? Finally, what are the long-term effects of study skills instruction? Do improvements in this area generalize across subjects and maintain over time? Is periodic monitoring and instruction in this functioning area necessary to ensure more durable improvements? Does study skill instruction make a difference in the eventual academic outcome of students with ADHD? Answers to these questions will certainly aid helping these students in this crucial area of competence for independent learning.

In a related area of concern, as a function of their impulsivity, youngsters with ADHD frequently do not consider the long-term consequences of their actions nor do they plan ahead with any consistency. Thus, students with this disorder often require greater guidance in planning for post-secondary school activities (i.e., entering the workforce or college). Although vocational and educational counseling are typically preferred to all secondary level students at varying levels of intensity, it is particularly crucial for individuals with ADHD to receive ongoing, intensive advising in this area. The identification of interests and strengths at an earlier age than other children may be necessary for students with this disorder. This should not be an effort to "pigeonhole" a child into one track (e.g., vocational education) versus another (e.g., college preparatory courses), but rather to encourage the student to develop a focus or interest area that will maintain their motivation for continuing their schooling. One of the greatest risks facing this population is a loss of interest in education resulting in leaving school prematurely. Thus, helping the child to look ahead and plan for the future may spur an interest in school, even if such interest is limited to selected subject areas. Beginning in middle school and continuing through each high school grade, students with ADHD should meet regularly with their guidance counselors or related personnel to receive continuous assessment and programming related to vocational/collegiate aspirations.

As in the case of study skills, limited empirical work has been conducted in the area of vocational programming for students with this disorder. We need information as to methods of career and academic counseling that are best suited to students with attention problems. How early in the child's educational program should interest assessment and vocational counseling take place? How frequent and specific must this counseling be to ensure greater success? What are the possible iatrogenic effects (e.g., premature determination of post-secondary plans) of career guidance and how may these be minimized? What methods may be used to encourage youngsters to take greater levels of responsibilty for their own future? Even though most professionals working with these students would agree that this is a crucial area of investigation, to date it has received scant empirical attention.

The Use of a School-Based Case Manager

The successful treatment of ADHD frequently requires coordination of services among parents, student, teachers, other school professionals, physicians, and community-based service providers (e.g., clinical child psychologists). All too often, service providers associated with a given student's treatment program work independently of each other with limited consistent communication occurring among them. This state of affairs increases the potential for redundancy of services or, worse still, the provision of conflicting treatment advice to parents and children. It seems reasonable to assume that effective communication among treatment team members and coordination of services could be enhanced by the efforts of one person serving in the role of a case manager. As children with ADHD spend much of their day in school settings, one cost-effective possibility is for a school-based professional to take on case manager responsibilities.

An effective case manager would provide the following services to the child and treatment team:

1. Serve as the liaison between the school and home by communicating on a regular basis with the student's teachers and parents. In addition, the case manager would have regular contact with all community-based professionals (e.g., physician) working with the student.

2. Coordinate school-based programming among teachers at the middle, junior high, or senior high school level. The case manager would either meet with each teacher individually or lead team meetings on a regular basis. This process would facilitate consistency in programming across classrooms while preventing potential miscommunication leading to ineffective treatment.

3. Coordinate home–school contingency management programming. When home-based contingencies are tied to a child's school performance, consistent communication between the student's parents and teachers is crucial. Also, it is important that all participants in the program are cognizant of their responsibilities and adhere to the tenets of the intervention. This awareness and adherence may be facilitated by the case manager maintaining contact with parents and teachers, as well as periodically convening team meetings to assess progress and make changes in the format or content of the home–school program.

4. Communicate with physicians regarding medication effects on school behavior and academic performance. The importance of school-based data in determining a child's medication response as well as delineating an individual's optimal dose was discussed in Chapter 5. Having a designated person who serves as the link between the physician and the school greatly enhances the probability of effective medication monitoring and, therefore, improved outcomes. Thus, the case manager would collate and communicate information regarding changes in the child's school performance to the physician during the initial evaluation of medication response (see Appendices 7.4 and 7.5). In addition, he or she could apprise the physician and/or parents of any unusual changes in the child's behavior that may be occurring as a result of long-term medication administration. Also, any changes in the child's medication or dosage could be communicated by the parent or physician to members of the student's school-based team through the case manager.

5. Serve as a child advocate to facilitate obtaining appropriate school- and community-based services. The case manager should develop an overview of the types of services that a student with ADHD may require versus those currently available. When gaps are found between existing and necessary services, the case manager should advocate for changes in the child's educational and community-based programming with appropriate members of the treatment team (e.g., school administrators, parents). In addition, advocacy for greater professional attention to student outcomes may be warranted.

The above list of case manager responsibilities is not intended to be exhaustive as there may be other roles that the case manager could serve depending upon the child's needs. Further, each of these responsibilities may be inapplicable in some cases. Nevertheless, there is a strong need for a single person to coordinate services on an ongoing basis. In many cases, this should be a school-based professional who can follow a child's education across grade levels (e.g., school psychologist, guidance counselor). School-based professionals have the advantage of daily contact with the child's teachers as well as the opportunity to make contacts with parents and community-based members of the child's treatment team. Ongoing coordination of services and communication among team members is assumed to enhance the overall efficacy of long-term treatment of this disorder.

Preservice Training in ADHD

One of the most frequent complaints voiced by parents of children with ADHD is that their children's teachers do not appear to have any background in working with students who have this disorder. Many teachers, particularly those in general education classrooms, readily acknowledge their limitations in working with these students. To address this problem, school systems have endeavored to provide in-service training to their staff on ways to identify, teach, and manage these children in both general and special education settings. Unfortunately, there are no empirical data to indicate that brief, didactic training in how to work with children who have ADHD is effective in enhancing the knowledge and skills of educators. In fact, it appears that many teachers are not adequately prepared to work effectively with such children even after attending in-service workshops or reading the relevant professional literature.

Given this state of affairs, instruction in how to meet the educational and behavioral needs of children with ADHD should occur at the preservice level of training (i.e., prior to receiving teacher certification) for all teachers in training, as well as other school personnel. This training would afford the opportunity to provide not only didactic instruction in ADHD, but also supervised practice in effective teaching and behavior management strategies. The fact that every educator will typically work with at least one student who has ADHD per school year would warrant that this proposal receive serious consideration. Unfortunately, at the present time, intensive training in working with such children usually does not occur at the preservice level.

Although it seems reasonable to assume that preservice training in ADHD will enhance educators' skills in working with these children, there are currently no empirical data to support this claim. Thus, the efficacy of preservice training in ADHD should be examined in detail. Specifically, what training activities lead to greater levels of understanding of this disorder and an enhancement of teaching and management skills? Will the combination of didactic instruction, assigned readings, and supervised practice be sufficient to prepare teachers to work effectively with this population? Are other training modalities (e.g., practicum placement in school for children with behavior disorders) necessary to teach adequate levels of skills in this area? These are important questions as adequate preservice training for teachers represents a proactive (i.e., preventive) model of service delivery for students with ADHD and ultimately could reduce the need for more costly, intensive programming at a later date.

School-Based Research on ADHD

Although various behavioral and cognitive-behavioral interventions for ADHD have been found to be effective in empirical studies, there is still a great deal to be learned about how to enhance the school performance of students who have this disorder (for review see Fiore, Becker, & Nero, 1993). Relative to the voluminous research literature examining stimulant medication treatment of this disorder, consideration of school-based psychosocial and instructional interventions is in its infancy. There are many directions that could be taken in this area; some of the more practice-relevant dimensions for future research are identified below.

Behavioral interventions that have been employed for ADHD are quite diverse in scope, content, and intensity. Little is known about the relative efficacies of intervention components (e.g., token reinforcement vs. reponse cost). What are the sufficient components of behavioral interventions for ADHD and how much should programming vary as a function of individual (e.g., age, gender, severity of the disorder) and environmental (e.g., general education vs. special education placement, level of teacher stress) factors? Practitioners need to know not only whether an intervention will work, but also which treatment will be most effective under a given set of circumstances.

Most of the intervention research has focused on manipulating consequences to change the behavior of students with ADHD. There is a dearth of information on what antecedent events can be used to reduce problematic behaviors and enhance academic performance. What are the most effective ways to present academic material to students with ADHD? Will the efficacy of various modes of instruction vary as a function of the behavioral and academic profile of the child? How can we improve children's attention to task directions? Are there ways that we can alter the stimulation level of academic material such that children with ADHD will be more likely to complete their work in a timely and accurate fashion? Greater knowledge of effective ways to manipulate antecedent events would presumably aid in preventing and/or reducing the severity of many of the behavioral control difficulties associated with this disorder, while enhancing academic skill achievement and performance.

Even though behavioral interventions have been found to be effective for ADHD, these treatments often are not employed in classrooms.

Despite their effectiveness, teachers frequently find such procedures unacceptable due to time constraints, lack of resources, or philosophical differences with the approach to intervening (Witt & Elliott, 1985). In other words, many interventions that work well in a research paradigm are not perceived as very practical, particularly when implemented in general education classrooms. Thus, we need to know how to increase the acceptability of effective interventions. It is not enough to establish that a treatment works, we also must know if it is acceptable to the "consumers" (i.e., teachers, parents, and students) of these interventions. Are there modifications that can be made to currently available interventions that will increase their acceptability and hence their adoption into practice? How can the efficacy of interventions that have greater levels of acceptability, such as self-management strategies, be increased? The true test of whether research in this area contributes to practice will be the degree to which teachers and other school personnel actually implement empirically valid procedures on a consistent basis over lengthy time periods.

Researchers in the field of ADHD must develop and evaluate other methods for working with these children in school settings. This work should be aimed at directly enhancing educational outcomes, rather than primarily controlling student problem behaviors. For example, procedures discussed in Chapter 6 included peer-mediated interventions and CAI. These technologies have great promise for students with ADHD, but have not been studied in any great detail. The search for intervention strategies that are effective in ameliorating ADHD symptoms *and* are acceptable to school practitioners must continue in earnest.

Finally, with the recent changes in the interpretation of federal regulations for special education, there is a great need to establish how and under what conditions children with ADHD might qualify for special services. Currently, the guidelines are quite vague as to how qualification decisions might be made. School systems are left to determine on their own how students with ADHD may be eligible for special education services. In an ideal world, there would be empirical guidelines available to facilitate eligibility decisions and to lead to effective programming. Under what conditions might students with ADHD benefit from special education? What assessment measures should be used to determine eligibility? What role do community-based professionals (e.g., physicians) play in making such decisions? What components should be included in a special education program for these students? Are these interventions different from what is currently available for students identified with learning disabilities and SED? Certainly, these issues deserve further investigation.

CONCLUSIONS

It is quite humbling to realize that although our understanding of ADHD has greatly advanced over the last several decades, children with this disorder continue to encounter significant difficulties in succeeding in our schools. To correct this situation, gains must be made in two major areas. First, practitioners in the fields of psychology and education must increase their awareness and understanding of the limitations of students with this disorder. Those professionals possessing expertise in working with such children must educate their colleagues to be similarly proficient. Children with this disorder are encountered in every type of school setting, therefore all educators should possess at least minimal competencies in identifying these children and designing effective educational programming to meet their needs and help them to become successful, productive citizens. Second, the technology of assessing and treating children with ADHD must be improved. Assessment methodologies must be developed that go beyond the reports of significant others so as to enhance the ecological validity of the evaluation process. Further, treatment modalities that are effective on the one hand, while cost-efficient and acceptable to consumers on the other, are sorely needed. Thus, the challenge is for research to lead to effective practice such that long-term improvements in school performance are attained for all children with ADHD. Until that goal is reached, however, the many suggestions contained herein may serve as starting points for guiding current practices to improve educational outcomes for these students.

References

Abikoff, H. (1985). Efficacy of cognitive training intervention in hyperactive children: A critical review. *Clinical Psychology Review, 5*, 479–512.

Abikoff, H., & Gittelman, R. (1985a). Hyperactive children treated with stimulants: Is cognitive training a useful adjunct? *Archives of General Psychiatry, 42*, 953–961.

Abikoff, H., & Gittelman, R. (1985b). The normalizing effects of methylphenidate on the classroom behavior of ADDH children. *Journal of Abnormal Child Psychology, 13*, 33–44.

Abikoff, H., Gittelman-Klein, R., & Klein, D. (1977). Validation of a classroom observation code for hyperactive children. *Journal of Consulting and Clinical Psychology, 45*, 772–783.

Abikoff, H., & Klein, R. G. (1992). Attention-deficit hyperactivity disorder and conduct disorder: Comorbidity and implications for treatment. *Journal of Consulting and Clinical Psychology, 60*, 881–892.

Abramowitz, A. J., Eckstrand, D., O'Leary, S. G., & Dulcan, M. K. (1992). ADHD children's responses to stimulant medication and two intensities of a behavioral intervention. *Behavior Modification, 16*, 193–203.

Abramowitz, A. J., & O'Leary, S. G. (1991). Behavioral interventions for the classroom: Implications for students with ADHD. *School Psychology Review, 20*, 220–234.

Abramowitz, A., O'Leary, S. G., & Rosen, L. A. (1987). Reducing off-task behavior in the classroom: A comparison of encouragement and reprimands. *Journal of Abnormal Child Psychology, 15*, 153–163.

Achenbach, T. M. (1991). *Manual for the Child Behavior Checklist and Revised Child Behavior Profile*. Burlington, VT: T. M. Achenbach.

Ackerman, P. T., Dykman, R. A., & Peters, J. E. (1977). Teenage status of hyperactive and nonhyperactive learning disabled boys. *American Journal of Orthopsychiatry, 47*, 577–596.

Adduci, L. (1991, September 2). My child couldn't pay attention. *Woman's Day*, pp. 102–106.

American Psychiatric Association. (1980). *Diagnostic and statistical manual of mental disorders* (3rd ed.). Washington, DC: Author.

American Psychiatric Association. (1987). *Diagnostic and statistical manual of mental disorders* (3rd ed., rev.). Washington, DC: Author.

American Psychiatric Association. (1991). *DSM-IV options book: Work in progress.* Washington, DC: Author.

American Psychiatric Association. (in press). *Diagnostic and statistical manual of mental disorders* (4th ed.). Washington, DC: Author.

Anastopoulos, A. D., & Barkley, R. A. (1988). Biological factors in attention-deficit hyperactivity disorder. *Behavior Therapist, 11,* 47–53.

Anastopoulos, A. D., & Barkley, R. A. (1990). Counseling and training parents. In R. A. Barkley, *Attention-Deficit Hyperactivity Disorder: A handbook for diagnosis and treatment* (pp. 397–431). New York: Guilford Press.

Anastopoulos, A. D., Shelton, T. L., DuPaul, G. J., & Guevremont, D. C. (1993). Parent training for attention deficit hyperactivity disorder: Its impact on parent functioning. *Journal of Abnormal Child Psychology, 21,* 581–596.

Anderson, R. C., Hiebert, E. H., Scott, J. A., & Wilkinson, I. A. G. (1985). *Becoming a nation of readers: The report of the commission on reading.* Washington, DC: National Institute of Education, U.S. Department of Education. Available from the Center for the Study of Reading, University of Illinois, Champaign, IL.

Anesko, K. M., Schoiock, G., Ramirez, R., & Levine, F. M. (1987). The Homework Problem Checklist: Assessing children's homework difficulties. *Behavioral Assessment, 9,* 179–185.

Archer, A., & Gleason, M. (1989). *Skills for school success (grades 3–6).* North Billerica, MA: Curriculum.

Atkeson, B. M., & Forehand, R. (1979). Home-based reinforcement programs designed to modify classroom behavior: A review and methodological evaluation. *Psychological Bulletin, 86,* 1298–1308.

Atkins, M. S., & Pelham, W. E. (1991). School-based assessment of attention-deficit hyperactivity disorder. *Journal of Learning Disabilities, 24,* 197–204.

Atkins, M. S., Pelham, W. E., & Licht, M. H. (1985). A comparison of objective classroom measures and teacher ratings of Attention Deficit Disorder. *Journal of Abnormal Child Psychology, 13,* 155–167.

August, G. J., & Garfinkel, G. D. (1989). Behavioral and cognitive subtypes of ADHD. *Journal of the American Academy of Child and Adolescent Psychiatry, 28,* 739–748.

August, G. J., & Garfinkel, G. D. (1990). Comorbidity of ADHD and reading disability among clinic-referred children. *Journal of Abnormal Child Psychology, 18,* 29–45.

August, G. J., & Holmes, C. S. (1984). Behavior and academic achievement in hyperactive subgroups and learning-disabled boys. *American Journal of Diseases in Children, 138,* 1025–1029.

Ayllon, T., Layman, D., & Kandel, H. (1975). A behavioral-educational alternative to drug control of hyperactive children. *Journal of Applied Behavior Analysis, 8,* 137–146.

Bacon, J. (1988, February 17). What's the best medicine for hyper kids? *USA Today,* p. 4D.

Bardon, J. I. (1988). Alternative educational approaches: Implications for school psychology. In J. L. Graden, J. E. Zins, & M. J. Curtis (Eds.), *Alternative educational delivery systems: Enhancing instructional options for all students* (pp. 563–571). Washington, DC: National Association of School Psychologists.

Barkley, R. A. (1977). The effects of methylphenidate on various measures of activity level and attention in hyperkinetic children. *Journal of Abnormal Child Psychology, 5,* 351–369.

Barkley, R. A. (1979). Using stimulant drugs in the classroom. *School Psychology Digest, 8,* 412–425.

Barkley, R. A. (1981). *Hyperactive children: A handbook for diagnosis and treatment.* New York: Guilford Press.

Barkley, R. A. (1987). *Defiant children: A clinician's manual for parent training.* New York: Guilford Press.

Barkley, R. A. (1988a). Attention-Deficit Hyperactivity Disorder. In E. J. Mash & L. G. Terdal (Eds.), *Behavioral assessment of childhood disorders* (2nd ed., pp. 69–104). New York: Guilford Press.

Barkley, R. A. (1988b). Child behavior rating scales and checklists. In M. Rutter, A. H. Tuma, & I. S. Lann (Eds.), *Assessment and diagnosis in child psychopathology* (pp. 113–155). New York: Guilford Press.

Barkley, R. A. (1989). Attention-Deficit Hyperactivity Disorder. In E. J. Mash & R. A. Barkley (Eds.), *Treatment of childhood disorders* (pp. 39–72). New York: Guilford Press.

Barkley, R. A. (1990). *Attention-Deficit Hyperactivity Disorder: A handbook for diagnosis and treatment.* New York: Guilford Press.

Barkley, R. A. (1991a). The ecological validity of laboratory and analogue assessment methods of ADHD symptoms. *Journal of Abnormal Child Psychology, 19,* 149–178.

Barkley, R. A. (1991b). *Attention-Deficit Hyperactivity Disorder: A clinical workbook.* New York: Guilford Press.

Barkley, R. A. (1992, October). *Is EEG neurofeedback an effective treatment for ADHD?* Paper presented at the annual conference of Children with Attention Deficit Disorders (CH.A.D.D.), Chicago, IL.

Barkley, R. A. (in press). Impaired delayed responding: A unified theory of attention-deficit hyperactivity disorder. In D. K. Routh (Ed.), *Disruptive behavior disorders in childhood: Essays honoring Herbert C. Quay.* New York: Plenum Press.

Barkley, R. A., Anastopoulos, A. D., Guevremont, D. C., & Fletcher, K. E. (1991). Adolescents with attention-deficit hyperactivity disorder: Patterns of behavioral adjustment, academic functioning, and treatment utilization. *Journal of the American Academy of Child and Adolescent Psychiatry, 30,* 752–861.

Barkley, R. A., Anastopoulos, A. D., Guevremont, D. C., & Fletcher, K. E. (1992). Attention-deficit hyperactivity disorder in adolescents: Mother-adolescent interactions, family beliefs and conflicts, and maternal psychopathology. *Journal of Abnormal Child Psychology, 20,* 263–288.

Barkley, R. A., Copeland, A., & Sivage, C. (1980). A self-control classroom for hyperactive children. *Journal of Autism and Developmental Disorders, 10,* 75–89.

Barkley, R. A., & Cunningham, C. E. (1978). Do stimulant drugs improve the academic performance of hyperkinetic children? A review of outcome research. *Journal of Clinical Pediatrics, 17,* 85-92.

Barkley, R. A., DuPaul, G. J., & Costello, A. (1993). Stimulants. In J. S. Werry & M. G. Aman (Eds.), *Practitioners guide to psychoactive drugs for children and adolescents* (pp. 205-237). New York: Plenum Press.

Barkley, R. A., DuPaul, G. J., & McMurray, M. B. (1990). A comprehensive evaluation of attention deficit disorder with and without hyperactivity as defined by research criteria. *Journal of Consulting and Clinical Psychology, 58,* 775-789.

Barkley, R. A., DuPaul, G. J., & McMurray, M. B. (1991). Attention Deficit Disorder with and without Hyperactivity: Clinical response to three dose levels of methylphenidate. *Pediatrics, 87,* 519-531.

Barkley, R. A., Fischer, M., Edelbrock, C. S., & Smallish, L. (1990). The adolescent outcome of hyperactive children diagnosed by research criteria: I. An 8-year prospective follow-up study. *Journal of the American Academy of Child and Adolescent Psychiatry, 29,* 546-557.

Barkley, R. A., Fischer, M., Newby, R., & Breen, M. (1988). Development of a multi-method clinical protocol for assessing stimulant drug responses in ADHD children. *Journal of Clinical Child Psychology, 17,* 14-24.

Barkley, R. A., Grodzinsky, G., & DuPaul, G. J. (1992). Frontal lobe functions in attention deficit disorder with and without hyperactivity: A review and research report. *Journal of Abnormal Child Psychology, 20,* 163-188.

Barkley, R. A., Guevremont, D. C., Anastopoulos, A. D., & Fletcher, K. E. (1992). A comparison of three family therapy programs for treating family conflicts in adolescents with attention-deficit hyperactivity disorder. *Journal of Consulting and Clinical Psychology, 60,* 450-462.

Barkley, R. A., Karlsson, J., Strzelecki, E., & Murphy, J. (1984). Effects of age and Ritalin dosage on the mother–child interactions of hyperactive children. *Journal of Consulting and Clinical Psychology, 52,* 750-758.

Barkley, R. A., McMurray, M. B., Edelbrock, C. S., & Robbins, K. (1989). The response of aggressive and non-aggressive ADHD children to two doses of methylphenidate. *Journal of the American Academy of Child and Adolescent Psychiatry, 28,* 873-881.

Barkley, R. A., McMurray, M. B., Edelbrock, C. S., & Robbins, K. (1990). The side effects of Ritalin in ADHD children: A systematic placebo-controlled evaluation of two doses. *Pediatrics, 86,* 184-192.

Barlow, D. (Ed.). (1981). *Behavioral assessment of adult disorders.* New York: Guilford Press.

Barrios, B., & Hartmann, D. P. (1986). The contributions of traditional assessment: Concepts, issues, and methodologies. In R. O. Nelson & S. C. Hayes (Eds.), *Conceptual foundations of behavioral assessment* (pp. 81-110). New York: Guilford Press.

Beck, A. T., Ward, C. H., Mendelson, M., Mock, J., & Erbaugh, J. (1961). An inventory for measuring depression. *Archives of General Psychiatry, 4,* 561-571.

Beck, I. L., Perfetti, C. A., & McKeown, M. E. (1982). The effects of long-term vocabulary instruction on lexical access and reading comprehension. *Journal of Educational Psychology, 74,* 506-521.

Beitchman, J. H., Wekerle, C., & Hood, J. (1987). Diagnostic continuity from preschool to middle childhood. *Journal of the American Academy of Child and Adolescent Psychiatry, 26,* 694–699.

Bell, R. Q., & Harper, L. (1977). *Child effects on adults.* New York: Wiley.

Bergan, J. R., & Kratochwill, T. R. (1990). *Behavioral consultation and therapy.* New York: Plenum Press.

Berliner, D. C. (1987). Simple views of effective teaching and a simple theory of classroom instruction. In D. C. Berliner & B. V. Rosenshine (Eds.), *Talks to teachers: A festschrift for N. L. Gage* (pp. 93–110). New York: Random House.

Berliner, D. C., & Rosenshine, B. V. (Eds.). (1987). *Talks to teachers: A festschrift for N. L. Gage.* New York: Random House.

Bersoff, D. N., & Hofer, P. T. (1990). The legal regulation of school psychology. In T. B. Gutkin & C. R. Reynolds (Eds.), *The handbook of school psychology* (2nd ed., pp. 939–961). New York: Wiley.

Biederman, J. (1991). Sudden death in children treated with a tricyclic antidepressant. *Journal of the American Academy of Child and Adolescent Psychiatry, 30,* 495–498.

Biederman, J., Baldessarini, R. J., Wright, V., Knee, D., & Harmatz, J. S. (1989). A double-blind placebo-controlled study of desipramine in the treatment of ADHD: I. Efficacy. *Journal of the American Academy of Child and Adolescent Psychiatry, 28,* 777–784.

Biederman, J., Munir, K., Knee, D., Armentano, M., Autor, S., Waternaux, C., & Tsuang, M. (1987). High rate of affective disorders in probands with attention deficit disorders and in their relatives: A controlled family study. *American Journal of Psychiatry, 144,* 330–333.

Braswell, L., & Bloomquist, M. L. (1991). *Cognitive-behavioral therapy with ADHD children: Child, family, and school interventions.* New York: Guilford Press.

Breen, M. J., & Barkley, R. A. (1988). Child psychopathology and parenting stress in girls and boys having attention deficit disorder with hyperactivity. *Journal of Pediatric Psychology, 13,* 265–280.

Bremness, A. B., & Sverd, J. (1979). Methylphenidate-induced Tourette syndrome: Case report. *American Journal of Psychiatry, 136,* 1334–1335.

Bronowski, J. (1977). Human and animal languages. In *A sense of the future* (pp. 104–131). Cambridge, MA: MIT Press.

Brown, R. T., & Borden, K. A. (1986). Hyperactivity at adolescence: Some misconceptions and new directions. *Journal of Clinical Child Psychology, 15,* 194–209.

Brown, R. T., & Sleator, E. K. (1979). Methylphenidate in hyperkinetic children: Differences in dose effects on impulsive behavior. *Pediatrics, 64,* 408–411.

Budoff, M., Thormann, J., & Gras, A. (1984). *Microcomputers in special education.* Cambridge, MA: Brookline Books.

Buhrmester, D., Whalen, C. K., Henker, B., MacDonald, V., & Hinshaw, S. P. (1992). Prosocial behavior in hyperactive boys: Effects of stimulant medication and comparison with normal boys. *Journal of Abnormal Child Psychology, 20,* 103–122.

Campbell, S. B. (1990). *Behavior problems in preschool children: Clinical and developmental issues.* New York: Guilford Press.

Cantwell, D. P. (1986). Attention deficit disorder in adolescents. *Clinical Psychology Review, 6,* 237–247.

Cantwell, D. P., & Baker, L. (1991). Association between attention-deficit hyperactivity disorder and learning disorders. *Journal of Learning Disabilities, 24,* 88–95.

Cantwell, D. P., & Satterfield, J. H. (1978). The prevalence of academic underachievement in hyperactive children. *Journal of Pediatric Psychology, 3,* 168–171.

Carnine, D., Kameenui, E., & Silbert, J. (1990). *Direct instruction reading.* Columbus, OH: Merrill.

Carnine, D., & Kinder, D. (1985). Teaching low performing students to apply generative and schema strategies to narrative and expository material. *Remedial and Special Education, 6,* 20–30.

Casat, C. D., Pleasants, D. Z., Schroeder, D. H., & Parler, D. W. (1989). Bupropion in children with attention deficit disorder. *Psychopharmacology Bulletin, 25,* 198–201.

Chall, J. S. (1983). Literacy: Trends and explanations. *Educational Researcher, 12,* 3–8.

Chelune, G. J., Ferguson, W., Koon, R., & Dickey, T. O. (1986). Frontal lobe disinhibition in attention deficit disorder. *Child Psychiatry and Human Development, 16,* 221–234.

Christenson, S. L., Rounds, T., & Gorney, D. (1992). Family factors and student achievement: An avenue to increase students' success. *School Psychology Quarterly, 7,* 178–206.

Cohen, M., Becker, M. G., & Campbell, R. (1990). Relationships among four methods of assessment of children with attention-deficit hyperactivity disorder. *Journal of School Psychology, 28,* 189–202.

Colvin, G. T., & Sugai, G. M. (1988). Proactive strategies for managing social behavior problems: An instructional approach. *Education and Treatment of Children, 11,* 341–348.

Comings, D. E., & Comings, B. G. (1984). Tourette's syndrome and attention deficit disorder with hyperactivity: Are they genetically related? *Journal of the American Academy of Child and Adolescent Psychiatry, 23,* 138–146.

Cone, J. D. (1986). Idiographic, nomothetic, and related perspectives in behavioral assessment. In R. O. Nelson & S. C. Hayes (Eds.), *Conceptual foundations of behavioral assessment* (pp. 111–128). New York: Guilford Press.

Conners, C. K. (1980). *Food additives and hyperactive children.* New York: Plenum Press.

Conners, C. K., & Wells, K. C. (1985). ADD-H adolescent self-report scale. *Psychopharmacology Bulletin, 21,* 921–922.

Copeland, L., Wolraich, M., Lindgren, S., Milich, R., & Woolson, R. (1987). Pediatricians' reported practices in the assessment and treatment of Attention Deficit Disorders. *Developmental and Behavioral Pediatrics, 8,* 191–197.

Cunningham, C. E., & Barkley, R. A. (1979). The interactions of hyperactive and normal children with their mothers during free play and structured task. *Child Development, 50,* 217–224.

Cunningham, C. E., Siegel, L. S., & Offord, D. R. (1985). A developmental dose response analysis of the effects of methylphenidate on the peer interactions of attention deficit disordered boys. *Journal of Child Psychology and Psychiatry, 26,* 955–971.

Davila, R. R., Williams, M. L., & MacDonald, J. T. (1991, September 16). *Clarification of policy to address the needs of children with attention deficit disorders within general and/or special education.* Unpublished letter to chief state school officers, U.S. Department of Education.

Denckla, M. B., & Rudel, R. G. (1978). Anomalies of motor development in hyperactive boys. *Annals of Neurology, 3,* 231–233.

Denckla, M. B., Rudel, R. G., Chapman, C., & Krieger, J. (1985). Motor proficiency in dyslexic children with and without attentional disorders. *Archives of Neurology, 42,* 228–231.

DeRisi, W. J., & Butz, G. (1975). *Writing behavioral contracts: A case simulation practice manual.* Champaign, IL: Research Press.

Deshler, D. D., & Schumaker, J. B. (1988). An instructional model for teaching students how to learn. In J. L. Graden, J. E. Zins, & M. J. Curtis (Eds.), *Alternative educational delivery systems: Enhancing instructional options for all students* (pp. 391–411). Washington, DC: National Association of School Psychologists.

Diener, R. M. (1991). Toxicology of Ritalin. In L. L. Greenhill & B. B. Osman (Eds.), *Ritalin: Theory and patient management* (pp. 34–43). New York: Mary Ann Liebert.

Donnelly, M., & Rapoport, J. L. (1985). Attention deficit disorders. In J. M. Wiener (Ed.), *Diagnosis and psychopharmacology of childhood and adolescent disorders* (pp. 179–197). New York: Wiley.

Douglas, V. I. (1980). Higher mental processes in hyperactive children: Implications for training. In R. Knights & D. Bakker (Eds.), *Treatment of hyperactive and learning disordered children* (pp. 65–92). Baltimore: University Park Press.

Douglas, V. I. (1984). The psychological processes implicated in ADD. In L. M. Bloomingdale (Ed.), *Attention deficit disorder: Diagnostic, cognitive, and therapeutic understanding* (pp. 147–162). New York: Spectrum.

Douglas, V. I., Barr, R. G., O'Neill, M. E., & Britton, B. G. (1986). Short term effects of methylphenidate on the cognitive, learning, and academic performance of children with Attention Deficit Disorder in the laboratory and the classroom. *Journal of Child Psychology and Psychiatry, 27,* 191–211.

Douglas, V. I., Barr, R. G., O'Neill, M. E., & Britton, B. G. (1988). Dosage effects and individual responsivity to methylphenidate in attention deficit disorder. *Journal of Child Psychology and Psychiatry, 29,* 453–475.

Dulcan, M. K. (1990). Using psychostimulants to treat behavioral disorders of children and adolescents. *Journal of Child and Adolescent Psychopharmacology, 1,* 7–20.

DuPaul, G. J. (1991a). Parent and teacher ratings of ADHD symptoms: Psychometric properties in a community-based sample. *Journal of Clinical Child Psychology, 20,* 245–253.

DuPaul, G. J. (1991b). Attention-deficit hyperactivity disorder: Classroom intervention strategies. *School Psychology International, 12,* 85–94.

DuPaul, G. J. (1992). How to assess attention-deficit hyperactivity disorder within school settings. *School Psychology Quarterly, 7,* 60–74.

DuPaul, G. J., Anastopoulos, A. D., Shelton, T. L., Guevremont, D. C., & Metevia, L. (1992). Multimethod assessment of attention-deficit hyperactivity disorder: The diagnostic utility of clinic-based tests. *Journal of Clinical Child Psychology, 21,* 394–402.

DuPaul, G. J., & Barkley, R. A. (1990). Medication therapy. In R. A. Barkley, *Attention-Deficit Hyperactivity Disorder: A handbook for diagnosis and treatment* (pp. 573–612). New York: Guilford Press.

DuPaul, G. J., & Barkley, R. A. (1992a). Situational variability of attention problems: Psychometric properties of the revised home and school situations questionnaires. *Journal of Clinical Child Psychology, 21,* 178–188.

DuPaul, G. J., & Barkley, R. A. (1992b). Social interaction of children with attention deficit hyperactivity disorder: Effects of methylphenidate. In J. McCord & R. E. Tremblay (Eds.), *Preventing antisocial behavior: Interventions from birth through adolescence* (pp. 89–116). New York: Guilford Press.

DuPaul, G. J., & Barkley, R. A. (1993). Behavioral contributions to pharmacotherapy: The utility of behavioral methodology in medication treatment of children with attention deficit hyperactivity disorder. *Behavior Therapy, 24,* 47–65.

DuPaul, G. J., & Eckert, T. L. (in press). The effects of social skills curricula: Now you see them, now you don't. *School Psychology Quarterly,*

DuPaul, G. J., Guevremont, D. C., & Barkley, R. A. (1991a). Attention-deficit hyperactivity disorder in adolescence: Critical assessment parameters. *Clinical Psychology Review, 11,* 231–245.

DuPaul, G. J., Guevremont, D. C., & Barkley, R. A. (1991b). Attention-deficit hyperactivity disorder. In R. J. Morris & T. R. Kratochwill (Eds.), *The practice of child therapy* (2nd ed., pp. 115–144). New York: Pergamon Press.

DuPaul, G. J., Guevremont, D. C., & Barkley, R. A. (1992). Behavioral treatment of attention-deficit hyperactivity disorder in the classroom: The use of the Attention Training System. *Behavior Modification, 16,* 204–225.

DuPaul, G. J., & Henningson, P. N. (1993). Peer tutoring effects on the classroom performance of children with attention-deficit hyperactivity disorder. *School Psychology Review, 22,* 134–143.

DuPaul, G. J., Kwasnik, D., Anastopoulous, A. D., & McMurray, M. B. (1993). *The effects of methylphenidate on self-report ratings of attention deficit hyperactivity disorder symptoms.* Unpublished manuscript, Lehigh University, Bethlehem, PA.

DuPaul, G. J., & Rapport, M. D. (1993). Does methylphenidate normalize the classroom performance of children with attention deficit disorder? *Journal of the American Academy of Child and Adolescent Psychiatry, 32,* 190–198.

DuPaul, G. J., Rapport, M. D., & Perriello, L. M. (1991). Teacher ratings of academic skills: The development of the Academic Performance Rating Scale. *School Psychology Review, 20,* 284–300.

DuPaul, G. J., Stoner, G., Tilly, W. D., & Putnam, D. (1991). Interventions for attention problems. In G. Stoner, M. Shinn, & H. Walker (Eds.), *Interventions for achievement and behavior problems* (pp. 685–714). Silver Spring, MD: National Association of School Psychologists.

Dykman, R. A., & Ackerman, P. T. (1991). Attention deficit disorder and specific learning disability: Separate but often overlapping disorders. *Journal of Learning Disabilities, 24,* 96–103.

Elia, J., & Rapoport, J. L. (1991). Ritalin versus dextroamphetamine in ADHD: Both should be tried. In L. L. Greenhill & B. B. Osman (Eds.), *Ritalin: Theory and patient management* (pp. 69–74). New York: Mary Ann Liebert.

Elliott, S. L., Witt, J. C., & Kratochwill, T. R. (1991). Selecting, implementing, and evaluating classroom interventions. In G. Stoner, M. R. Shinn, & H. M. Walker (Eds.), *Interventions for achievement and behavior problems* (pp. 99–135). Silver Spring, MD: National Association of School Psychologists.

Ellis, E. S., Deshler, D. D., & Schumaker, J. B. (1989). Teaching adolescents with learning disabilities to generate and use task specific strategies. *Journal of Learning Disabilities, 22,* 108–119, 130.

Epstein, J. L. (1986). Parents' reactions to teacher practices of parent involvement. *Elementary School Journal, 86,* 277–294.

Evans, I. M., & Meyer, L. H. (1985). *An educative approach to behavior problems.* Baltimore: Paul H. Brookes.

Evans, R. W., Gualtieri, C. T., & Amara, I. (1986). Methylphenidate and memory: Dissociated effects in hyperactive children. *Psychopharmacology, 90,* 211–216.

Evans, S. W., & Pelham, W. E. (1991). Psychostimulant effects on academic and behavioral measures for ADHD junior high school students in a lecture format classroom. *Journal of Abnormal Child Psychology, 19,* 537–552.

Feingold, B. (1975). *Why your child is hyperactive.* New York: Random House.

Feldman, S., Denhoff, E., & Denhoff, E. (1979). The attention disorders and related syndromes outcome in adolescence and young adult life. In E. Denhoff & L. Stern (Eds.), *Minimal brain dysfunction: A developmental approach* (pp. 133–148). New York: Musson.

Felton, R. H., Wood, F. B., Brown, I. S., Campbell, S. K., & Harter, M. R. (1987). Separate verbal memory and naming deficits in attention deficit disorder and reading disability. *Brain and Language, 31,* 171–184.

Fergusson, D. M., & Horwood, L. J. (1992). Attention deficit and reading achievement. *Journal of Child Psychology and Psychiatry, 33,* 375–385.

Fielding, L. T., Murphy, R. J., Reagan, M. W., & Peterson, T. L. (1980). An assessment program to reduce drug use with the mentally retarded. *Hospital and Community Psychiatry, 31,* 771–773.

Fiore, T. A., Becker, E. A., & Nero, R. C. (1993). Educational interventions for students with ADD. *Exceptional Children, 60,* 163–173.

Fitzpatrick, P. A., Klorman, R., Brumaghim, J. T., & Borgstedt, A. D. (1992). Effects of sustained-release and standard preparations of methylphenidate on attention deficit disorder. *Journal of the American Academy of Child and Adolescent Psychiatry, 31,* 226–234.

Flicek, M. (1992). Social status of boys with both academic problems and attention-deficit hyperactivity disorder. *Journal of Abnormal Child Psychology, 20,* 353–366.

Forehand, R. L., & McMahon, R. J. (1981). *Helping the noncompliant child: A clinician's guide to parent training.* New York: Guilford Press.

Fowler, M. (1992). *Ch.A.D.D. educators manual: An in-depth look at attention deficit disorders from an educational perspective.* Plantation, FL: Ch.A.D.D.

Frick, P. J., Kamphaus, R. W., Lahey, B. B., Loeber, R., Christ, M. A. G., Hart, E. L., & Tannenbaum, L. E. (1991). Academic underachievement and the disruptive behavior disorders. *Journal of Consulting and Clinical Psychology, 59,* 289–294.

Frick, P. J., & Lahey, B. B. (1991). Nature and characteristics of Attention- deficit Hyperactivity Disorder. *School Psychology Review, 20,* 163–173.

Fuerst, D. R., Fisk, J. L., & Rourke, B. P. (1989). Psychosocial functioning of learning-disabled children: Replicability of statistically derived subtypes. *Journal of Consulting and Clinical Psychology, 57,* 275–280.

Fuster, J. M. (1989). A theory of prefrontal functions: The prefrontal cortex and the temporal organization of behavior. In J. M. Fuster (Ed.), *The prefrontal cortex: Anatomy, physiology, and neuropsychology of the frontal lobe* (pp. 157–196). New York: Raven Press.

Gadow, K. D. (1981). Drug therapy for hyperactivity: Treatment procedures in natural settings. In K. D. Gadow & J. Loney (Eds.), *Psychosocial aspects of drug treatment for hyperactivity* (pp. 325–378). Boulder, CO: Westview Press.

Gadow, K. D. (1986). *Children on medication: Vol. 1. Hyperactivity, learning disabilities, and mental retardation.* Boston: Little, Brown.

Gadow, K. D. (1993). A school-based medication evaluation program. In J. L. Matson (Ed.), *Handbook of hyperactivity in children* (pp. 186–219). Boston: Allyn & Bacon.

Gadow, K. D., Nolan, E. E., Paolicelli, L. M., & Sprafkin, J. (1991). A procedure for assessing the effects of methylphenidate on hyperactive children in public school settings. *Journal of Clinical Child Psychology, 20,* 268–276.

Gadow, K. D., Nolan, E. E., Sverd, J., Sprafkin, J., & Paolicelli, L. (1990). Methylphenidate in aggressive-hyperactive boys: I. Effects on peer aggression in public school settings. *Journal of the American Academy of Child and Adolescent Psychiatry, 29,* 710–718.

Garmezy, N. (1978). DSM-III: Never mind the psychologists; Is it good for children? *Clinical Psychologist, 31,* 1, 4–6.

Gittelman, R. (1985). Self-evaluation (teenager's) self-report. *Psychopharmacology Bulletin, 21,* 925–926.

Gittelman, R., & Kanner, A. (1986). Psychopharmacotherapy. In H. C. Quay & J. S. Werry (Eds.), *Psychopathological disorders of childhood* (3rd ed., pp. 455–495). New York: Wiley.

Gittelman, R., Mannuzza, S., Shenker, R., & Bonagura, N. (1985). Hyperactive boys almost grown up. *Archives of General Psychiatry, 42,* 937–947.

Gittelman, R., Abikoff, H., Pollack, E., Klein, D., Katz, S., & Mattes, J. (1980). A controlled trial of behavior modification and methylphenidate in hyperactive children. In C. Whalen & B. Henker (Eds.), *Hyperactive children: The social ecology of identification and treatment* (pp. 221–246). New York: Academic Press.

Gittelman-Klein, R., & Klein, D. F. (1987). Pharmacotherapy of childhood hyperactivity: An update. In H. Y. Meltzer (Ed.), *Psychopharmacology: The third generation of progress* (pp. 1215–1221). New York: Raven Press.

Gleason, M. M., Colvin, G., & Archer, A. L. (1991). Interventions for improving study skills. In G. Stoner, M. R. Shinn, & H. M. Walker (Eds.), *Interven-*

tions for achievement and behavior problems (pp. 137–160). Silver Spring, MD: National Association of School Psychologists.

Goldstein, S., & Ingersoll, B. (1992). Controversial treatments for children with attention deficit hyperactivity disorder. *Ch.A.D.D.ER, 6*, 19–22.

Goldstein, S., & Ingersoll, B. (1993). Controversial treatments for ADHD: Essential information for clinicians. *ADHD Report, 1*(4), 4–5.

Gordon, M. (1986). How is a computerized attention test used in the diagnosis of attention deficit disorder? *Journal of Children in Contemporary Society, 19*, 53–64.

Goyette, C. H., Conners, C. K., & Ulrich, R. F. (1978). Normative data on Revised Conners Parent and Teacher Rating Scales. *Journal of Abnormal Child Psychology, 6*, 221–236.

Greene, R. (1993). Hidden factors affecting the educational success of ADHD students. *ADHD Report, 1*(2), 8–9.

Greenhill, L. L. (1984). Stimulant related growth inhibition in children: A review. In L. Greenhill & B. Shopsin (Eds.), *The psychobiology of childhood* (pp. 135–157). New York: Spectrum.

Greenwood, C. R., Carta, J. J., & Hall, R. V. (1988). The use of tutoring strategies in classroom management and educational instruction. *School Psychology Review, 17*, 258–275.

Greenwood, C. R., Delquadri, J., & Carta, J. J. (1988). *Classwide peer tutoring.* Seattle: Educational Achievement Systems.

Greenwood, C. R., Maheady, L., & Carta, J. J. (1991). Peer tutoring programs in the regular education classroom. In G. Stoner, M. R. Shinn, & H. M. Walker (Eds.), *Interventions for achievement and behavior problems* (pp. 179–200). Silver Spring, MD: National Association of School Psychologists.

Gresham, F. M. (1989). Assessment of treatment integrity in school consultation and prereferral intervention. *School Psychology Review, 18*, 37–50.

Gresham, F. M. (1991). Conceptualizing behavior disorders in terms of resistance to intervention. *School Psychology Review, 20*, 23–36.

Gresham, F. M., & Elliott, S. N. (1990). *Social skills rating system.* Circle Pines, MN: American Guidance Service.

Gresham, F. M., & Gansle, K. A. (1992a). Misguided assumptions of DSM-III-R: Implications for school psychological practice. *School Psychology Quarterly, 7*, 79–95.

Gresham, F. M., & Gansle, K. A. (1992b). Misological or misconstrued? Rejoinder to Reynolds and Hynd. *School Psychology Quarterly, 7*, 108–111.

Gross, M. D., Tofanelli, M. S., Butzirus, S. M., & Snodgrass, E. (1987). The effect of diets rich in and free from additives on the behavior of children with hyperkinetic and learning disorders. *Journal of the American Academy of Child and Adolescent Psychiatry, 26*, 53–55.

Grossen, B., & Carnine, D. (1991). Strategies for maximizing reading success in the regular classroom. In G. Stoner, M. R. Shinn, & H. M. Walker (Eds.), *Interventions for achievement and behavior problems* (pp. 333–355). Silver Spring, MD: National Association of School Psychologists.

Gualtieri, C. T., Hicks, R. E., & Mayo, J. P. (1983). Hyperactivity and homeostasis. *Journal of the American Academy of Child and Adolescent Psychiatry, 22*, 382–384.

Guevremont, D. C. (1990). Social skills and peer relationship training. In R. A. Barkley, *Attention-Deficit Hyperactivity Disorder: A handbook for diagnosis and treatment* (pp. 540–572). New York: Guilford Press.

Guevremont, D. C., DuPaul, G. J., & Barkley, R. A. (1990). Diagnosis and assessment of attention-deficit hyperactivity disorder in children. *Journal of School Psychology, 28,* 51–78.

Guevremont, D. C., DuPaul, G. J., & Barkley, R. A. (1993). Behavioral assessment of attention-deficit hyperactivity disorder. In J. L. Matson (Ed.), *Handbook of hyperactivity in children* (pp. 150–168). Boston: Allyn & Bacon.

Guevremont, D. C., & Foster, S. L. (1993). Impact of social problem-solving training on aggressive boys: Skill acquisition, behavior change, and generalization. *Journal of Abnormal Child Psychology, 21,* 13–28.

Haenlein, M., & Caul, W. F. (1987). Attention deficit disorder with hyperactivity: A specific hypothesis of reward dysfunction. *Journal of the American Academy of Child and Adolescent Psychiatry, 26,* 356–362.

Hakola, S. (1992). Legal rights of students with attention deficit disorder. *School Psychology Quarterly, 7,* 285–297.

Halperin, J. M., Gittelman, R., Klein, D. F., & Rudel, R. G. (1984). Reading-disabled hyperactive children: A distinct subgroup of Attention Deficit Disorder with Hyperactivity? *Journal of Abnormal Child Psychology, 12,* 1–14.

Halperin, J. M., Sharma, V., Greenblatt, E., & Schwartz, S. T. (1991). Assessment of the continuous performance test: Reliability and validity in a non-referred sample. *Psychological Assessment: A Journal of Consulting and Clinical Psychology, 3,* 603–608.

Hamlett, K. W., Pellegrini, D. S., & Conners, C. K. (1987). An investigation of executive processes in the problem-solving of attention deficit disorder-hyperactive children. *Journal of Pediatric Psychology, 12,* 227–240.

Hammer, E. F. (1975). *The clinical application of projective drawings.* Springfield, IL: Charles C. Thomas.

Hartsough, C. S., & Lambert, N. M. (1985). Medical factors in hyperactive and normal children: Prenatal, developmental, and health history findings. *American Journal of Orthopsychiatry, 55,* 190–210.

Hasselbring, T. S., Goin, L. I., & Bransford, J. D. (1988). Developing math automaticity in learning handicapped children: The role of computerized drill and practice. *Focus on Exceptional Children, 20*(6), 1–7.

Haynes, S. N. (1986). The design of intervention programs. In R. O. Nelson & S. C. Hayes (Eds.), *Conceptual foundations of behavioral assessment* (pp. 386–429). New York: Guilford Press.

Hersen, M., & Barlow, D. H. (1982). *Single case experimental designs: Strategies for studying behavior change.* Elmsford, NY: Pergamon Press.

Heward, W. L., Heron, T. E., Gardner, R., & Prayzer, R. (1991). Two strategies for improving students' writing skills. In G. Stoner, M. R. Shinn, & H. M. Walker (Eds.), *Interventions for achievement and behavior problems* (pp. 379–398). Silver Spring, MD: National Association of School Psychologists.

Hinshaw, S. P. (1987). On the distinction between attentional deficits/hyperactivity and conduct problems/aggression in child psychopathology. *Psychological Bulletin, 101,* 443–463.

Hinshaw, S. P. (1991). Stimulant medication and the treatment of aggression in children with attentional deficits. *Journal of Clinical Child Psychology, 20,* 301–312.

Hinshaw, S. P. (1992a). Externalizing behavior problems and academic underachievement in childhood and adolescence: Causal relationships and underlying mechanisms. *Psychological Bulletin, 111,* 127–155.

Hinshaw, S. P. (1992b). Academic underachievement, attention deficits, and aggression: Comorbidity and implications for intervention. *Journal of Consulting and Clinical Psychology, 60,* 893–903.

Hinshaw, S. P., Henker, B., & Whalen, C. K. (1984). Self-control in hyperactive boys in anger-inducing situations: Effects of cognitive-behavioral training and of methylphenidate. *Journal of Abnormal Child Psychology, 12,* 55–77.

Hinshaw, S. P., Henker, B., Whalen, C. K., Erhardt, D., & Dunnington, R. E., Jr. (1989). Aggressive, prosocial, and nonsocial behavior in hyperactive boys: Dose effects of methylphenidate in naturalistic settings. *Journal of Consulting and Clinical Psychology, 57,* 636–643.

Holborow, P. L., & Berry, P. S. (1986). Hyperactivity and learning difficulties. *Journal of Learning Disabilities, 19,* 426–431.

Hops, H., & Greenwood, C. R. (1988). Social skills deficits. In E. J. Mash & L. G. Terdal (Eds.), *Behavioral assessment of childhood disorders* (2nd ed., pp. 263–316). New York: Guilford Press.

Horn, W. F., Ialongo, N., Popovich, S., & Peradotto, D. (1987). Behavioral parent training and cognitive-behavioral self-control therapy with ADD-H children: Comparative and combined effect. *Journal of Clinical Child Psychology, 16,* 57–68.

Horner, R. H., Albin, R. W., & O'Neill, R. E. (1991). Supporting students with severe intellectual disabilities and severe challenging behaviors. In G. Stoner, M. R. Shinn, & H. M. Walker (Eds.), *Interventions for achievement and behavior problems* (pp. 269–287). Silver Spring, MD: National Association of School Psychologists.

Horner, R. H., Dunlap, G., & Koegel, R. L. (1988). *Generalization and maintenance: Lifestyle changes in applied settings.* Baltimore: Paul H. Brookes.

Hoy, E., Weiss, G., Minde, K., & Cohen, H. (1978). The hyperactive child at adolescence: Cognitive, emotional, and social functioning. *Journal of Abnormal Child Psychology, 6,* 311–324.

Hoza, B., Pelham, W. E., Sams, S. E., & Carlson, C. (1992). An examination of the "dosage" effects of both behavior therapy and methylphenidate on the classroom performance of two ADHD children. *Behavior Modification, 16,* 164–192.

Humphrey, L. L. (1982). Children's and teacher's perspectives on children's self-control: The development of two rating scales. *Journal of Consulting and Clinical Psychology, 50,* 624–633.

Hunt, R. D., Lau, S., & Ryu, J. (1991). Alternative therapies for ADHD. In L. L. Greenhill & B. B. Osman (Eds.), *Ritalin: Theory and patient management* (pp. 75–95). New York: Mary Ann Liebert.

Hunt, R. D., Mindera, R. B., & Cohen, D. J. (1985). Clonidine benefits children with Attention-Deficit Disorder and Hyperactivity: Report of a double-blind placebo-crossover therapeutic trial. *Journal of the American Academy of Child and Adolescent Psychiatry, 24,* 617–629.

Hynd, G. (1992). Misrepresentation or simply misinformed? Comment on Gresham and Gansle. *School Psychology Quarterly, 7,* 100–103.

Jacob, R. G., O'Leary, K. D., & Rosenblad, C. (1978). Formal and informal classroom settings: Effects on hyperactivity. *Journal of Abnormal Child Psychology, 6,* 47–59.

Jacobsen, N. S., & Truax, P. (1991). Clinical significance: A statistical approach to defining meaningful change in psychotherapy research. *Journal of Consulting and Clinical Psychology, 59,* 12–19.

Jenson, W. R., Clark, E., Walker, H. M., & Kehle, T. (1991). Behavior disorders: Training needs for school psychologists. In G. Stoner, M. R. Shinn, & H. M. Walker (Eds.), *Interventions for achievement and behavior problems* (pp. 763–787). Silver Spring, MD: National Association of School Psychologists.

Johnson, R. A., Kenney, J. B., & Davis, J. B. (1976, November). Developing school policy for use of stimulant drugs for hyperactive children. *School Review,* pp. 78–96.

Johnston, C., Pelham, W. E., Hoza, J., & Sturges, J. (1987). Psychostimulant rebound in Attention Deficit Disordered boys. *Journal of the American Academy of Child and Adolescent Psychiatry, 27,* 806–810.

Johnston, J. M., & Pennypacker, H. S. (1980). *Strategies and tactics of human behavioral research.* Hillsdale, NJ: Erlbaum.

Kagan, J. (1966). Reflection-impulsivity: The generality and dynamics of conceptual tempo. *Journal of Abnormal Psychology, 71,* 17–24.

Kameenui, E. J., & Simmons, D. C. (1990). *Designing instructional strategies: The prevention of academic learning problems.* Columbus, OH: Merrill.

Kavale, K. A., & Mattson, P. D. (1983). One jumped off the balance beam: Meta-analysis of perceptual-motor training. *Journal of Learning Disabilities, 16,* 165–173.

Kazdin, A. E. (1988). *Child psychotherapy: Developing and identifying effective treatments.* Elmsford, NY: Pergamon Press.

Kazdin, A. E. (1989). *Behavior modification in applied settings* (4th ed.). Homewood, IL: Dorsey Press.

Kazdin, A. E. (1992). *Research design in clinical psychology* (2nd ed.). Boston: Allyn & Bacon.

Kelley, M. L. (1990). *School–home notes: Promoting children's classroom success.* New York: Guilford Press.

Kendall, P. C., & Braswell, L. (1985). *Cognitive-behavioral therapy for impulsive children.* New York: Guilford Press.

Keogh, B. A. (1971). Hyperactivity and learning disorders: Review and speculation. *Exceptional Children, 38,* 101–109.

Klingman, A., Melamed, B. G., Cuthbert, M. I., & Hermecz, D. A. (1984). Effects of participant modeling on information acquisition and skill utilization. *Journal of Consulting and Clinical Psychology, 52,* 414–422.

Klorman, R. (1986). Attention deficit disorder in adolescence. In R. A. Feldman & A. R. Stiffman (Eds.), *Advances in adolescent mental health* (Vol. 1, pp. 19–62). Greenwich, CT: JAI Press.

Klorman, R., Brumaghim, J. T., Salzman, L. F., Strauss, J., Borgsted, A. D., McBride, M. C., & Loeb, S. (1988). Effects of methylphenidate on Attention-Deficit Hyperactivity Disorder with and without aggressive/noncompliant features. *Journal of Abnormal Psychology, 97,* 413–422.

Kohler, F. W., Schwartz, I., Cross, J., & Fowler, S. A. (1989). The effects of two alternating intervention roles on independent work skills. *Education and Treatment of Children, 12,* 205–218.

Kohler, F. W., & Strain, P. S. (1990). Peer-assisted interventions: Early promises, notable achievements, and future aspirations. *Clinical Psychology Review, 10,* 441–452.

Kupietz, S. S. (1991). Ritalin blood levels and their correlations with measures of learning. In L. L. Greenhill & B. B. Osman (Eds.), *Ritalin: Theory and patient management* (pp. 247–255). New York: Mary Ann Leibert.

LaGreca, A. M. (1990). *Through the eyes of the child.* Boston: Allyn & Bacon.

Lahey, B. B. (1993, February). *Results of DSM-IV field trials for attention-deficit hyperactivity disorder.* Paper presented at the annual meeting of the Professional Group for ADD and Related Disorders, Santa Fe, NM.

Lahey, B. B., & Carlson, C. (1992). Validity of the diagnostic category of attention deficit disorder without hyperactivity: A review of the literature. In S. E. Shaywitz & B. A. Shaywitz (Eds.), *Attention deficit disorder comes of age: Toward the twenty-first century* (pp. 119–144). Austin, TX: Pro-Ed.

Lahey, B. B., Piacentini, J. C., McBurnett, K., Stone, P., Hartdagen, S., & Hynd, G. (1988). Psychopathology in the parents of children with conduct disorder and hyperactivity. *Journal of the American Academy of Child and Adolescent Psychiatry, 27,* 163–170.

Lambert, N. M., & Sandoval, J. (1980). The prevalence of learning disabilities in a sample of children considered hyperactive. *Journal of Abnormal Child Psychology, 8,* 33–50.

Landau, S., Milich, R., & Widiger, T. A. (1991). Conditional probabilities of child interview symptoms in the diagnosis of attention deficit disorder. *Journal of Child Psychology and Psychiatry, 32,* 501–513.

Levin, H., Glass, G., & Meister, G. (1984). *Cost-effectiveness of four educational interventions* (Report No. 84–A11). Stanford, CA: Institute for Research in Educational Finance and Governance, Stanford University.

Levine, M. D., Busch, B., & Aufseeser, C. (1982). The dimension of inattention among children with school problems. *Pediatrics, 70,* 387–395.

Lindsley, O. R. (1991). From technical jargon to plain English for application. *Journal of Applied Behavior Analysis, 24,* 449–458.

Livingston, R. (1990). Psychiatric comorbidity with reading disability: A clinical study. *Advances in Learning and Behavioral Disabilities, 6,* 143–155.

Lochman, J. E., & Curry, J. F. (1986). Effects of social problem-solving and self-instruction training with aggressive boys. *Journal of Clinical Child Psychology, 15,* 159–164.

Loney, J., & Milich, R. (1982). Hyperactivity, inattention, and aggression in clinical practice. In D. Routh & M. Wolraich (Eds.), *Advances in developmental and behavioral pediatrics* (Vol. 3, pp. 113–147). Greenwich, CT: JAI Press.

Lou, H. C., Henriksen, L., & Bruhn, P. (1984). Focal cerebral hypoperfusion in children with dysphasia and/or Attention Deficit Disorder. *Archives of Neurology, 41,* 825–829.

Lou, H. C., Henriksen, L., Bruhn, P., Borner, H., & Nielsen, J. B. (1989). Striatal dysfunction in attention deficit and hyperkinetic disorder. *Archives of Neurology, 46,* 48–52.

Lovejoy, M. C., & Rasmussen, N. H. (1990). The validity of vigilance tasks in differential diagnosis of children referred for attention and learning problems. *Journal of Abnormal Child Psychology, 18,* 671–681.

Lubar, J. (1992, October). *Is EEG neurofeedback an effective treatment for ADHD?* Paper presented at the CH.A.D.D. fourth annual conference, Chicago, IL.

Madsen, C. H., Becker, W. C., & Thomas, D. R. (1968). Rules, praise, and ignoring: Elements of elementary classroom control. *Journal of Applied Behavior Analysis, 1,* 139–150.

Marston, D. B. (1989). A curriculum-based measurement approach to assessing academic performance: What it is and why do it. In M. R. Shinn (Ed.), *Curriculum-based measurement: Assessing special children* (pp. 18–78). New York: Guilford Press.

Martens, B. K. (1992). The difference between a good theory and a good treatment is a matter of degree. *School Psychology Quarterly, 7,* 104–107.

Martens, B. K., & Kelly, S. Q. (1993). A behavioral analysis of effective teaching. *School Psychology Quarterly, 8,* 10–26.

Matson, J. L. (Ed.). (1993). *Handbook of hyperactivity in children.* Boston: Allyn & Bacon.

Mattes, J. A., & Gittelman, R. (1983). Growth of hyperactive children on maintenance regimen of methylphenidate. *Archives of General Psychiatry, 40,* 317–321.

McConaughy, S. H., Achenbach, T. M., & Gent, C. L. (1988). Multiaxial empirically based assessment: Parent, teacher, observational, cognitive, and personality correlates of child behavior profile types for 6- to 11-year- old boys. *Journal of Abnormal Child Psychology, 16,* 485–509.

McConaughy, S. H., Mattison, R. E., & Peterson, R. (in press). Behavioral/emotional problems of children with serious emotional disturbance and learning disabilities. *School Psychology Review.*

McConnell, S. R., & Hecht, M. (1991). Instructional problems and interventions: Training needs for school psychologists. In G. Stoner, M. R. Shinn, & H. M. Walker (Eds.), *Interventions for achievement and behavior problems* (pp. 741–761). Silver Spring, MD: National Association of School Psychologists.

McGee, R., & Share, D. L. (1988). Attention deficit disorder-hyperactivity and academic failure: Which comes first and what should be treated? *Journal of the American Academy of Child and Adolescent Psychiatry, 27,* 318–325.

McGee, R., Williams, S., & Silva, P. A. (1984). Behavioral and developmental characteristics of aggressive, hyperactive, and aggressive–hyperactive boys. *Journal of the American Academy of Child and Adolescent Psychiatry, 23,* 270–279.

McMahon, R. J., & Wells, K. C. (1989). Conduct disorders. In E. J. Mash & R. A. Barkley (Eds.), *Treatment of childhood disorders* (pp. 73–132). New York: Guilford Press.

Meichenbaum, D., & Goodman, J. (1971). Training impulsive children to talk to themselves: A means of developing self-control. *Journal of Abnormal Psychology, 77*, 115–126.

Mendelson, L., Johnson, N., & Stewart, M. A. (1971). Hyperactive children as teenagers: A follow-up study. *Journal of Nervous and Mental Disease, 153*, 273–279.

Meyer, L. H., & Evans, I. M. (1989). *Nonaversive interventions for behavior problems: A manual for home and community.* Baltimore: Paul H. Brookes.

Milich, R., Carlson, C. L., Pelham, W. E., Jr., & Licht, B. G. (1991). Effects of methylphenidate on the persistence of ADHD boys following failure experiences. *Journal of Abnormal Child Psychology, 19*, 519–536.

Milich, R., & Kramer, J. (1984). Reflections on impulsivity: An empirical investigation of impulsivity as a construct. In K. Gadow & I. Bialer (Eds.), *Advances in learning and behavioral disabilities* (Vol. 3, pp. 117–150). Greenwich, CT: JAI Press.

Milich, R., & Landau, S. (1982). Socialization and peer relations in hyperactive children. In K. D. Gadow & I. Bialer (Eds.), *Advances in learning and behavioral disabilities* (Vol. 1, pp. 283–339). Greenwich, CT: JAI Press.

Milich, R., Wolraich, M., & Lindgren, S. (1986). Sugar and hyperactivity: A critical review of empirical findings. *Clinical Psychology Review, 6*, 493–513.

Minuchin, S. (1974). *Families and family therapy.* Cambridge, MA: Harvard University Press.

Moffitt, T. E., & Silva, P. A. (1988). Self-reported delinquency, neuropsychological deficit, and history of attention deficit disorder. *Journal of Abnormal Child Psychology, 16*, 553–569.

Murray, H. A. (1943). *Thematic apperception test.* Cambridge, MA: Harvard University Press.

National Association of School Psychologists. (1992a, May). Position statement on students with attention deficits. *NASP Communique, 20*, 5.

National Association of School Psychologists. (1992b). *Professional Conduct Manual: Principles for Professional Ethics. Standards for the Provision of School Psychological Services.* Silver Spring, MD: Author.

Nussbaum, N. L., Grant, M. L., Roman, M. J., Poole, J. H., & Bigler, E. (1990). Attention deficit disorder and the mediating effect of age on academic and behavioral variables. *Developmental Behavioral Pediatrics, 11*, 22–26.

Office of Technology Assessment. (1988). *Power on! New tools for teaching and learning* (OTA-SET-379). Washington, DC: U.S. Government Printing Office.

Okyere, B. A., & Heron, T. E. (1991). Use of self-correction to improve spelling in regular education classrooms. In G. Stoner, M. R. Shinn, & H. M. Walker (Eds.), *Interventions for achievement and behavior problems* (pp. 399–413). Silver Spring, MD: National Association of School Psychologists.

Olympia, D., Jenson, W. R., Clark, E., & Sheridan, S. (1992). Training parents to facilitate homework completion: A model of home–school collaboration. In S. L. Christenson & J. C. Conoley (Eds.), *Home-school collaboration: Building a fundamental educational resource* (pp. 309–331). Silver Spring, MD: National Association of School Psychologists.

O'Leary, K. D. (1980). Pills or skills for hyperactive children. *Journal of Applied Behavior Analysis, 13*, 191–204.

O'Leary, K. D., Pelham, W. E., Rosenbaum, A., & Price, G. H. (1976). Behavioral treatment of hyperkinetic children: An experimental evaluation of its usefulness. *Clinical Pediatrics, 15*, 510–515.

O'Malley, J. E., & Eisenberg, L. (1973). The hyperkinetic syndrome. *Seminars in Psychiatry, 5*, 95–103.

O'Shea, L. J., Sindelar, P. T., & O'Shea, D. J. (1987). The effects of repeated readings and attentional cues on the reading fluency and comprehension of learning disabled readers. *Learning Disabilities Research, 2*, 103–109.

Paine, S. C., Radicchi, J., Rosellini, L. C., Deutchman, L., & Darch, C. B. (1983). *Structuring your classroom for academic success*. Champaign, IL: Research Press.

Pany, D., Jenkins, J. R., & Schreck, J. (1982). Vocabulary instruction: Effects on word knowledge and reading comprehension. *Learning Disability Quarterly, 5*, 202–214.

Parker, H. C. (1992). *The ADD hyperactivity handbook for schools: Effective strategies for identifying and teaching students with attention deficit disorders in elementary and secondary schools*. Plantation, FL: Impact.

Parker, J. G., & Asher, S. R. (1987). Peer relations and later personal adjustment: Are low-accepted children at risk? *Psychological Bulletin, 102*, 357–389.

Patterson, G. R. (1976). The aggressive child: Victim and architect of a coercive system. In E. Mash, L. Hamerlynck, & L. Handy (Eds.), *Behavior modification and families* (pp. 267–316). New York: Brunner/Mazel.

Pelham, W. E. (1989). Behavior therapy, behavioral assessment, and psychostimulant medication in treatment of attention deficit disorders: An interactive approach. In J. Swanson & L. Bloomingdale (Eds.), *Attention deficit disorders IV: Current concepts and emerging trends in attentional and behavior disorders of childhood* (pp. 169–195). London: Pergamon Press.

Pelham, W. E., & Bender, M. E. (1982). Peer relationships in hyperactive children: Description and treatment. In K. D. Gadow & I. Bialer (Eds.), *Advances in learning and behavioral disabilities* (Vol. 1, pp. 365–436). Greenwich, CT: JAI Press.

Pelham, W. E., Bender, M. E., Caddell, J., Booth, S., & Moorer, S. H. (1985). Methylphenidate and children with attention deficit disorder. *Archives of General Psychiatry, 42*, 948–952.

Pelham, W. E., Carlson, C., Sams, S. E., Vallano, G., Dixon, M. J., & Hoza, B. (1993). Separate and combined effects of methylphenidate and behavior modification on boys with attention-deficit hyperactivity disorder in classroom. *Journal of Consulting and Clinical Psychology, 61*, 506–515.

Pelham, W. E., & Hoza, J. (1987). Behavioral assessment of psychostimulant effects on ADD children in a summer day treatment program. In R. Prinz (Ed.), *Advances in behavioral assessment of children and families* (Vol. 3, pp. 3–33). Greenwich, CT: JAI Press.

Pelham, W. E., McBurnett, K., Harper, G. W., Milich, R., Murphy, D. A., Clinton, J., & Thiel, C. (1990). Methylphenidate and baseball playing in ADHD children: Who's on first? *Journal of Consulting and Clinical Psychology, 58*, 130–133.

Pelham, W. E., & Milich, R. (1991). Individual differences in response to Ritalin in classwork and social behavior. In L. L. Greenhill & B. B. Osman (Eds.), *Ritalin: Theory and patient management* (pp. 203–221). New York: Mary Ann Liebert.

Pelham, W. E., Murphy, D. A., Vannatta, K., Milich, R., Licht, B. G., Gnagy, E. M., Greenslade, K. E., Greiner, A. R., & Vodde-Hamilton, M. (1992). Methylphenidate and attributions in boys with attention-deficit hyperactivity disorder. *Journal of Consulting and Clinical Psychology, 60,* 282–292.

Pelham, W. E., & Murphy, H. A. (1986). Attention deficit and conduct disorders. In M. Hersen (Ed.), *Pharmacological and behavioral treatment: An integrative approach* (pp. 108–148). New York: Wiley.

Pelham, W. E., Sturges, J., Hoza, J., Schmidt, C., Biijlsma, J. J., Milich, R., & Moorer, S. (1987). Sustained release and standard methylphenidate effects on cognitive and social behavior in children with Attention Deficit Disorder. *Pediatrics, 80,* 491–501.

Pelham, W. E., Vodde-Hamilton, M., Murphy, D. A., Greenstein, J. L., & Vallano, G. (1991). The effects of methylphenidate on ADHD adolescents in recreational, peer group, and classroom settings. *Journal of Clinical Child Psychology, 20,* 293–300.

Peterson, L., Homer, A. L., & Wonderlich, S. A. (1982). The integrity of independent variables in behavior analysis. *Journal of Applied Behavior Analysis, 15,* 477–492.

Pfiffner, L. J., & Barkley, R. A. (1990). Educational placement and classroom management. In R. A. Barkley, *Attention-Deficit Hyperactivity Disorder: A handbook for diagnosis and treatment* (pp. 498–539). New York: Guilford Press.

Pfiffner, L. J., & O'Leary, S. G. (1987). The efficacy of all-positive management as a function of the prior use of negative consequences. *Journal of Applied Behavior Analysis, 20,* 265–271.

Pfiffner, L. J., & O'Leary, S. G. (1993). School-based psychological treatments. In J. L. Matson (Ed.), *Handbook of hyperactivity in children.* Boston: Allyn & Bacon.

Pfiffner, L. J., O'Leary, S. G., Rosen, L. A., & Sanderson, W. C., Jr. (1985). A comparison of the effects of continuous and intermittent response cost and reprimands in the classroom. *Journal of Clinical Child Psychology, 14,* 348–352.

Physicians' Desk Reference. (1993). Oradell, NJ: Medical Economics.

Piers, E. V. (1984). *Piers–Harris Children's Self-Concept Scale: Revised manual.* Los Angeles: Western Psychological Services.

Platzman, K. A., Stoy, M. R., Brown, R. T., Coles, C. D., Smith, I. E., & Falek, A. (1992). Review of observational methods in attention deficit hyperactivity disorder (ADHD): Implications for diagnosis. *School Psychology Quarterly, 7,* 155–177.

Pliszka, S. R. (1987). Tricyclic antidepressants in the treatment of children with Attention Deficit Disorder. *Journal of the American Academy of Child and Adolescent Psychiatry, 26,* 127–132.

Pliszka, S. R. (1991). Antidepressants in the treatment of child and adolescent psychopathology. *Journal of Clinical Child Psychology, 20,* 313–320.

Prout, H. T., & Ferber, S. M. (1988). Analogue assessment: Traditional personality assessment measures in behavioral assessment. In E. S. Shapiro & T. R. Kratochwill (Eds.), *Behavioral assessment in schools: Conceptual foundations and practical applications* (pp. 322–350). New York: Guilford Press.

Rapoport, J. L. (1986). Antidepressants in childhood attention deficit disorder and obsessive-compulsive disorder. *Psychosomatics, 27,* 30–36.

Rapoport, J., Buchsbaum, M., Weingartner, H., Zahn, T., Ludlow, C., Bartko, J., Mikkelson, E., Langer, D., & Bunney, W. (1980). Dextroamphetamine: Cognitive and behavioral effects in normal and hyperactive boys and normal adult males. *Archives of General Psychiatry, 37,* 933–946.

Rapport, M. D. (1987a). Attention-deficit disorder with hyperactivity. In M. Hersen & V. B. Van Hasselt (Eds.), *Behavior therapy with children and adolescents* (pp. 325–361). New York: Wiley.

Rapport, M. D. (1987b). *The Attention Training System: User's manual.* DeWitt, NY: Gordon Systems.

Rapport, M. D., Carlson, G. A., Kelly, K. L., & Pataki, C. (1993). Methylphenidate and desipramine in hospitalized children: I. Separate and combined effects on cognitive function. *Journal of the American Academy of Child and Adolescent Psychiatry, 32,* 333–342.

Rapport, M. D., DuPaul, G. J., & Kelly, K. L. (1989). Attention-Deficit Hyperactivity Disorder and methylphenidate: The relationship between gross body weight and drug response in children. *Psychopharmacology Bulletin, 25,* 285–290.

Rapport, M. D., DuPaul, G. J., Stoner, G., & Jones, J. T. (1986). Comparing classroom and clinic measures of attention deficit disorder: Differential, idiosyncratic, and dose-response effects of methylphenidate. *Journal of Consulting and Clinical Psychology, 54,* 334–341.

Rapport, M. D., Jones, J. T., DuPaul, G. J., Kelly, K. L., Gardner, M. J., Tucker, S. B., & Shea, M. S. (1987). Attention Deficit Disorder and methylphenidate: Group and single-subject analyses of dose effects on attention in clinic and classroom settings. *Journal of Clinical Child Psychology, 16,* 329–338.

Rapport, M. D., & Kelly, K. L. (1991). Psychostimulant effects on learning and cognitive function: Findings and implications for children with Attention-deficit Hyperactivity Disorder. *Clinical Psychology Review, 11,* 61–92.

Rapport, M. D., Murphy, A., & Bailey, J. S. (1980). The effects of a response cost treatment tactic on hyperactive children. *Journal of School Psychology, 18,* 98–111.

Rapport, M. D., Murphy, A., & Bailey, J. S. (1982). Ritalin vs. response cost in the control of hyperactive children: A within subject comparison. *Journal of Applied Behavior Analysis, 15,* 205–216.

Rapport, M. D., Stoner, G., DuPaul, G. J., Birmingham, B. K., & Tucker, S. (1985). Methylphenidate in hyperactive children: Differential effects of dose on academic, learning, and social behavior. *Journal of Abnormal Child Psychology, 13,* 227–244.

Rapport, M. D., Stoner, G., DuPaul, G. J., Kelly, K. L., Tucker, S. B., & Schoeler, T. (1988). Attention deficit disorder and methylphenidate: A multilevel analysis of dose-response effects on children's impulsivity across settings. *Journal of the American Academy of Child and Adolescent Psychiatry, 27,* 60–69.

Rapport, M. D., Tucker, S. B., DuPaul, G. J., Merlo, M., & Stoner, G. (1986). Hyperactivity and frustration: The influence of size and control over rewards in delaying gratification. *Journal of Abnormal Child Psychology, 14,* 191–204.

Redman, C. A., & Zametkin, A. J. (1991). Ritalin and brain metabolism. In L. L. Greenhill & B. B. Osman (Eds.), *Ritalin: Theory and patient management* (pp. 301–308). New York: Mary Ann Liebert.

Reeve, E., & Garfinkel, B. (1991). Neuroendocrine and growth regulation: The role of sympathomimetic medication. In L. L. Greenhill & B. B. Osman (Eds.), *Ritalin: Theory and patient management* (pp. 289–300). New York: Mary Ann Liebert.

Reid, J. B., & Patterson, G. R. (1991). Early prevention and intervention with conduct problems: A social interactional model for the integration of research and practice. In G. Stoner, M. R. Shinn, & H. M. Walker (Eds.), *Interventions for achievement and behavior problems* (pp. 715–739). Silver Spring, MD: National Association of School Psychologists.

Reith, H., Bahr, C., Polsgrove, L., Okolo, C., & Eckert, R. (1987). The effects of microcomputers on the secondary special education classroom ecology. *Journal of Special Education Technology, 8*, 36–45.

Reith, H. J., & Semmel, M. I. (1991). Use of computer-assisted instruction in the regular classroom. In G. Stoner, M. R. Shinn, & H. M. Walker (Eds.), *Interventions for achievement and behavior problems* (pp. 215–239). Silver Spring, MD: National Association of School Psychololgists.

Reschly, D. J. (1988). Special education reform: School psychology revolution. *School Psychology Review, 17*, 459–475.

Reynolds, C. R. (1992). Misguided epistemological shifting, misdirected misology, and dogma in diagnosis. *School Psychology Quarterly, 7*, 96–99.

Reynolds, M. C. (1988). Alternative educational approaches: Implications for school psychology. In J. L. Graden, J. E. Zins, & M. J. Curtis (Eds.). *Alternative educational delivery systems: Enhancing instructional options for all students* (pp. 555–562). Washington, DC: National Association of School Psychologists.

Reynolds, W. M. (1987). *Reynolds Adolescent Depression Scale: Professional manual.* Odessa, FL: Psychological Assessment Resources.

Rhode, G., Morgan, D. P., & Young, K. R. (1983). Generalization and maintenance of treatment gains of behaviorally handicapped students from resource rooms to regular classrooms using self-evaluation procedures. *Journal of Applied Behavior Analysis, 16*, 171–188.

Robin, A. L. (1990). Training families with ADHD adolescents. In R. A. Barkley, *Attention-Deficit Hyperactivity Disorder: A handbook for diagnosis and treatment* (pp. 462–497). New York: Guilford Press.

Robin, A. L., & Foster, S. L. (1989). *Negotiating parent–adolescent conflict: A behavioral–family systems approach.* New York: Guilford Press.

Robinson, P. W., Newby, T. J., & Ganzell, S. L. (1981). A token system for a class of underachieving hyperactive children. *Journal of Applied Behavior Analysis, 14*, 307–315.

Rose, T. L., & Sherry, L. (1984). Relative effects of two previewing procedures on LD adolescents' oral reading performance. *Learning Disability Quarterly, 7*, 39–44.

Rosen, L. A., O'Leary, S. G., Joyce, S. A., Conway, G., & Pfiffner, L. J. (1984).

The importance of prudent negative consequences for maintaining the appropriate behavior of hyperactive students. *Journal of Abnormal Child Psychology*, *12*, 581–604.

Rosenshine, B. V. (1987). Explicit teaching. In D. C. Berliner & B. V. Rosenshine (Eds.), *Talks to teachers: A festschrift for N. L. Gage* (pp. 75–92). New York: Random House.

Ross, D. M., & Ross, S. A. (1982). *Hyperactivity: Current issues, research and theory* (2nd ed.). New York: Wiley.

Rosvold, H. E., Mirsky, A. F., Sarason, I., Bransome, E. D., & Beck, L. H. (1956). A continuous performance test of brain damage. *Journal of Consulting Psychology*, *20*, 343–350.

Rourke, B. P. (1988). Socioemotional disturbances of learning disabled children. *Journal of Consulting and Clinical Psychology*, *56*, 801–810.

Routh, D. K., Schroeder, C. S., & O'Tuama, L. A. (1974). Development of activity level in children. *Developmental Psychology*, *10*, 163–168.

Rowe, K. J., & Rowe, K. S. (1992). The relationship between inattentiveness in the classroom and reading achievement (Part B): An explanatory study. *Journal of the American Academy of Child and Adolescent Psychiatry*, *31*, 357–368.

Ryan, N. D. (1990). Pharmacotherapy of adolescent major depression: Beyond TCAs. *Psychopharmacology Bulletin*, *26*, 75–79.

Safer, D. J., & Krager, J. M. (1988). A survey of medication treatment for hyperactive/inattentive students. *Journal of the American Medical Association*, *260*, 2256–2258.

Sallee, F. R., Stiller, R. L., & Perel, J. M. (1992). Pharmacodynamics of pemoline in attention deficit disorder with hyperactivity. *Journal of the American Academy of Child and Adolescent Psychiatry*, *31*, 244–251.

Salvia, J., & Ysseldyke, J. E. (1991). *Assessment* (5th ed.). Boston: Houghton Mifflin.

Samuels, S. J. (1979). The method of repeated readings. *Reading Teacher*, *32*, 403–408.

Satterfield, J. H., Hoppe, C. M., & Schell, A. M. (1982). A prospective study of delinquency in 110 adolescent boys with attention deficit disorder and 88 normal adolescent boys. *American Journal of Psychiatry*, *139*, 795–798.

Satterfield, J. H., Satterfield, B. T., & Schell, A. M. (1987). Therapeutic interventions to prevent delinquency in hyperactive boys. *Journal of the American Academy of Child and Adolescent Psychiatry*, *26*, 56–64.

Saudargas, R. A., & Creed, V. (1980). *State-event classroom observation system*. Knoxville, TN: University of Tennessee, Department of Psychology.

Schachar, R., Rutter, M., & Smith, A. (1981). The characteristics of situationally and pervasively hyperactive children: Implications for syndrome definition. *Journal of Child Psychology and Psychiatry*, *22*, 375–392.

Schacht, T., & Nathan, P. E. (1977). But is it good for the psychologists?: Appraisal and status of DSM-III. *American Psychologist*, *32*, 1017–1025.

Schaughency, E. A., & Rothlind, J. (1991). Assessment and classification of Attention-deficit hyperactive disorders. *School Psychology Review*, *20*, 187–202.

Schrag, P., & Divoky, D. (1975). *The myth of the hyperactive child.* New York: Pantheon.

Schwartz, I. S., & Baer, D. M. (1991). Social validity assessments: Is current practice state of the art? *Journal of Applied Behavior Analysis, 24,* 189–204.

Semrud-Clikeman, M., Biederman, J., Sprich-Buckminster, S., Lehman, B. K., Faraone, S. V., & Norman, D. (1992). Comorbidity between ADDH and learning disability: A review and report in a clinically referred sample. *Journal of the American Academy of Child and Adolescent Psychiatry, 31,* 439–448.

Shapiro, E. S. (1989). *Academic skills problems: Direct assessment and intervention.* New York: Guilford Press.

Shapiro, E. S. (Ed.). (1992). Response/dialogue: The social maladjustment exclusion clause [Special issue]. *School Psychology Review, 21,* 11–44.

Shapiro, E. S., & Cole, C. L. (1994). *Self-management interventions for classroom behavior change.* New York: Guilford Press.

Shapiro, E. S., & Kratochwill, T. R. (Eds.). (1988). *Behavioral assessment in schools: Conceptual foundations and practical applications.* New York: Guilford Press.

Shaywitz, S. E., & Shaywitz, B. A. (1991). Attention deficit disorder: Diagnosis and role of Ritalin in management. In L. L. Greenhill & B. B. Osman (Eds.), *Ritalin: Theory and patient management* (pp. 45–67). New York: Mary Ann Liebert.

Shelton, T. L., & Barkley, R. A. (1990). Clinical, developmental, and biopsychosocial considerations. In R. A. Barkley, *Attention-Deficit Hyperactivity Disorder: A handbook for diagnosis and treatment* (pp. 209–231). New York: Guilford Press.

Shinn, M. R. (Ed.). (1989). *Curriculum-based measurement: Assessing special children.* New York: Guilford Press.

Silver, L. B. (1981). The relationship between learning disabilities, hyperactivity, distractibility, and behavioral problems. *Journal of the American Academy of Child and Adolescent Psychiatry, 20,* 385–397.

Silver, L. B. (1990). Attention-deficit hyperactivity disorder: Is it a learning disability or a related disorder? *Journal of Learning Disabilities, 23,* 394–397.

Simeon, J. G., Ferguson, H. B., & Van Wyck Fleet, J. (1986). Bupropion effects in attention deficit and conduct disorders. *Canadian Journal of Psychiatry, 31,* 581–585.

Sindelar, P. T., & Stoddard, K. (1991). Teaching reading to mildly disabled students in regular classes. In G. Stoner, M. R. Shinn, & H. M. Walker (Eds.), *Interventions for achievement and behavior problems* (pp. 357–378). Silver Spring, MD: National Association of School Psychologists.

Smith, D. J., Young, K. R., Nelson, J. R., & West, R. P. (1992). The effect of a self-management procedure on the classroom academic behavior of students with mild handicaps. *School Psychology Review, 21,* 59–72.

Smith, L. (1975). *Your child's behavior chemistry.* New York: Random House.

Solanto, M. V. (1984). Neuropharmacological basis of stimulant drug action in attention deficit disorder with hyperactivity: A review and synthesis. *Psychological Bulletin, 95,* 387–409.

Solanto, M. V. (1991). Dosage effects of Ritalin on cognition. In L. L. Greenhill & B. B. Osman (Eds.), *Ritalin: Theory and patient management* (pp. 233–245). New York: Mary Ann Liebert.

Solanto, M. V., & Wender, E. H. (1989). Does methylphenidate constrict cognitive functioning? *Journal of the American Academy of Child and Adolescent Psychiatry, 28,* 897–902.

Spencer, T., Biederman, J., Wilens, T., Steingard, R., & Geist, D. (1993). Nortriptyline treatment of children with attention-deficit hyperactivity disorder and tic disorder or Tourette's syndrome. *Journal of the American Academy of Child and Adolescent Psychiatry, 32,* 205–210.

Spencer, T., Biederman, J., Wright, V., & Danon, M. (1992). Growth deficits in children treated with desipramine: A controlled study. *Journal of the American Academy of Child and Adolescent Psychiatry, 31,* 235–243.

Spivack, G., & Shure, M. B. (1974). *Social adjustment of young children: A cognitive approach to solving real-life problems.* San Francisco: Jossey-Bass.

Sprafkin, J., Grayson, P., Gadow, K. D., Nolan, E. E., & Paolicelli, L. M. (1986). *Code for Observing Social Activity (COSA).* Stony Brook, NY: State University of New York, Department of Psychiatry and Behavioral Science.

Sprague, R. K., & Sleator, E. K. (1977). Methylphenidate in hyperkinetic children: Differences in dose effects on learning and social behavior. *Science, 198,* 1,274–1,276.

Sprick, R. S., & Nolet, V. (1991). Prevention and management of secondary-level behavior problems. In G. Stoner, M. R. Shinn, & H. M. Walker (Eds.), *Interventions for achievement and behavior problems* (pp. 519–538). Silver Spring, MD: National Association of School Psychologists.

Stokes, T. F., & Baer, D. M. (1977). An implicit technology of generalization. *Journal of Applied Behavior Analysis, 10,* 349–367.

Stokes, T. F., & Osnes, P. G. (1989). An operant pursuit of generalization. *Behavior Therapy, 20,* 337–355.

Stoner, G., & Carey, S. P. (1992). Serving students with ADD: Avoiding deficits in professional attention. *School Psychology Quarterly, 7,* 302–307.

Stoner, G., & Green, S. K. (1992a). *A pilot study of instruction in and understanding of classroom rules in the primary grades.* Unpublished manuscript, University of Oregon, Eugene, OR.

Stoner, G., & Green, S. K. (1992b). Reconsidering the scientist-practitioner model for school psychology practice. *School Psychology Review, 21,* 154–165.

Stoner, G., Shinn, M. R., & Walker, H. M. (Eds.). (1991). *Interventions for achievement and behavior problems.* Silver Spring, MD: National Association of School Psychologists.

Sulzer-Azaroff, B., & Mayer, G. R. (1977). *Applying behavior analysis procedures with children and youth.* Fort Worth, TX: Holt, Rinehart, & Winston.

Sulzer-Azaroff, B., & Mayer, G. R. (1986). *Achieving educational excellence using behavioral strategies.* Fort Worth, TX: Holt, Rinehart, & Winston.

Sulzer-Azaroff, B., & Mayer, G. R. (1991). *Behavior analysis for lasting change.* Fort Worth, TX: Holt, Rinehart, & Winston.

Swanson, J. M. (1988). Measurement of serum concentrations and behavioral response in ADDH children to acute doses of methylphenidate. In L. B. Bloomingdale (Ed.), *Attention deficit disorder: New research in attention, treatment, and psychopharmacology* (pp. 107–126). New York: Pergamon Press.

Swanson, J. M. (1992). *School-based assessments and interventions for ADD students.* Irvine CA: K.C.

Swanson, J., & Kinsbourne, M. (1975). Stimulant-related state-dependent learning in hyperactive children. *Science, 192,* 1354-1357.

Swanson, J., & Kinsbourne, M. (1980). Food dyes impair performance of hyperactive children on a laboratory learning test. *Science, 207,* 1485-1486.

Szatmari, P., Offord, D. R., & Boyle, M. H. (1989). Ontario child health study: Prevalence of attention deficit disorder with hyperactivity. *Journal of Child Psychology and Psychiatry, 30,* 219-230.

Tant, J. L., & Douglas, V. I. (1982). Problem solving in hyperactive, normal, and reading-disabled boys. *Journal of Abnormal Child Psychology, 10,* 285-306.

Taylor, E., Schachare, R., Thorley, G., Wieselberg, H. M., Everitt, B., & Rutter, M. (1987). Which boys respond to stimulant medication? A controlled trial of methylphenidate in boys with disruptive behavior. *Psychological Medicine, 17,* 121-143.

Taylor, J. A. (1951). The relationship of anxiety to the conditioned eyelid response. *Journal of Experimental Psychology, 42,* 183-188.

Toufexis, A. (1989, January 16). Worries about overactive kids: Are too many youngsters being misdiagnosed and medicated? *Time,* p. 65.

Turnbull, A. P., & Turnbull, H. R. (1986). *Families, professionals, and exceptionality: A special partnership.* Columbus, OH: Merrill.

Ullman, D. G., Barkley, R. A., & Brown, H. W. (1978). The behavioral symptoms of hyperkinetic children who successfully responded to stimulant drug treatment. *American Journal of Orthopsychiatry, 48,* 425-437.

Ullmann, R. K., Sleator, E. K., & Sprague, R. L. (1985). Introduction to the use of the ACTeRS. *Psychopharmacology Bulletin, 21,* 915-920.

Vatz, B. C. (1990, April). *Behavioral subtypes of learning disabled children.* Paper presented at the annual convention of the National Association of School Psychologists, San Francisco.

Voelker, S. L., Carter, R. A., Sprague, D. J., Gdowski, C. L., & Lachar, D. (1989). Developmental trends in memory and metamemory in children with attention deficit disorder. *Journal of Pediatric Psychology, 14,* 75-88.

Vyse, S. A., & Rapport, M. D. (1989). The effects of methylphenidate on learning in children with ADDH: The stimulus equivalence paradigm. *Journal of Consulting and Clinical Psychology, 57,* 425-435.

Walker, H. M., & McConnell, S. R. (1988). *Walker-McConnell Scale of Social Competence and School Adjustment.* Austin, TX: Pro-Ed.

Walker, H. M., & Severson, H. (1988). *Systematic screening for behavior disorders assessment system.* Longmont, CO: Sopris West.

Wallander, J. L., Schroeder, S. R., Michelli, J. A., & Gualtieri, C. T. (1987). Classroom social interactions of Attention Deficit Disorder with Hyperactivity children as a function of stimulant medication. *Journal of Pediatric Psychology, 12,* 61-76.

Weiss, B., Williams, J. H., Margen, S., Abrams, B., Caan, B., Citron, L., Cox, C., McKibben, J., Ogar, D., & Schultz, S. (1980). Behavioral responses to artificial food colors. *Science, 207,* 1487-1488.

Weiss, G., & Hechtman, L. (1993). *Hyperactive children grown up* (2nd ed.): *ADHD in children, adolescents, and adults.* New York: Guilford Press.

Weiss, G., Kruger, E., Danielson, U., & Elman, M. (1975). Effects of long-term treatment of hyperactive children with methylphenidate. *Canadian Medical Association Journal, 112,* 159–165.

Weiss, G., Minde, K., Werry, J. S., Douglas, V., & Nemeth, E. (1971). Studies on the hyperactive child. VII: Five year follow-up. *Archives of General Psychiatry, 24,* 409–414.

Werry, J. S., Elkind, G. S., & Reeves, J. C. (1987). Attention deficit, conduct, oppositional, and anxiety disorders in children: III. Laboratory differences. *Journal of Abnormal Child Psychology, 15,* 409–428.

Werry, J. S., Sprague, R. L., & Cohen, M. N. (1975). Conners' Teacher Rating Scale for use in drug studies with children—An empirical study. *Journal of Abnormal Child Psychology, 3,* 217–229.

Whalen, C. K., Collins, B. E., Henker, B., Alkus, S. R., Adams, D., & Stapp, J. (1978). Behavior observations of hyperactive children and methylphenidate (Ritalin) effects in systematically structured classroom environments: Now you see them, now you don't. *Journal of Pediatric Psychology, 3,* 177–187.

Whalen, C. K., & Henker, B. (Eds.). (1980). *Hyperactive children: The social ecology of identification and treatment.* New York: Academic Press.

Whalen, C. K., Henker, B., Buhrmester, D., Hinshaw, S. P., Huber, A., & Laski, K. (1989). Does stimulant medication improve the peer status of hyperactive children? *Journal of Consulting and Clinical Psychology, 57,* 545–549.

Whalen, C. K., Henker, B., Collins, B. E., Finck, D., & Dotemoto, S. (1979). A social ecology of hyperactive boys: Medication effects in structured classroom environments. *Journal of Applied Behavior Analysis, 12,* 65–81.

Whalen, C. K., Henker, B., & Dotemoto, S. (1981). Teacher response to methylphenidate (Ritalin) versus placebo status of hyperactive boys in the classroom. *Child Development, 52,* 1005–1014.

Whalen, C. K., Henker, B., Hinshaw, S. P., Heller, T., & Huber-Dressler, A. (1991). Messages of medication: Effects of actual versus informed medication status on hyperactive boys' expectancies and self-evaluations. *Journal of Consulting and Clinical Psychology, 59,* 602–606.

Whalen, C. K., Henker, B., Swanson, J. M., Granger, D., Kliewer, W., & Spencer, J. (1987). Natural social behaviors in hyperactive children: Dose effects of methylphenidate. *Journal of Consulting and Clinical Psychology, 55,* 187–193.

White, M. A. (1975). Natural rates of teacher approval and disapproval in the classroom. *Journal of Applied Behavior Analysis, 8,* 367–372.

Wielkiewicz, R. M. (1990). Interpreting low scores on the WISC-R third factor: It's more than distractibility. *Psychological Assessment: A Journal of Consulting and Clinical Psychology, 2,* 91–97.

Wirt, R. D., Lachar, D., Klinedinst, J. K., & Seat, P. D. (1977). *Multidimensional description of child personality: A manual for the Personality Inventory for Children.* Los Angeles: Western Psychological Services.

Witt, J. C., & Elliott, S. N. (1985). Acceptability of classroom management strategies. In T. R. Kratochwill (Ed.), *Advances in school psychology* (Vol. 4, pp. 251–288). Hillsdale, NJ: Erlbaum.

Witt, J. C., & Martens, B. K. (1988). Problems with problem-solving consultation: A re-analysis of assumptions, methods, and goals. *School Psychology Review, 17,* 211–226.

Wixon, K. K. (1986). Vocabulary instruction and children's comprehension of basal stories. *Reading Research Quarterly, 21,* 317–329.

Woodward, J., Carnine, D., & Collins, M. T. (1986). *Closing the performance gap in secondary education.* Unpublished manuscript, University of Oregon, Eugene.

Ysseldyke, J. E., & Christenson, S. L. (1987). *The Instructional Environment Scale.* Austin, TX: Pro-Ed.

Ysseldyke, J. E., & Christenson, S. L. (1988). Linking assessment to intervention. In J. L. Graden, J. E. Zins, & M. J. Curtis (Eds.), *Alternative educational delivery systems: Enhancing instructional options for all students* (pp. 91–110). Washington, DC: National Association of School Psychologists.

Zametkin, A., Rapoport, J. L., Murphy, D. L., Linnoila, M., & Ismond, D. (1985). Treatment of hyperactive children with monoamine oxidase inhibitors: I. Clinical efficacy. *Archives of General Psychiatry, 42,* 962–966.

Zentall, S. S. (1985). A context for hyperactivity. In K. D. Gadow & I. Bialer (Eds.), *Advances in learning and behavioral disabilities* (Vol. 4, pp. 273–343). Greenwich, CT: JAI Press.

Zentall, S. S. (1988). Production deficiencies in elicited language but not in the spontaneous verbalizations of hyperactive children. *Journal of Abnormal Child Psychology, 16,* 657–673.

Zentall, S. S., & Meyer, M. J. (1987). Self-regulation of stimulation for ADD-H children during reading and vigilance task performance. *Journal of Abnormal Child Psychology, 15,* 519–536.

Zirkel, P. A. (1992, December 15). A checklist for determining legal eligibility of ADD/ADHD students. *Special Educator, 8*(7), 93–97.

Index